BROMPTON
BICYCLE

EXCELLENT BOOKS

EXCELLENT BOOKS
richardpeacecycling.com
richardpeace6@gmail.com
4th edition printed 2024

Text © David Henshaw 2009-2024
Photographs and illustrations © David Henshaw / Brompton Bicycle Ltd / Richard Peace except where indicated otherwise

ISBN 978-1901464 42 9

Front cover design: Diana Powell dianampowell@gmail.com
Rear cover photo: Once Bromptons only came in red - today's colour range is vast
Frontispiece: Electric Nano-Brompton with SP trailer bike and child seats

With thanks to: Will Butler-Adams Brompton Bicycle MD, Alan Clarke of Sturmey-Archer Europe BV, Steve Grosvenor, Tim Guinness, Tony Hadland, Adam Hart-Davis, Gary Lovell, Juliane Neuß, Tim Reeves and Andrew Ritchie
And to photo contributors:
Paul Bader, Andy & Sue Black, Vincent Burgeon, Tony Castles, Ben Cooper, ETS Design, Dave Holladay, Marcus Jackson-Baker, Carl Kamenzind, Paul Lenton, Phil O'Connor, Tony L. Oliver, Philipp Onori, Olivier Pascaud, Antoine Pethers, Len Rubin, Mark Sanders, Andrew Stevenson, Jos Vromen, Thomas Wiegold, Matthias Witte and Ken Yanoviak
Thanks to David Walker for retouching work on the inside rear cover photo

Author's Dedication:
To Julian Vereker, who would have enjoyed a Brompton book.

The Brompton won Best Product award at Cyclex in 1987 - a big step forward for the company at the time. Julian's delight is obvious.

Contents

Foreword i

The Author and his Brompton iii

A Short History of Folding Bikes 1

Getting Brompton Off the Ground 19

Going it Alone and the Mark 1 Bike 33

Mark 2 Bikes 43

Competition Hots Up - the Mark 3s 65

Into the New Millennium 81

Brompton Electric and International Turmoil 107

The All Titanium Bike and New Horizons 139

The World of Brompton Specials 153

Using and Maintaining a Brompton 181

Brompton People & Places 220

Making a Brompton 222

Appendices 224

Index 241

Foreword

During the 1990s I presented a television series called Local Heroes, in which I cycled around this country (and a few others), mainly on a mountain bike, talking about dead scientists and inventors, and showing what they had done. We transported the mountain bike from Land's End to John O'Groats (literally) – and beyond – and were constantly aware that it might come to grief (or get nicked) and leave us stranded; so I decided to acquire a standby machine – and a folding bike was the obvious choice.

I can't remember who pointed me in the direction of the Brompton, but it may well have been David Henshaw; I met him and his wife Jane at some bike event. Anyway, I persuaded Andrew Ritchie to make me a pink-and-yellow machine for the TV series; I rode it to an early meeting of the Folding Society at Weymouth, and it travelled with me and the TV crew for many thousands of miles, appearing on television in Sicily (where I broke the back axle at the top of Mt Etna), in Egypt (where I used it to show how Eratosthenes had measured the size of the Earth) and in sundry other exotic locations. I even rode it round the demonstration desk at the Royal Institution and through the corridors of the BBC offices at White City.

Sadly that lovely machine was stolen. I was invited to be interviewed about folding bikes on Radio 4's *You and Yours* programme at Broadcasting House in London. The producer told me not to bring my Brompton into the studio, which was cramped, but to lock it up outside. I did as I was told, but when I came out again it was gone. Now I have a smart green one with only two gears, which is fine, because this is my London transport, and London has no hills (well, almost none).

The Brompton is an ideal bike for any city and for commuting. It folds easily and quickly, and can go in a train, the tube, or a bus; it's not too heavy to carry, and it's a good ride. The really important thing is that I can take it in with me; it is welcome at the British Library, the Science Museum, the Royal Society, and even the Dog and Duck, and once inside a building it is unlikely to be stolen.

I find the Brompton the most reliable way to get around London; regardless of traffic, strikes, or security threats, I know just how long it will take me to get from A to B, and I can easily carry what I need in the bag on the front.

This book is splendid; David writes clearly and amusingly, and I was delighted to find out about the tortuous history of this superb bicycle. I have visited Andrew Ritchie and been shown around the factory, but he is modest about his achievements, and tends to hide his light under a bushel. I hope this book will go some way to hauling it out again. In any case I am sure you will enjoy reading it.

Adam Hart-Davis 2009

The Author and his Brompton

I can honestly say the Brompton changed my life. In the early 1990s, my wife Jane and I were house-sitting - generally in London and the busy southeast - and filling spare moments writing books and articles about cars and trains. But like many people at the time, we were becoming concerned about the way transport was going - Twyford Down, Bathampton, the news seemed to be full of stories of apparently unwanted trunk roads being foisted on unwilling communities. Working much of the time in London, and driving a fairly high mileage, we started to look for ways of reducing our car mileage, with the rather vague idea that if everyone did the same, the need for new roads would be reduced and we'd all be happier.

The rail network, despite being ravaged by politicians of all shades, is generally competitive with car journeys between city centres, but what about those awkward journeys ten miles from the nearest railhead? I began sketching ideas for a personal transport machine on the back of an envelope. Some sort of bicycle seemed to fit the bill, but it would need to fold to go on trains and buses, be light enough to carry, and strong enough to transport one person and enough luggage for six weeks for maybe ten miles.

I didn't know it at the time, but I had sketched a Bickerton, a British invention of the 1960s and in many ways the granddaddy of the modern folding bike. The Bickerton was good enough, but it was wobbly and idiosyncratic to ride, and no doubt my invention would have been even wobblier. While leafing through *New Cyclist* (a new and vaguely avant-garde cycle magazine) early in 1991, I came across an advertisement for a neat and compact folding bike. I happened to be in London the following week, and called at Cyclecare Olympia, the shop that had placed the advertisement, and one of very few cycle shops stocking the Brompton at the time.

It turned out to be an amazing machine, and capable far beyond my wildest dreams. A bit heavy perhaps, but neat, easy to fold after a few trial runs, and eminently practical for rail commuting, with clip-on luggage that made light work of 10kg loads, and equipped with other sensible things like mudguards and lights.

I bought a Brompton on the spot and rode it the short distance to Kensington Olympia station, folding it behind a pillar to avoid any embarrassing folding faux pas. I still have that Brompton L3, although like a well-used vintage motor car, there aren't many original parts on it after 40,000 miles. That same night, I threw away the back-of-an-envelope sketches and became an enthusiastic Brompton owner. It was too good to be made in the Far East. Perhaps it was American? The brochure said Brentford. I popped out there a few weeks later, and instead of a distribution warehouse I found a couple of railway arches, a charming intellectual-looking chap, two men in blue overalls, and an office girl. At the time, that *was* Brompton Bicycle. If the product was so fantastic, why was the company so small? The world, it seemed, had yet to discover the Brompton, but eventually it did.

Within a year we had established The Folding Society, nominally a forum for all folding bikes, but built around our enthusiasm for the Brompton, and the folding bike club gradually grew with the bike manufacturer. By October 1993, the Folding Society had its own magazine, which became The Folder, and metamorphosed in August 1997 into *A to B* magazine. It was much the same - similarly tongue-in-cheek, but with a broader transport base, touching on bike carriage by rail, sea and air, and later electric bikes too, but always coming home to the folding bike concept.

Writing in 2024, I still edit A to B, and I still ride that original black L3 Brompton, and both have shaped my life. In a quarter of a century, Brompton has changed too, from a tiny workshop under a railway arch to a major British exporter, and one of the biggest industrial employers in West London. Back then, ownership of a Brompton was considered to be either absurd, or faintly elitist, depending on your point of view, but today the little bikes have become everyday transport for everyman and everywoman, and quite right too.

The Brompton really was years ahead of its time in 1991. Back then, most trains still offered luggage space, and the concept of folding bike commuting was a new and rather radical idea. Brompton fought for years to get cycle shops on side, and even longer to win round sceptical rail companies, but it all came right in the end. Transport operators are largely onside now, but space on trains, ferries and especially aircraft is in ever greater demand. We used to take Bromptons on the train for family holidays, but no more. The challenge to produce smaller and lighter bikes remains and Brompton continues to lead the field.

For me, this look back at the development, and ultimately the triumph, of the Brompton folding bicycle is something of a personal pilgrimage. I feel privileged to have met Andrew in the early days, and watched from the sidelines as the three employees become thousands, the turnover multi-millions, and the little folding bike a global icon.

David Henshaw 2024

A Short History of Folding Bikes

Top - An early spur to development of folding bikes was the concept of military use. Here pre-WWI French troops experiment with folding bikes. Their high command was said to be quite receptive to the idea, hoping the bikes would make troops more mobile in any forthcoming conflict.

Above - C.H. Clark's tiny-wheeler of 1919 reportedly spawned some folders in the US.

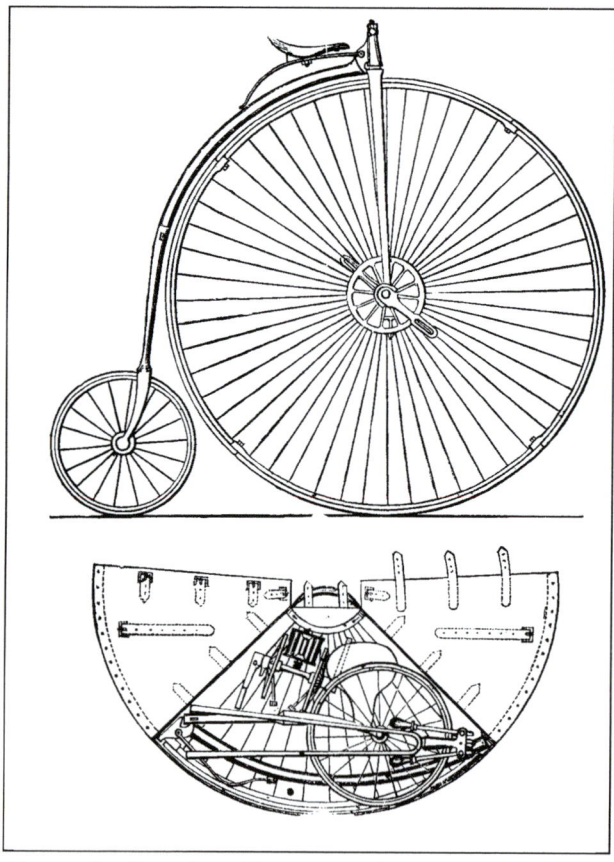

Above - the Grout Portable attempted to overcome the obstacle to folding that large wheels posed, with a front wheel that split down into four quadrants.

A Short History of Folding Bikes

"The idea of putting a bicycle into a bag is, indeed, a queer one, but of considerable value for all that, in these days of high railway charges."
Henry Sturmey 'The "Indispensable" Bicyclist's Handbook' 1881

The 19th Century to WWII

Folding bicycles (and indeed tricycles) have existed at various levels of sophistication since bicycles first appeared. The bicycle was a revolutionary machine in the late 19th century, but relatively cumbersome, and many inventors would try to reduce its size for transport or storage. When cyclists today talk about restrictions on carrying bicycles by train, they tend to treat this as a modern phenomenon, but bicycles were just as unwelcome aboard trains in Victorian times. In the mid-1880s, it typically cost a shilling (£4.90 today[1]) to carry a bicycle 50 miles by train, but in south-east England, the price could be twice that. To take a bike 250 miles by train could cost from 3 shillings and 6 pence to a whopping 7 shillings (£17.05 to £34.10 today[1]). Clearly, a Brompton would have paid for itself very quickly, had it been available!

Before the invention of the compact chain-driven 'safety' bicycle in the 1890s, bicycles had a huge driven wheel of anything up to 150cm in diameter. These 'high bicycles' (popularly known as penny-farthings) were big, heavy and awkward to transport.

A recurring theme with folding bikes is small wheels, because no matter how clever the folding mechanism, the final folded height can never be less than the diameter of the wheel. As the high bicycle was little taller than its enormous front wheel, the only way to produce a smaller package for transport was to 'fold' the wheel itself, something that was achieved in 1878 by one William Grout, inventor of the Grout Portable. The Grout was a clever design, the front wheel separating to produce four quadrants that packed together in a bag, together with the rear wheel, cranks, saddle, folded handlebars and frame. The latter split into two parts, which fitted neatly into the bag with everything else. Little is known about the Grout, not even its weight, which must have been considerable, but at £19 to £23 (£1,660 to £2,010 today[1]) - when a skilled craftsman earned less than £2 a week - it was expensive, and it took a claimed ten minutes to fold, probably a good deal longer in practice. It was not a success, and no examples are thought to survive.

In any event, the Grout Portable was rendered obsolete within a few years by the arrival of the safety bicycle. This innovation put the pedal cranks in the middle of the frame, linked to a relatively small back wheel by a chain or (rather less successfully) a belt. A 'safety' could be ridden just as fast as a high bicycle because the chain drive allowed higher gearing, so the same comfortable pedal speed would spin the back wheel faster, giving the advantages of a large wheel without the inconvenience. Much later, the same technique would be applied to even smaller wheels on ever more compact folding bikes, but in the 1880s the safety bicycle settled down with wheels of 26 to 30 inches in diameter, and was to remain more or less unchanged until the modern era. The remarkable longevity of the classic diamond-frame safety bicycle helps to explain why acceptance of small-wheeled folding bikes a century later was a little reluctant. The bicycle had hardly changed for four generations, making bicycle shops rather conservative establishments, but in reality the modern small-wheeled folding bike was simply a radical application of the 'safety' principles - that is, smaller wheels with more extreme gearing.

Small wheels took a long time to arrive, but manufacturers continued to experiment with folding frames, generally doing the obvious thing and putting a vertical hinge in the middle of the main frame tube, allowing the wheels to fold around and sit side-by-side. One of the first was the Faun, patented

[1] See text note on page 241

in 1896. This was quite a neat 'fold in half' design, producing an acceptably compact folded package that wouldn't look out of place on a commuter train today. But these early folders were expensive. The Faun cost 28 to 30 guineas (£3,070 to £3,290 today[1]), a considerable sum, making it accessible only to the very wealthy.

At the time, all bicycles were expensive, but within a few years, the price of a no-frills non-folding machine had tumbled, thanks to mass production and growing demand, although they remained expensive by modern standards. Folding bikes cost even more to make, and their limited sales made it difficult to realize the economies of scale available to manufacturers of simpler, cruder machines - nothing has changed! In the late Victorian era, a folding bicycle would have been extremely useful for a working man commuting by rail or tram, but the high prices meant they were only within reach for the wealthy, who generally had carriages - increasingly of the horseless variety - to get to and from the station. For these reasons, the market remained very limited.

By the early 20th century, the folding bicycle had become little more than a curiosity, though several attempts were made to revive the genre, principally for military use. In the days when soldiers slogged their way forward on foot, military theorists reasoned that a folding bike could be carried easily across rough ground, and unfolded for rapid advancement (and, of course, retreat) when the opportunity presented itself.

The most interesting machine of this type was the Dursley-Pedersen, produced by Mikael Pedersen, a Danish engineer who had settled in England. The Pedersen was constructed of a light, rigid lattice of steel tubes, with a suspended hammock-like seat. Most models didn't fold, but in 1900, at the height of the second Boer War, Pedersen introduced a separable version with a detachable front wheel and steering assembly. Sadly, it was ignored by the military top brass, and sold only fitfully to the public, before being withdrawn five years later.

With the demise of Pedersen's folder, the trail goes cold until the advent of the First World War, when armament (and bicycle) manufacturer BSA was instructed to produce a folding bike for military use. These were heavy, unsophisticated machines, folding in half around a vertical bar mid-frame. Quite how many went into service and how useful they proved in combat is not known, but BSA went on to produce another folding machine during the Second World War. This was a rather more elegant design, with twin curved frame tubes fitted with hinged joints mid-way, the joints being secured by wing-nuts. This time, the folding bicycle did at last seem to have found a genuinely useful role.

WWI saw folding bikes developed as (theoretically) a mobility aid on the battlefield, though those demonstrated on the left by the high-mobility Italian Bersaglieri corps appear more of a hindrance to quick movement when mounted on the back for carrying over rough terrain.

© www.oldbike.eu

[1] See text note on page 241

The unusual Pedersen (above) was aimed at Boer War troops but largely ignored by those in power.
The BSA (below) was most certainly used in WWII - but exactly how and where remains unclear.

According to military vehicle expert Colin Stevens, analysis of the serial numbers indicates that over 70,000 BSA folders were manufactured during the Second World War. Though often referred to as "parabikes" by collectors, this term more properly applies to a non-folding postwar model, sold to the public and trading on wartime mythology as a marketing tool - actual training manuals tended to refer to the original military folder as the "airborne bicycle".

Contemporary military instruction manuals show how the 'airborne' really did become airborne. Used independently of individual soldiers, the bikes could float to earth under their own mini-parachutes that were released in flight. Alternatively, and seemingly highly perilously, they could also be attached to the parachutist by suspension lines (see below left), and accompany him on his descent. The potential for serious injuries or worse from entanglement, or actually landing on the bike itself, don't seem to have been at the forefront of the military planners' minds.

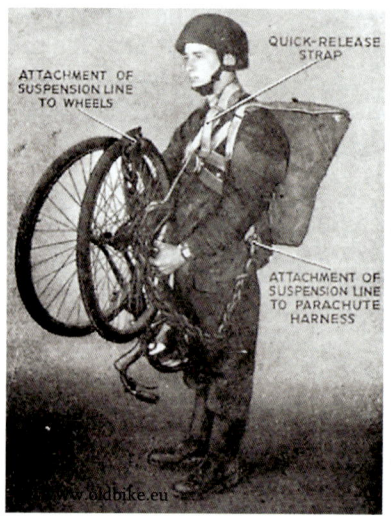

BSA's WWII 'airborne' folder certainly looked the part strapped to a parachutist (far left) or ridden in the 'drop zone' (near left.).

In reality many were hauled through the uninviting waters of the English Channel in the face of fierce German resistance - as the D-Day battle scene (left) shows. Here the folder's main advantage was to make best use of the storage space in the landing craft. Apparently many were abandoned within a few miles of going ashore.

Folding Bikes in the US - the 19th Century to WWII

The early history of folding bikes in the US appears to have been the realm of lone inventors and small-scale manufacturers rather than mass market orientated companies - despite the fact that the country was in the midst of a well-documented bicycle craze in the late 19th century. One of the largest early US manufacturers of bikes, the Pope Manufacturing Company, built nearly 50,000 bikes in 1881, yet seems to have totally overlooked folders.

And so it fell to an individual to introduce folders to America's bicycle hungry populace in the late 19th century. In 1893 Michael B. Ryan patented a folding bicycle and a New York Times entry from 1897 makes it clear the bicycles were already in very limited production; 'a decided novelty at the show was the display of military folding bicycles, made by the Dwyer Folding Bicycle Company of Danbury Conn...a ladies folding bicycle is also shown and will be sure to attract much attention from the women'. Despite the newspaper terming the bikes 'military', the US military seem to have shown little interest in folders at this time, in stark contrast to many contemporary European armed forces.

In 1919 Scientific American magazine featured 'a new model of bicycle invented by Mr C.H. Clark... whose wheels had apparently shrunk to the size of a dinner plate.' The bike was claimed to have held its own against conventional bikes in a New York City race, though reportedly losing some ground due to difficulty cornering. The tiny small-wheeler was taken in a lift into the offices of Scientific American. Although the bike didn't fold, a later, tantalisingly undated report on the 1919 article states 'One can still spot these "city bicycles" today, now made with the advantage of being able to be folded for easier storage.'

A photo from Scientific American in 1919 shows C.H. Clark's groundbreaking use of small wheels.

Around half a century after their first appearance in the US the military placed its first official order for folding bicycles - or more accurately demountables; in 1941 Westfield-Columbia Compax 'folding' bikes were delivered to a Paramarines training camp in Lakehurst, New Jersey.

With US-Japanese tension mounting, the Westfield-Columbia Manufacturing Company had seemingly foreseen a future need for a military folder and designed what the 1940 patent calls a 'collapsible bicycle'. As sales catalogues from the time make clear, the initial version of the Compax was aimed squarely at civilians who wanted all the advantages of a bike that packed down quickly, which the Compax (actually branded the Compax Sports Traveler for the non-military market) appears to have done. A single-bladed wing nut allowed the handlebars to swing down to one side of the frame whilst a wing-nutted collar held the two halves of the single mainframe together. Quick the process may have been, but the disassembled package appears to have lacked any means of holding the two halves together and adverts from the time show the two sections being carried separately. A single-speed rear hub featured coaster braking.

Though there are no recorded sales figures during peacetime for what was claimed to be 'America's first folding bicycle' it seems safe to assume - with an effective sales period of only six months before wartime austerity brought an end to such fripperies - that the figures were relatively small. The first urgent shipments of bikes to the military still bore the civilian paint job, but this was later changed and the spec beefed up to include balloon tyres amongst other things. Despite the Paramarines being the first to take delivery of the bikes there is no recorded evidence of them arriving in a war zone by parachute. Indeed, the exact use of US military folding bikes in action remains cloaked in mystery, despite the evidence suggesting the military took delivery of several large shipments.

The Compax was aimed initially at civilians, with marketing suggesting use in boats, buses and trains. However, true mass production only became feasible with large contracts to supply the military.

Post WWII - the Moulton Era

Clearly civilian folding bikes remained rare in the first half of the 20th century, and it was not until the 1960s, with the arrival of the Moulton, that the technology began to find its feet. Moultons are often described as folding bikes, but in fact Dr. Moulton never produced a folding machine. Most were completely rigid, although the Stowaway variant split in two with the application of an Allen key to a central joint. Even that was a car boot job, and certainly not the sort of thing you would carry on a commuter train or in a small boat.

Dr. Alex Moulton was an engineer specialising in automotive suspension, and as such, he did a great deal of work for British car manufacturers, principally developing rubber and rubber/gas suspensions. But his expertise in suspension technology also led Moulton to challenge the orthodoxy of the 26-inch wheel safety bicycle, reasoning that a bicycle with suspension could give an acceptable ride with wheels about half the normal size.

Why use small wheels if the bicycle was not to fold? There is a popular misconception that small-wheeled bicycles are wobbly, slow and hard to ride, but that is by no means always the case, and Moulton soon realized that smaller wheels brought a number of key advantages: the wheels were lighter, increasing acceleration and - assuming the bicycle had decent suspension - reducing unsprung weight, beneficial to both ride and handling. A small wheel also offered a smaller frontal area, reducing wind resistance, and the shorter spokes produced less turbulence, both factors making the bike easier to pedal at speed. And where most of a conventional bicycle is unusable dead space, a small-wheeled machine offered plenty of room front and rear for carrying luggage.

The downside of small wheels is increased tyre rolling resistance. There are two main reasons for this - smaller wheels tend to be deflected up and down on bumps and holes more than big wheels, producing energy-sapping vibration (this can be largely solved with suspension), and the sharper radius of the small tyres results in a greater degree of flexure where the tyre meets the road. Quite simply, the road is flat, and the tyre curved. As the tyre revolves it is continually being deformed and springing back into shape, flexure that absorbs quite a bit of energy. The smaller the wheel, the greater the deformation and the greater the loss of power. In a series of experiments, Dr. Moulton succeeded in minimizing this effect, chiefly by utilizing high tyre pressures, reducing the size of the 'flat' area where the tyre hits the road.

Using his considerable influence, Moulton persuaded Dunlop to develop improved high pressure bicycle tyres, and although he might not have realized it at the time, by choosing the existing 16" x 13/8" (ISO 37-349mm) tyre, Moulton had set the pattern for the future development of the folding bike. The 349mm tyre was primarily used on children's bikes, but, more or less by chance, it was close to ideal for use on a folding bike - small enough to produce a low folded package, but large enough to deal with potholes, particularly when aided by suspension, of course.

By the postwar period, bicycle tyre sizes, like many international standards, had developed into a haphazard mishmash of imperial and metric sizes. Traditionally tyre sizes were measured in either metric or imperial in terms of overall diameter and width, so a 16" x 13/8" would be roughly 16 inches tall by 13/8 inches wide (in practice most examples are closer to 17 inches tall).

However, this system tells us nothing about the rim diameter the tyre will fit, and by the 1950s, the bicycle tyre trade was collapsing into farce, with different countries offering different rims and different systems of measurement, so that an apparently over-size tyre might prove too small for a given wheel rim, and vice-versa.

It's a winner

Since its announcement in 1962, the Moulton has won four major design awards. The 1964 Design Centre award. A gold medal at the International Milan Triennale. The F. H. Bidlake Memorial Trophy. The Ambassador Award for achievement in industry. The Moulton has also won the day in the field of sport. It holds the Cardiff - London record of 6 hrs. 43 mins. at an average speed of 24 m.p.h. In 1965 Vic Nicholson riding a Moulton won fifteen major time trials.

You can take it anywhere

The Moulton Stowaway has a quick and simple dismantling action. It fits easily into any car boot (— even a Mini!). Campers and yachtsmen also find the Stowaway particularly useful for collecting provisions, etc. Flat dwellers can dismantle the bicycle and store it indoors.

There's no end to the uses of the Stowaway.

All images © Moulton Developments

Although the classic Moulton didn't fold, the Stowaway variant broke in two for carriage in a car boot, as above. This Stowaway version of the smaller Moulton Mini was the nearest Dr. Moulton ever came to producing a compact folding bike, but although it appeared in the 1967 brochure, it never went into production. Also note the bike is being placed in the boot of a Morris 1100 with Moulton Hydrolastic suspension

Some sanity arrived with the formation of the European Tyre & Rim Technical Organization, or ETRTO, in 1964. ETRTO introduced a metric 'bead seat diameter' system, which was later adopted by the International Standards Organization. The tyre code (sometimes described as ETRTO and sometimes ISO) classifies a tyre by its width, and the diameter between the two opposing sides of the 'bead' - the steel or nylon cables in the root of the tyre that secure it over the wheel rim. To prevent the tyre falling off, the ISO size is slightly smaller than the rim diameter, which is nominally 360mm on the Moulton or Brompton tyre. Dr. Moulton went on to develop an even better 17-inch (ETRTO 369mm) tyre in cooperation with Dunlop, based on a pre-existing tubular racing tyre, but this size remained something of an oddity, used only on Moulton bikes. It is for his work in proving and developing the 37-349mm tyre that Dr. Moulton will be remembered in the folding bicycle world.

The Moulton bicycles were extremely clever machines, giving a conventional riding position, improved performance (thanks to the inherent advantages of 16-inch wheels and suspension) and better load-carrying. There have been few transport revolutions quite as complete as the advancement (and subsequent retrenchment) of the Moulton bicycle in the 1960s. From a standing start in 1963, sales peaked at 1,000 a week in 1965, making Moulton the second biggest single brand cycle manufacturer in the country. Quite by chance, this radical 'mini' bicycle had caught the mood of the times, becoming as much an icon of the swinging '60s as the miniskirt and the mini car. The stratospheric sales curve caused utter panic among established manufacturers, still producing bicycles whose appearance and technology had changed little since Edwardian days. There followed a wild stampede to introduce rival small-wheelers, most of which were knocked out in a few weeks by unwilling draughtsmen, who knew little of the technological principles involved and - one suspects - cared less.

As Moulton had the patents on suspension, his rivals had to find other means of giving their bikes a compliant ride. Dawes chose a larger tyre size, opting initially for a wide, low-pressure

Despite its small wheels, the Moulton's clever design kept the riding position and much of the bike's geometry in a similar layout to the standard big wheelers - giving a reassuringly comfortable yet fast ride

The classic Moulton design (bottom right)- small wheels with their own unique suspension system, meaning plenty of luggage room front and rear. As with the later Brompton, car boot portability was seen as major selling point (right).

metric 500A tyre, of about 20 1/2 inches in diameter, with a bead seat diameter of 440mm. The Dawes Kingpin, launched in 1964, proved quite a successful machine, although only about 10% were true folders with hinged frames, the resulting package being arguably more cumbersome than the rigid bike. But although heavy and cumbersome, the Kingpin was well made, and stayed in production well into the 1980s. On some versions, such as the Newpin, Dawes used the British format 20" x 1 3/8", or 451mm tyre. Where the 349mm tyre was the ideal basis round which to build a compact folding bike, the 500A and 451mm sizes were particularly well suited to larger fold-in-half machines, and this general layout evolved into the standard folding bike of the 1960s and early '70s.

The Raleigh RSW Compact, illustrated in a Swiss retail catalogue from the time. Even in its folded form it occupies much of the Mercedes' capacious boot.

British bikes, such as the Raleigh 20 range, tended to use the 451, whereas European machines were typically fitted with 500A. Some export Raleigh 20s were fitted with the North American 406mm rim and the BMX craze later introduced this slightly smaller tyre to the UK. Subsequently most 20-inch wheel bikes have used the 406mm tyre. Unfortunately, most bikes of this type were heavy, undergeared and - lacking the Moulton's sophisticated geometry and suspension - hard work to ride. Increasingly produced in Eastern Europe and the Far East and sold through popular magazines, the 'shopper' turned a generation against folding bikes. When the Brompton arrived twenty years later, bicycle shops would - reasonably enough - argue with Andrew Ritchie, its designer, that if the 20-inch shopper was poor, logically his 16-inch machine would be even worse.

This jaundiced view was reinforced by Raleigh, which had actually been involved in the Moulton bicycle project in the early days, but pulled out prior to the launch. Desperate to get a bit of the small-wheel action, Raleigh developed a 16-inch Moulton-esque bicycle, known as the RSW16. To get round the suspension patent, the company opted for wide low pressure tyres, which gave a soft ride and appalling rolling resistance. Raleigh came to the party a bit late, launching the RSW16 in July 1965, but it spent £100,000 on publicity, and took many sales from Moulton. Like the Moulton, the original RSW16 didn't fold, but it was soon joined by the Compact variant, possibly the worst folding bike ever produced. The RSW Compact hinged upwards mid-frame, bringing the two wheels together, while the handlebars hinged down. Almost 100cm long when folded, it really was easier to transport when unfolded, especially when the sinew-challenging weight of 18kg (40lb) was taken into account. The RSW Compact was an absurd bike, but thanks to Raleigh's marketing muscle and national dealer network, it stayed in production until 1968, while the slightly more practical non-folding version was still available in 1974, albeit with slimmer tyres.

The cheap and cheerful 20-inch shopper bikes and dreary RSW did terrible damage to the reputation of small wheels. Within a few short years, all the good work done by Moulton had been undone, the folder becoming synonymous with shoddily made, short-range bicycles. The public soon forgot that Dr. Moulton's 16- and 17-inch machines held a number of speed and endurance records, some of which remain unbeaten to this day.

The public might have been put off, but the poor riding and folding performance of contemporary folding bikes brought about a number of new designs, all - interestingly enough - aimed at the car boot rather than rail commuter, cars being very much the modern thing in the late 1960s. One early example was the Newland, designed by engineering lecturer David Newland. He set out to produce a bike that would fit in the boot of a Mini and weigh around 9kg (20lb). In practice, the 'productionized' prototype built by Raleigh weighed 12.9kg (28$\frac{1}{2}$lb), but although it was ready for production by 1967, a downturn in small-wheeled sales, and Raleigh's subsequent purchase of Moulton, scuppered the project. As the Moulton itself had been extinguished within a few years, one gets the distinct impression that Raleigh was only interested in folding bikes to the extent of protecting its traditional territory. With the Moulton out of the way, Raleigh's big-wheel diamond-frame bicycles (and the Raleigh 20 fold-in-half machine) would not be seriously challenged for another twenty years. Although it didn't even reach production, the Newland is important in any history of the folding bike because it pointed the way to the future by folding in three places. Admittedly all the folds were in the same plane, so the resulting package was rather large at 127cm x 91cm x 33cm, with a volume of 381 litres (13$\frac{1}{2}$ cubic feet), but it is said to have folded and ridden well, despite diminutive 12-inch wheels.

The Bickerton

In the 1970s, the folding bike finally hit the big time in terms of sales, if not rideability, with the arrival of the Bickerton. Harry Bickerton was an aeronautical engineer who had learnt his craft squeezing horse-power out of the Spitfire's Rolls-Royce Merlin engine, and keeping the plane one step ahead of the Messerschmidt. It was arguably one of the most critical jobs undertaken by anyone in the Second World War.

After a varied post-war career, he found himself banned from driving in the late 1960s after an accident in Dorset. To help stay mobile, Harry bought a Puch Pic-Nic, a reasonably competent 20-inch shopper of the day, but he detested the machine, describing it as 'a heap of scrap iron'. Like all good engineers, he decided that he could do better, and set about designing himself a smaller, lighter bicycle that could be used to link or 'integrate' other forms of transport. The Bickerton didn't share many traits with the Merlin engine, but Harry's aeronautical background made itself felt in his use of light alloys, and bolts, dowels or resin bonding in place of welds. As so often before and since, this completely fresh approach to what a bicycle should do, and how it was made, was to yield some interesting results.

Like David Newland, Harry Bickerton aimed high with the specification - a bike that would fit in the boot of a Mini and weigh 8.2kg (18lbs). In the event, it satisfied the first requirement, but weighed a little more - 9.1kg in single-speed form, 10kg for a 3-speed version, and 10.4kg for the Sturmey 5-speed model. Like the Moulton, the Bickerton was built around the excellent 37-349mm tyre, or at least the back wheel was, the front being a smaller 14-inch tyre, also used by Dr. Moulton on his 7/8-size Mini Moulton range.

The Bickerton horrified conventional cyclists by flexing and wobbling like a jelly, but if you adopted a smooth riding technique it went quite well and could be ridden considerable distances. If you rode with gusto, something usually broke, as many riders found to their cost. Harry, who seems not to have minced his words, emphasized in an early brochure that the bike was, 'designed for intelligent, competent human beings - not gorillas'. For all its failings, the Bickerton folded into a compact package reasonably quickly and was lighter than anything that had come before. And so it was that Harry's driving ban kicked the folding bike industry into gear. The engineer had needed a machine light and compact enough to carry by bus and train, and his little bike pushed the technology far beyond its 'chuck in a car boot' brethren to achieve this.

Like many other folding bikes, the Bickerton had a single mainframe tube, although in this case, it was made of rectangular aluminium alloy rather than steel tube, with a folding joint roughly midway, allowing the rear wheel to fold around to meet the front wheel. Before this could be done, the handlebars had to be realigned by loosening four quick-release joints, allowing the grips to twist inwards and the whole assembly to turn through 90°, ending up sandwiched between the two wheels. Another quick-release allowed the saddle to be dropped, but if you really wanted a compact package, the saddle and pillar had to be removed and squidged in with the other bits.

There were several howling disadvantages to this arrangement. The frame and tall spindly handlebars flexed all over the place, and if you forgot to tighten any of the many joints and clips, you could end up in a heap on the ground. Unlike most folders, the oily chain was sandwiched between the frames when the bike was folded, but it still protruded far enough to smear the clothes and luggage of fellow travellers on the train. And as the frame halves and handlebars didn't clip into place, the bike was liable to unfold while being carried. The

Bickerton was launched in 1970, and sales grew rapidly, until the small company was producing more than 500 bikes a year. Still very small beer to the likes of Raleigh and Moulton, but respectable enough.

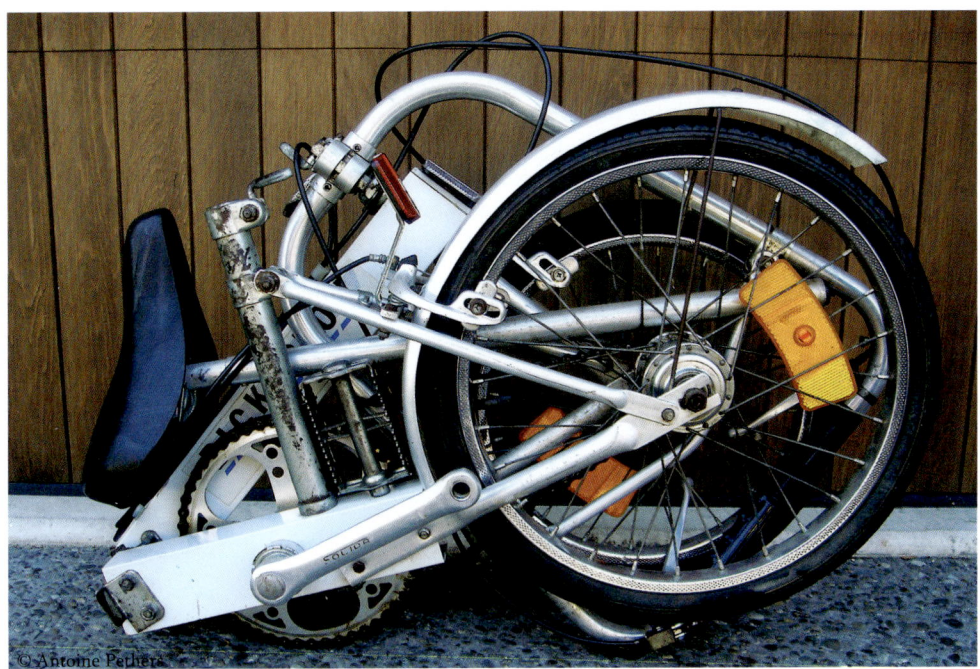

A Bickerton Classic - with its trademark huge handlebars and angular mainframe.
It folded down surprisingly compactly and quickly - certainly better than anything that had come before, and in this respect was groundbreaking.

In 1975, Bickerton licensed production to engineering company TCK, but in generally gloomy economic conditions, the new licence-holder went bankrupt just two years later in 1977. The rights were transferred once again to an Australian company, which went on to build another 50,000 bikes in the next few years, but in 1982, this company also got into difficulties, and being owed £60,000, Harry Bickerton took the rights back. The wheel then turned full circle, Harry Bickerton teaming up with his son Mark and former MD of TCK Steve Rowlinson to set up a folding bike factory of their own. The Bickerton-Rowlinson years were the most stable for the Bickerton, but it was by now an elderly machine, and after Harry's retirement in 1987, Mark found himself in control of a shrinking business selling a single ageing product, and surrounded by new and much better folding bikes.

Although the Brompton wasn't yet being manufactured in big numbers, it was very much on the scene, as was the cruder, but mass-market Dahon, fresh in from Taiwan. Mark responded by introducing the Bickerton Country, a larger, heavier variant, equipped, rather absurdly, with knobbly 406mm BMX tyres to appeal to a younger audience.

A Bickerton Californian - Bickerton effectively ditched the 'wobbly wonder' that was their original creation and went with the more rigidly engineered style of Dahon.

A Short History of Folding Bikes

All the Country succeeded in doing was ditching the Bickerton's only strengths, its compact size and light weight. In 1989, Mark Bickerton made a last desperate attempt to develop a completely new bike, teaming up with the National Engineering Laboratory in East Kilbride. The project got underway, but for various reasons, Mark decided to pull the plug before the bike went into production and the factory was closed in 1991. Bickerton-Rowlinson was already marketing a 'badge-engineered' Dahon model as the Bickerton Dahon (later the Californian). Badge-engineering - the production of a 'new' model by rebadging a machine made by someone else - was still rare, but it would become an increasingly common route for product-starved British manufacturers. Mark Bickerton went on to sell Klein mountain bikes for a few years, but came back to folding bikes in 1995 as Dahon's UK agent.

  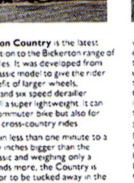 

The Bickerton Classic (left), was joined by the Country (right) in the late 1980s. Aimed at a younger off-road market, it added weight, but little else, to the original Bickerton design.

Dahon

There are probably more myths surrounding the Dahon than any other folding bike. From its first stirrings with the Grout Portable to the 1960s, the folding bike story had been a predominantly British affair. From the 1960s to the 1980s, European manufacturers had joined the party, mass-producing fold-in-half bikes in large numbers, but the Dahon was to turn the folding bicycle into a global phenomenon.

First, the myths: Dahon might be an anagram of Honda, but only by chance! It is actually a contraction of the name of David Hon, the founder of the company. Hon was a physicist working for the Hughes Aircraft Corporation in America, and a specialist in laser technology, with several patents to his name. He is also credited with designing the NASA moon buggy, which appears not to be true, although he certainly had some involvement with the moon landings, as part of the general mobilization of the US scientific community. Another myth has it that the Dahon is a US-made machine, but it has always been made in the Far East, the Stars & Stripes on the frame referring rather tenuously to the country in which it was designed.

The turning point for Dr. Hon came with the Arab oil embargo of the early 1970s, and the ensuing oil supply crisis that almost brought the car-based US transport system to its knees. Might a bicycle not offer an alternative? Not the heavy, bulky bicycles of Hon's youth, but light, foldable machines that could be carried by bus, train or car. Designing a prototype took several years, and it was not until 1982 in the wake of the second oil crisis provoked by the Iranian revolution, that Dr. Hon finally introduced a bike.

Hon had hoped to hand the design over to a manufacturer, but as with the Bickerton (and as we shall see, the Brompton), things didn't work out quite so smoothly, and he was shown the door by all the major bicycle manufacturers. Undaunted, Hon gathered together $3 million in venture capital backing and set up a factory in Taiwan to produce the bike himself, the first machines appearing in 1983, two years behind the Brompton, but in much greater numbers.

Dahon today produces an almost bewildering variety of bikes - but at the heart of most models is a mid-frame hinge dating back to Dahon's earliest designs - still no rival to the Brompton's compact 'fold-in-three'. Here are some of their more varied recent offerings:

* Helios SL - At 7.6kg claimed to be the 'lightest production line folder in the world' - at the time. In fact, the Panasonic Traincle was much lighter and produced in fair numbers for Japan.

* Curve - touted as a 16" wheeled, sub- 10kg competitor to the Brompton

* Cadenza - a fast 26" wheeled road bike

* Ciao - an easy to ride town bike, complete with rack and dynamo lights

* Jack - big tyres and rigid construction for town and trail

On the face of it, the Dahon was a simple fold-in-half bike, built around 16 x 1¾" (ISO 44-305mm) tyres. Although nominally 16 inches like the British 349mm, this was in reality closer to 15 inches in overall diameter, which helped to produce a lower folded package, but increased the rolling resistance of the tyres proportionately. Unlike the clumsy 20-inch fold-in-half bikes of the 1960s, the Dahon featured a folding handlebar stem, and was quite compact (if a little long) and easy to fold. Early models were quite heavy, but Hon and his team gradually refined the bikes, going on to produce around two million in 25 years and dominating the folding bike market.

Most Dahons have the trademark fold-in-half frame, in a variety of wheel sizes, from 305mm to full-size, but the company came to specialize in 20-inch (406mm)-wheeled bicycles. As well as producing its own machines, Dahon also developed (or in some cases, 'badge-engineered') bikes for other major bicycle manufacturers, while licensing its older technology to cut-price Far Eastern manufacturers. But we're jumping some years ahead of our story, because Dr. Hon was not the only inventor working on a folding bike in the 1970s. In London, the Brompton was already taking shape.

Getting Brompton Off the Ground These photos date from 1977 and were incorporated into a brochure aimed at corporate investors, rather than consumers.

The bike is one of the 16-inch wheel prototypes, P3 or P4. Although the cow horn handlebars and clunky frame hinge look ungainly, it's clearly a Brompton, especially when part- or fully-folded.

Getting Brompton Off the Ground
1973-1977

"The plastic seat sleeve was made of old drainpipe, because I couldn't afford a mould."
ANDREW RITCHIE

Personal Background

On 15th March 1947, in Newdigate, Surrey, Andrew Ritchie was born, the youngest of three children, after Caroline and Jamie. Although the Ritchies were in many ways an archetypical English upper middle class family, Andrew's mother Sybilla (better known as Moppy throughout her life) was German, with the added complication that his maternal great grandmother had been Australian. Mary Beauchamp (a cousin of writer Katherine Mansfield) had - rather improbably, but romantically - fallen in love with a Prussian aristocrat, Count Henning von Arnim, while undertaking the fashionable Italian tour with her father.

Mary married the Count in 1891, and Elizabeth von Arnim, as she became known, went on to become a successful author, publishing a string of titles in the early years of the 20th century. The couple had five children, the third of whom (sometimes referred to as 'the April Baby') was Andrew Ritchie's grandmother.

Continuing in this rather exotic vein, Elizabeth later had an affair with H G Wells, and after the Count died in 1910, went on to marry John Francis Stanley Russell, the 2nd Earl Russell (and elder brother of Bertrand Russell), before fleeing to America from what seems to have been a deeply unhappy marriage.

Andrew's father, William (Bill), came from an equally interesting line. His grandfather Charles Thomas Ritchie was Scottish, and held high office in the Conservative government of 1900-1905, first as Home Secretary, then - from 1903-1905 - as Chancellor of the Exchequer. He is best known for introducing to parliament the Local Government Act, which established the County Council administrative system. He was made a peer when the government resigned in 1905, but sadly lived only another few days. Charles' brother, Alderman Sir James Thomson Ritchie, became Lord Mayor of London in 1903.

With characteristic precision (and indeed modesty), Andrew Ritchie simply describes himself as 3/8ths German, half English and 1/8th Australian, "quite a mixture". Whether the Scottish political nous, German aristocratic blood, and artistic flair of these forebears have had any influence on the engineering of the folding bicycle is a matter for conjecture!

Set against the flamboyance of the Edwardian literary set, Andrew Ritchie's father Bill Ritchie seems to have led a quiet and respectable life as an area manager for Barclays Bank, before joining stockbroker Galloway & Pearson as an analyst. Home life for the children followed a comfortably Betjemanesque pattern of parties, rugger matches and public school. For an intelligent young man from his social class, Cambridge University was more or less an assumption, and Andrew graduated in 1968 with a 2.1 Degree in Mechanical Sciences. At this time, engineering as a career was hardly a sexy option, and many of Ritchie's contemporaries (including Tim Guinness, who was later to play a pivotal role in the Brompton story) opted for jobs in the financial world, while the more adventurous chose the embryonic field of computing, the path taken by Andrew Ritchie.

In the late 1960s, of course, computers were very large, very expensive and fiendishly difficult to programme and operate. But the computer world was at the cutting edge of Harold Wilson's 'white heat of technology', and for a young engineering graduate of the day, arguably the engineering of the future.

Ritchie soon found himself in Borehamwood, Hertfordshire, working for Elliott Automation, a company that produced computers and computer programmes, mainly for government, the table-sized machines performing a variety of roles, including air traffic control and - with advancing miniaturization - avionics and military applications. By modern standards, where millions of transistors can be printed on a wafer the size of the proverbial pin head - these were clunking great machines, with laughably modest computing power, typically 16kb of memory at the time Andrew Ritchie joined the firm.

Trained in a rather different discipline, Andrew spent the first eight months getting to grips with the architecture and structure of the computer, time that seemed wasted to an ambitious youngster, but the exercise no doubt served to refine an already logical and analytical mind. With computers being such a new field, Elliott Automation was a little unsure how to recruit potential programmers, and what to do with potential recruits once it had found them. Some bright spark in the personnel department ("ex-army, affable, and pretty useless," according to Ritchie), came up with the idea of sending the young graduates to Colchester Technical College to study metal working for four months.

One might assume that a Cambridge graduate engineer would know all there was to know about engineering, but - in those days at least - graduates were sent out into the world with only the barest of practical skills, such as welding and lathe work. Graduates like Ritchie were the young technocrats who would design the roads, bridges and turbocharged boys' toys of the Thunderbirds era. They knew plenty about the theory of engineering - thermodynamics, the stresses and strains imposed on structures, and the behaviour of materials - but virtually nothing about the practice of metal-bashing.

And so it was, quite by chance, that Elliott Automation not only gave Andrew Ritchie a grounding in computers, but some essential 'hands on' mechanical skills. He could never have guessed it at the time, but these apparently unconnected multi-layered skills - engineering design, computer design, and practical metal bashing - were to serve him well in later years.

Ritchie seems to have enjoyed himself at Colchester, sharing a house with two Cambridge friends sent on the course by their respective employers, one of whom was Marcus Agius, an engineer destined to take the commercial route to fame and fortune, winding up as chairman of Barclays Bank.

Back at Borehamwood, Ritchie soon got itchy feet, and moved to Engineering Solutions, a software development company based in Croydon. The cold logic of software design seems to have suited him, and he soon became immersed in the development of an automated drawing machine for the civil engineering industry. Today, a £50 laser printer attached to a home PC could do the same job in a few seconds, albeit on a smaller scale, but for the chunky 16kb mainframes of the late 1960s, the idea was somewhat ahead of its time. Despite writing everything in basic machine code rather than memory-hungry high level language, and wrestling with the task for eighteen months, Ritchie left the company without producing a workable program, a rare failure that still rankles today. At the time, 32kb machines were just appearing, but to use something so sophisticated in a drawing machine would not have been economic. The episode might appear to have been a dead end, but after the high-flying theory of Cambridge, and 'money no object' government projects at Elliott Automation, the period at Engineering Solutions was Ritchie's first brush with the economics of the market place. For the first time, he had worked with the constraints of cost very much in mind. His next move was to take him even further down the entrepreneurial road.

Getting Brompton off the Ground 1973-1977

The Pot Plant Era

Quite why some people settle into a steady career, while others exhibit a certain restlessness, is not always clear. Andrew Ritchie had shown a flair for engineering design, but chose to move into computers; he had a talent for computer programming, but moved into the world of commerce.

At the age of 24, Ritchie left the computer industry, never to return, choosing instead to sell pot plants door-to-door. Why would anyone with such marketable skills opt for a career that many less qualified people could have mastered? After three years in large organizations, Ritchie seems to have felt the need for some independence, and he had been seduced by the profit potential, intrigued that a plant bought for £1 at 5am in Covent Garden could be sold a few hours later for £2 in Putney. It seemed like money for old rope, but perhaps only a Cambridge graduate engineer could have been naive enough to think that the world of market trading could be that simple.

With a Morris Minor van, Ritchie would drive to Covent Garden every morning, then west against the commuter flow, to "flog the plants to pretty housewives in Wimbledon, Putney and Barnes". Initially, Ritchie worked single-handedly with a single van, but with an injection of £3,000 of capital from his friend Tim Guinness, now doing rather well in the financial world, London House Plants briefly flourished. Within a couple of years the company had a fleet of five ex-GPO vans, and more than a dozen employees:

"I'd get up at 4.30am every morning to go to the market, then armed with a peddler's licence, hawk plants to the housewives of Barnes and Wimbledon. Then one thing led to another. Somebody said, 'Could you do a lawn?' I hadn't a clue how to lay turf or put up a trellis, but we ended up creating some biggish London gardens, doing displays in hotels and looking after pot-plants for all sorts of people, including the great and good of the day. There was plenty of opportunity."

1975: Andrew Ritchie and Tim Guinness with one of the ex-GPO London House Plants vans

21

But London House Plants was hardly marketing a unique product, and despite boundless youthful enthusiasm, Andrew seems to have rather lost interest in the scheme as his fertile mind began to burst with new and more exciting ideas. After four years ("chaos" according to Ritchie), the goodwill was sold off for next to nothing, Tim Guinness got most of his £3,000 back and London House Plants melted quietly away. But the retail experience had added another crucial talent to Ritchie's growing range of abilities, and by this time he was thinking much bigger thoughts.

At its height, the houseplant company had spawned a retail shop in Dawes Road, Fulham, and most days Ritchie would share a lunchtime pint with his friend and landlord Robert Newall, owner of a printing works in the same premises. Despite a brief flirtation with motorcycling, Andrew was a regular cyclist, the germ - as for so many graduates - being planted during his university days. One lunchtime the talk turned to bicycles: "Wouldn't it be wonderful if you had a bike which went with you wherever you wanted to go?", said Ritchie. This was in about 1973. It was the sort of light pub chatter that is soon forgotten, but Ritchie didn't forget, and his thoughts began to turn towards the problems of bicycle storage and use.

Other ideas came and went as London House Plants ran its course. One was an idea for a thermostatic shower mixer tap, something quite common today, but a leap of the imagination then. Ritchie decided that there were too many technical issues, and in any event, most people were perfectly happy with the ordinary mixer design, but the bicycle idea was to come back into focus after a chance meeting.

The Brompton Takes Shape

At this time, in 1975, Andrew's father Bill was working for city stockbrokers Galloway & Pearson, and it was there that he was approached by Bill Ingram, an Australian who had become involved with the Bickertons. Harry Bickerton was still building small numbers of folding bikes from a garage in Welwyn Garden City, and Bill, who was captivated by the principle of a portable bike, was trying to raise capital to expand the business. It's not entirely clear how he ended up at Bill Ritchie's door, but nevertheless, he did, and Bill Ritchie suggested a meeting with his son. We can't be sure quite how and why Ritchie senior thought Andrew's input would be helpful. His son was interested in engineering, and at something of a loose end at the time. In any event, it was to be a fateful meeting:

"Bill Ingram fetched up at my flat in 1975 with a Bickerton under his arm, and I thought on the one hand, 'Wow! Here's somebody who's done something about it', and then, 'Gosh, that's not a particularly clever approach'. After a chat, Bill went, but it seems we had established something of a rapport, because later he said, 'Do you think I should back you, with your intellect, and a foetal idea which doesn't even exist, or Harry Bickerton who's actually got a concrete thing, which works, and is there? Which way do I jump?'"

Ingram decided to go with the faintly Heath Robinson folding bike he knew, rather than back an enthusiastic young engineer who had yet to demonstrate a workable design. It was an understandable decision, but it turned out to be a big mistake. Even as the Australian left the flat above the Brompton Road, Ritchie was, unwittingly, embarking on what was to be a lifetime career. A folding bicycle seemed to be the ideal project: he recognised that he worked well on his own, and a folding bicycle was a modest enough undertaking to be managed by one person, rather than a team of engineers. Designing a folding bike would give him the independence he cherished, and make good use of the various skills he had acquired during his short, but peripatetic working career.

Andrew Ritchie was now 28, and convinced that he had at last found his niche. He scribbled down a few notes. Four things, he wrote, unavoidably have to stick out from a bicycle: the front wheel, back wheel, handlebars and saddle. The task was to fold these elements down quickly, safely and repeatably. This apparently straightforward problem had exercised some formidable minds, but for all sorts of reasons, Andrew Ritchie seems to have been the ideal man to finally solve it.

He immediately dismissed the long-established fold-in-half option, because it only partially solved the four folding objectives. A design where all four elements came into the middle made a lot more sense, but the key folding breakthroughs would take some time to arrive.

The first problem was money. London House Plants was still alive, working out a few long-term contracts in the hands of Tim Guinness's wife Beverley, but Ritchie would need backers if he was to spend months, or perhaps years, designing a folding bicycle from scratch. He talked the options through with a few friends, and one, Richard Goode, agreed to undertake a whip round among their mutual friends, persuading ten fledgling shareholders to put up £100 apiece. The long-suffering Tim Guinness was given an opportunity to come on board, but this time - in the nicest possible way - he refused to invest any money himself, and although the pair were to remain close friends, he was to have no further involvement in Brompton for nearly a quarter of a century: "I said to Andrew, 'You're not a businessman!'", Guinness later recalled, "and I think he agreed. That's why his plan was just to develop the prototype Brompton, outsource it and receive a royalty."

The directors of the company were Andrew Ritchie, Ritchie Senior, Richard Goode, George Brooksbank of Debenhams and Robert Woods (later a CBE and Chief Executive of P&O).

The ten shareholders would later be joined by two more, and in time Andrew would return to the group to call in another couple of thousand pounds, but the trust of those first ten backers was instrumental in getting the project off the ground. It helped, of course, that Ritchie had some fairly well-off friends with an investment philosophy and ready cash to risk a punt.

The prospectus, grandly entitled 'A Project for the Development of an Advanced Folding Bicycle' also included an early drawing of the Brompton design, sadly undated, but probably produced in early 1976. This sketch is interesting because it demonstrates the depth of detail Andrew had already put into the design. Although superficially very different to the Brompton, it included a few key features that would survive into production.

The bicycle was expected to have 18-inch wheels (although Ritchie suggested that more common 20-inch wheels would be feasible, if bulkier) and a 104cm wheelbase, which was pretty much as it ended up. By contrast, weight, with aluminium construction, was projected at 15 to 20lb (6.8 - 9.1kg), which represented a considerable degree of wishful thinking.

The handlebars and seat pillar were both to have telescopic sections, so as to reduce their height for folding, the collapsed pillar then folding forwards, and the front bars folding sideways to sit alongside the front wheel, a feature that would survive, as would the Moulton-style rubber block suspension, on the back at least.

Folding was interesting. The rear wheel would hinge forward to nestle between twin mainframe tubes, a trick made possible by lifting the bottom bracket bearing up and out of the way as the seat pillar folded. The front wheel/fork assembly was fitted with an angled (or asymmetrical) hinge, to fold under and back alongside its partner, with the folded handlebars on the outside. The various elements, including the bottom bracket, would be spring-loaded into the closed position and linked by a steel 'Bowden' cable, so that raising the seat pillar would cause everything to pop into place, and lowering it would (rather alarmingly) cause everything to collapse, including the rear rack, which folded neatly in from behind.

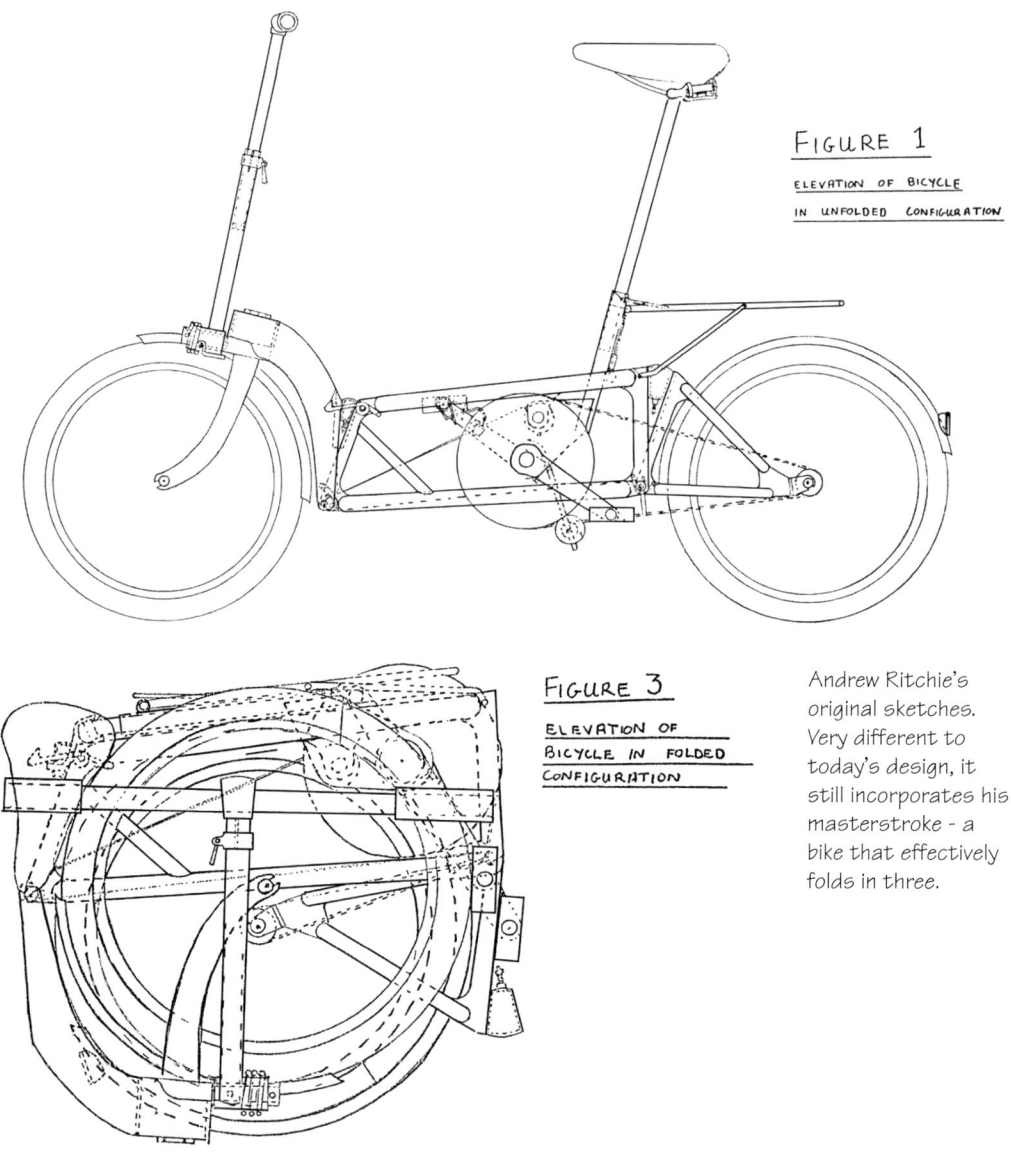

Andrew Ritchie's original sketches. Very different to today's design, it still incorporates his masterstroke - a bike that effectively folds in three.

Unlike the basic fold-in-half bikes of the day, this was, in effect, a bike that folded in three equal portions rather than two, and this means of reducing the length of the folded package was to be Ritchie's first masterstroke.

There wasn't enough money to fund even the most basic premises to build this machine, but with some rudimentary tools, Andrew began work on the first prototype in his flat. Stories about the man who designed and built a folding bicycle in his bedroom soon spread amongst friends and acquaintances. According to one early shareholder, Andrew allowed a mutual friend to take girls back to the flat when he wasn't at home, and on one memorable occasion a young lady fled in horror after discovering metal swarf in the bed!

The first prototype bicycle, P1, seems to have come together quite quickly. It was similar to the drawing, but differed in some key respects. The neat one-piece handlebar/stem assembly had been replaced with clever, but complicated, 'cow horn' bars that folded down either side of the front wheel. The front wheel assembly was similar to the drawing, folding under with an asymmetrical hinge to place the wheel alongside the frame tube, while the rear wheel folded under, but it now came up below a single large mainframe tube, rather than fitting between two thinner tubes, a crucial step forward.

The proposed Bowden cables survived onto P1, pulling the various elements apart when the seat pillar was raised, but it soon became clear that the idea was a non-starter: "...the cables broke pretty quickly under the considerable loads. I rode it a few times, but it was pretty wobbly! It eventually went into a skip." With the folding elements now falling more easily to hand, the need for the weight and complication of the cables was already looking questionable. It was one of those ideas that looked obvious on paper, but worked less well when translated into hardware. The idea was to make a reappearance on the Bike Friday Tikit, but only with respect to the simpler function of locking the handlebar stem clamp when the rear wheel was unfolded. With its big 18-inch wheels, the prototype was not yet obviously a linear ancestor of the Brompton, and it was heavier, but it was inching in the right direction.

On the second prototype, P2, the front end was completely redesigned, the suspension and skewed horizontal hinge being replaced with a vertical hinge, allowing the wheel to fold sideways to nestle against the mainframe. The handlebars were much simpler, but still rather ungainly, comprising two tubes which folded down either side of the front wheel. The steel cables had gone, and in most other respects, it was now looking quite Brompton-like.

One innovation was to become a quintessential Brompton feature. Instead of tipping forwards to fold, the seat pillar now telescoped straight down behind the folded rear frame, automatically locking the folded package together.

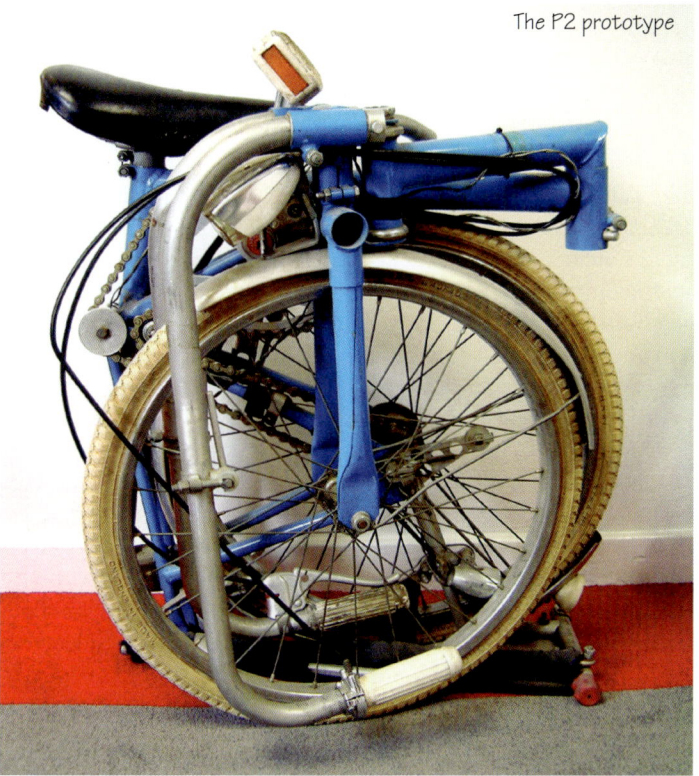

The P2 prototype

The rack was now firmly attached to the rear frame, and a nice touch was a couple of spring-loaded rollers from which two panels of cloth could be drawn up to enclose the folded package.

Quite when the Brompton name evolved is unclear, but Ritchie chose it because his flat was situated in the Brompton district of West London, with an eagle's eyrie view up and down the Cromwell Road and across to the Brompton Oratory. A mile or two east or west and the machine could have become the Kensington, the Belgravia, or even the Pimlico. Brompton - by pure chance - was an inspired choice. It had a timeless British ring to it, but without the implied snobbery of better-known West London addresses. It was smart, yet workaday. Ideal for a folding bike designed to appeal to everyday users.

The Brompton company was formally established in June 1976, registered to an address in Bowerdean Street, London SW6. Andrew Ritchie signed away his rights to the design in exchange for two thousand £1 Ordinary shares in the new company, a holding big enough to give him a controlling interest.

Even without the Bowden cables, the Brompton remained a complex design, but Ritchie set about refining and simplifying the machine, producing two more prototypes in his bedroom workshop by 1977. There were still many detail differences from the modern Brompton, but in terms of geometry and function, the identical prototypes P3 and P4 were effectively much the same as today's machine. The final crucial element was that both were built around the smaller 16-inch (349mm) tyre size, enabling the bike to pack even smaller, without compromising the wheelbase.

The company filed a provisional patent in 1976, and was granted a full British patent on 6th May 1977, the drawings showing a bicycle identifiably similar to the final product, with two important omissions: the handlebars still separated and folded down either side of the front wheel, and the front wheel still pivoted right around until it faced backwards, lying alongside the rear wheel, much the same as P2. But most of the other features were there: the rear wheel that folded under the frame, the rear suspension, the seat pillar locking the package together, and the chain tensioner taking up slack as the bike folded. These elements were successfully safeguarded in the 1977 patent, plus one or two other Brompton trademarks, including the rear rack that became a 'stand' under the bike when folded.

The design process had taken two and a half years, from conception to practical reality, and arguably could not have happened without the unique range of skills Andrew Ritchie had picked up in the preceding decade. He had produced a timeless classic, and from the reaction of friends and strangers alike, it was a consumer product that would take little selling. He could never have guessed that the battle to commercialise the bike was to be far more challenging.

Cold-shouldered by Industry

The board of Brompton Bicycle was split on the question of whether to establish a factory to build bicycles, or simply sell the design to an established manufacturer. The two big corporation men, Brooksbank and Woods, rather fancied the idea of setting up a small manufacturing plant as a diversion from the day-to-day tedium of running big business. The more pragmatic Richard Goode argued that it would be less risky, and more logical to pay Andrew to use his skills to design it, and put together a prototype or two to demonstrate the principles to a third party manufacturer with the tooling, financial muscle and skills to put the machine into production. The board would then sign a licensing agreement, and enjoy a steady flow of royalty payments as reward for setting the enterprise in motion.

It might have sounded a logical and sensible scenario, but for all sorts of reasons, it just wasn't going to work. British industry was going through hard times in the mid-1970s, and although one or two innovative products were inching into production, manufacturers were extremely wary. Lotus engineer Ron Hickman had developed the Workmate - a folding workstand with integral clamps - but his attempts to licence the product to either Stanley or Black & Decker had failed. It was only after Ron had found the capital to put the Workmate into limited production himself that Black & Decker eventually courted him, mass-producing the product from 1973, and ultimately turning Ron into a millionaire. Even for such an obvious and intuitive DIY product, targeted precisely at Black & Decker's existing customer base, getting the manufacturer on side

Getting Brompton off the Ground 1973-1977

The early Bromptons - P2, in blue, retains the 18-inch wheels and Bickerton-style handlebars, but the green P3 (top right) is much more Brompton-like, with 16-inch wheels. The only key elements still to be developed are the one-piece fold-down handlebars and the final piece in the puzzle, the geometry that enabled the front wheel to keep pointing forwards while the bike was folded - elements shown on the Mark 1 and Mark 2 bikes in red and black respectively.

had been an epic struggle. And bicycles were very much yesterday's news in the 1970s. The Moulton had injected some excitement into the genre a decade before (and briefly made small wheels respectable too), but it had peaked early and was now on the point of disappearing altogether.

In many ways, the Brompton was ahead of its time. Car boots were still reasonably cavernous, air travel far from commonplace, trains had guards vans, and bicycle theft was nowhere near as widespread or as sophisticated as it is today. Andrew Ritchie would be the first to admit that he was no salesman, leaving the Brompton to sell itself, rather than making a pitch to enthuse reluctant investors. But in 1977 even the most enthusiastic salesperson would have had trouble conjuring up an image of ranks of commuters unfolding their bikes at London Bridge station and riding into the city. A quarter of a century later it became fact, but in 1977 it would have been very hard to imagine such a scenario.

Several potential manufacturers reacted positively to Andrew's demonstrations but none were willing to offer backing or to build the bike under licence. The key targets were Raleigh - then still the British cycle industry's biggest brand - Dawes, another household name, and Black & Decker - not an obvious choice product-wise, but a company that had demonstrated innovation by championing the Workmate, albeit rather grudgingly.

Ritchie first contacted I H Phillips, the then Managing Director of Raleigh on February 8th 1977, offering to 'demonstrate and discuss the product'. The letter was duly passed to the desk of Mr A P Oakley, the Design Director, but Oakley was on an overseas tour and did not consider the offer until early March. It was not until Friday 1st April that Ritchie actually travelled up to Nottingham, demonstrated the prototype, and left it with the Raleigh engineers for a two-week examination. On the following Monday he wrote offering a few additional thoughts for Raleigh to digest, including the rather far-sighted observation that a battery-powered version might be feasible. This prediction might have seemed somewhat far-fetched in 1977, before the principle of electrically-assisted bicycles had even become enshrined in law, but again, it was to come true.

In due course, the prototype was returned to London, followed by a rejection letter on 21st April. According to Mr Oakley, the rejection was made on two counts: the Brompton would 'require a considerable degree of redesign', and - more damningly - Raleigh was 'not convinced that the device could open up a market of sufficiently high volume at the price it would have to be sold at.'

This caution might have been influenced by Raleigh's unhappy entanglement with Moulton. The manufacturer had initially rejected the design, then watched in horror as Dr. Moulton went it alone, taking a large slice of the declining bicycle market. Raleigh had then tried to spoil the market with its own inferior small-wheeler, and finally bought Moulton out, eventually phasing the machine out of existence.

In 1977, this expensive and troublesome foray into small wheels was still fresh in the minds of Raleigh's sales and marketing executives. Of course, by rejecting the Brompton, there was always the risk that Ritchie, or one of Raleigh's competitors, would do exactly what Moulton had done and swamp the market with an innovative new design. Mr Oakley must have been absolutely convinced that the Brompton had no widescale commercial merit whatsoever.

Interestingly, Andrew had approached Dr. Moulton while building the prototypes, and Moulton had been interested enough to make the long trek up from Bradford-upon-Avon to have a look. It must have been quite a meeting, the chauffeur-driven Bentley purring up to the pavement, and the guru of small wheels stepping out, and climbing the long flight of stairs to the flat where the young engineer was working on one of the prototypes. According to Dr. Moulton, Andrew asked straight out if he would consider building it, to which the reply was a flat "No". At this time, long after selling out to Raleigh, Moulton no longer had suitable production facilities, although he was considering going back into small-scale manufacture himself, the spaceframe AM series Moulton being launched a few years later. Both men were highly motivated, skilled engineers, but apart from the wheel size, their design philosophies were quite different. "I wouldn't have done it that way", says Moulton, "but I said, 'go on with it and do it yourself'. In no way did I discourage him from doing it." The two were not to meet again for some years, but they seem to have developed a mutual - if rather wary - respect.

With a growing pile of rejection letters, Andrew Ritchie started to consider small-scale production along the lines suggested by Brooksbank and Woods. This resulted in a split among the Brompton board, and as they (and indeed most of the other shareholders) were close friends, Richard Goode decided the best course of action was to resign, but he stayed close to Brompton, and remained a shareholder.

The plan now was to get enough venture capital behind the project to start production. After approaching several other firms, Brompton Bicycle began negotiations with venture capitalists ICFC (now known as 3Is), who eventually found some potential investors in Jersey. As the talks dragged on, Andrew stopped work on the project and took a delivery job with courier firm Fleet Street Flyers, using one of the old London House Plant delivery vans. He kept a bicycle in the back to reach congested parts of the city: "Whenever I had a run through Soho, I would just park the van - parking wasn't quite so onerous then - pop the bike out and do the errands while one's peers were still floundering in a traffic jam!" He was driving the van through Mayfair when the fateful message came through that after 18 months of negotiation, the ICFC deal had finally collapsed, and he was right back where he had started.

It was a major blow, but Andrew went back to work on the project, and in quite a short space of time made the final and decisive changes to the Brompton. The breakthrough was to re-engineer the fold so that the front wheel folded back on itself by pivoting around the headset bearings as the frame hinged back.

This was a brilliant bit of lateral thinking. The head bearings were already there, so there was no extra weight or complication involved, and the concertina-style double fold reduced the distance the wheel folded back, while increasing the distance it folded out.

© Brompton Bicycle Ltd

This eliminated the offset rear hinge, because the front wheel would now fit neatly against a centrally positioned rear wheel. The double fold also allowed the frame hinge to be moved back, reducing the length of the folded bike.

The final element in the Brompton design was the unique 'hinge, swivel and hook' system, where the front wheel kept pointing forwards instead of turning to face backwards, as it had done on the fold-in-half machines. It was a masterstroke - the front wheel now nestled comfortably against the rear wheel, with the chain sandwiched between the two, and the handlebars clipped against the outside.

The next logical move was to eliminate all the Bickerton-style quick-releases from the handlebars, put a single hinge at the base of the handlebar stem at 45° to the front wheel and fit a rigid bar/stem assembly that folded down against the outside of the front wheel. This made the package lighter, simpler and more compact. The skewed handlebar stem hinge was later patented in America by Dr. David Hon, although Andrew's early drawings seem to confirm that he had thought through this innovation first.

More or less by chance ("Careful design and good luck!", according to Ritchie), it emerged that the double fold and cantilevered handlebars suited the 16 x 13/8" tyre size almost perfectly. With frame elements scaled to suit a typical adult (not a tall one, but this would come later), the bike now folded down into a package little larger than its wheels and well under 30cm across. The folded Brompton had shrunk to a size that no-one had previously imagined possible, but without compromising the weight or strength of the bike.

"My heart sank in 1979 after the ICFC failure", said Ritchie, "but it was one of the best things that could have happened to Brompton. If I had got an institutional investor behind me and proceeded with an ill-thought through product, it would have sunk without trace." In the event, those few crucial extra months of design work had made all the difference.

Barring a few detail design changes, the Brompton was now equipped with all the innovations that would make it such a unique, practical and long-lived commercial product. It folded quickly and easily into a tiny package. Once folded, it was safe and clean to manoeuvre, as the chain and sprockets were on the inside, shielded between the wheels. Unfolded, the wheelbase was a generous 102cm - not quite up to conventional full-size bike standards, but almost miraculous from something that seconds before had been so small. The Brompton was more conjuring trick than folder, yet the generous wheelbase and rear suspension gave it excellent ride characteristics too. It was an engineering classic, but would it ever be built?

Steve Grosvenor's wife, Frances, demonstrates rather elegantly one of the keys to Brompton's success: portability. Whilst some subsequent folding bike designs were lighter or even folded to a smaller package, few were easy to carry when folded.

Getting Brompton off the Ground 1973-1977

The first Bromptons were born partly out of a perceived need to combine bike use with cars - indeed Andrew Ritchie's business plans emphasised this as a more ready market than coach and train travellers.
As these early publicity photos demonstrate, the Mark 1 Brompton coped well in both situations. As it happened, neither car boots nor coaches were to be as important as the bike/rail commuter market. While Andrew Ritchie does the folding, the bike is carried and ridden by Frances Grosvenor.

Going it Alone and the Mark 1 Bike Though the original plan was to sell the Brompton idea to a large scale manufacturer, inventor Andrew Ritchie found himself taking the lead role in producing the bikes almost single-handedly. It seems this was a stroke of luck, for in the process he was able to iron out initial weaknesses, ensuring the bike stood up well to the stresses and strains of daily use.

Going it Alone and the Mark 1 Bike
1978-1983

Brompton Goes it Alone

In 1978, while searching for capital and expertise to get the Brompton project underway, Andrew had been recommended to visit Lawrence-Tune, a company that built racy car conversions from premises in Ravenscourt Arches, Hammersmith, a few miles west of Brompton. The company wasn't able to help, but Andrew became friendly with Lawrence-Tune engineer Tim Reeve, a chance meeting that would prove significant later on.

If the mid-70s wasn't a very good time for launching a bicycle, it was a rotten time for selling souped-up sports cars. After the OPEC oil embargo of 1973-74, the writing was on the wall for firms like Lawrence-Tune, and soon after Andrew Ritchie arrived at the door, Chris Lawrence closed the business and started again in California, where he initially did rather well, trading as Lawrence-Tune West Inc.

Meanwhile, several of the bright young team of British engineers decided to branch out on their own. Tim Reeve and Steve Grosvenor set up an engineering design business in Barleymow Passage, Chiswick, while Nick Ouroussoff established an engineering workshop in nearby Kew. Ouroussoff was a designer too, but he had ended up with enough space to build things, and as the two companies often worked closely together, Grosvenor-Reeve tended to do the design and Nick Ouroussoff the engineering. These small West London engineering works were to play a significant role in getting Brompton off the ground.

Right from the start, Andrew Ritchie built his own jigs. In this early picture the steel tubes of a rear frame are held in position in the jig while being brazed. The techniques have changed little today.

After the collapse of the ICFC deal, Ritchie began to do occasional work for Grosvenor-Reeve and Nick Ouroussoff, who had recently left Lawrence-Tune. It is, perhaps, typical of Andrew Ritchie that his first move was to commission Ouroussoff to build a rig testing machine to endurance test the folding bikes, Brompton Bicycle thus paradoxically becoming Ouroussoff's first customer, at the same time as Andrew Ritchie became his first employee!

With the folding bike project more or less ready to go, and space available in Nick Ouroussoff's workshop, Ritchie scraped together basic funding by pre-selling a small batch of 30 bikes to shareholders for £250 a time. Building 30 machines would provide something tangible for his long-suffering investors, with a few demonstrators left over, plus a bike or two for Ritchie to test to destruction himself.

Building those first bikes in 1981 was a painfully slow process. Ritchie had little in the way of tooling, so most of the specialist parts had to be painfully crafted by hand. But there's no better way to improve and polish a product than to build a batch of 30 single-handedly. The 12 months allotted for the pre-production batch eventually stretched to 20 months and 50 bikes, but Ritchie admits that he learnt a tremendous amount in this period. Two relatively minor flaws came to light. The first 30 had plastic headset bearings: "I saw them in a catalogue and thought, 'If they're being marketed they must be all right. They were rubbish: all spongy and wobbly." Headset bearings were easily replaced. More problematic were the hinge assemblies, beautifully crafted eccentrics that gently pulled the frame and seat pillar sections together. Building 50 by hand proved very time-consuming, and they were just too complex for full production. A much simpler, more 'Brompton-style' solution would fall into place later on...

Despite a few niggles, the first bikes seem to have worked well and delighted their owners. Andrew Ritchie went on to ride 5,000 miles on his own machine before something cracked, revealing that further materials changes would be required on the next batch.

Ritchie's initial batch of bikes lined up in Nick Ouroussoff's workshop

With no obvious prospect of a licensing agreement, Ritchie began to think a little bigger. The first small run had helped iron out production problems, and generate enough cashflow to produce some rudimentary jigs and other tooling. What if he found bigger premises from which to build and sell a decent batch of bikes? Several hundred? Brompton was moving slowly and inexorably towards manufacture in its own right, but there was still a feeling that production of a bigger batch might encourage Raleigh or one of the other big players to invest.

Andrew Ritchie and his band of shareholders scraped together capital: £4,000 from a government-backed loan guarantee scheme and a further £8,000 of share capital, something that would probably not have been possible if the shareholders hadn't received their shiny new bikes! £12,000 wasn't much, but it was enough to buy basic machinery, produce some tooling and order stock.

Premises would have been a huge expense, and money was something Brompton Bicycle had very little of. But Ritchie still had his engineering know-how, and it was a very marketable asset. Having built a small number of bikes in Nick Ouroussoff's workshop, he moved back in with Tim Reeve and Steve Grosvenor, the design arm of the former Lawrence-Tune engineers, who had now moved from the cramped rooms at Barleymow Passage to the Old Powerhouse near Kew Gardens railway station, a substantial building with plenty of room to spare.

The agreement seems to have been that Ritchie would pay rent while building the batches of bikes, but there is some confusion over whether cash actually changed hands in practice, because Andrew also did quite a bit of design work for the company. Suffice to say, it was a friendly and amicable arrangement and it allowed Andrew to build bikes on a production line scale.

From their origins in designing souped-up motorcars, Grosvenor-Reeve was carving out a niche as a specialist engineering company - specialist in that many of its products were one-offs, and it was willing to talk to clients about anything. The deal worked out well for all concerned. Ritchie got the premises he needed, and Grosvenor-Reeve won the services of a designer with a flair for specialist engineering. According to Steve Grosvenor, "He even came with his own drawing board! He's a Cambridge graduate engineer, and the work he did for us was pretty impressive."

Ritchie designed a number of machines for Grosvenor-Reeve. Some, like the Turkish hazelnut skinning machine, have become the stuff of Brompton legend, but there were more mundane things too, like a machine for pressing plasterboard wall panels. The most interesting was a four-wheeled machine for loading and inspecting blast furnaces. This was normally front wheel drive and rear steer, enabling it to trundle up to the furnace, but at the flick of a switch all four wheels would swing through 90°, enabling it to move sideways, using, for example, the left pair of wheels for steering and the right for propulsion. The machine had a long manipulating arm that could be fitted with various tools and perform different functions under the control of a joystick, enabling it to take samples from the furnace, or skim impurities from the molten metal with some dexterity. This complex and sophisticated machine was controlled entirely by hydraulics, the drive system being designed by Andrew Ritchie. In the end, three were made, one going to Newcastle, and the others exported to Australia and New Zealand.

Intriguingly, he also worked on an electric traction motor designed by a young London engineer called Cedric Lynch. The motor was an unusually compact and efficient design, and the Greater London Council helped to fund basic tooling for a pre-production run, the tooling - including a machine for soldering the armature - being designed by Andrew Ritchie. For all its brilliance, the Lynch motor seems to have been rather ahead of its time. It was made for a while in the UK, then by Agni Motors in India. The turning point came when a Lynch motor powered an electric motorbike to victory in the inaugural Zero Emission Isle of Man TT race in 2009. In 2015, Agni

Left: Today the Old Powerhouse has an air of well-heeled luxury about it - a far cry from the brutish conditions in the early stages of Brompton production.

Above and left: Arguably Andrew Ritchie's most successful design whilst at Grosvenor-Reeve; the very complex drive system on this four-wheeled machine for loading and inspecting blast furnaces. This was normally front wheel drive and rear steer, enabling it to trundle up to the furnace, but at the flick of a switch all four wheels would swing through 90°, enabling it to move sideways, using, for example, the left pair of wheels for steering and the right for propulsion.
See **www.etsdesign.co.uk** for more detail.

Motors merged with Agility Global, and the resulting company, the Saietta Group, is firmly at the cutting-edge of electric motor design, with Cedric Lynch still very much involved.

The Lynch motor tooling was just one job of many, and between bouts of design work upstairs, Andrew Ritchie would be in the downstairs workshop building bikes. To help with the production of Bromptons, he had taken on his first employee, a dour Scot and occasional alcoholic, called Patrick, whose hours of work and behaviour could be a bit unpredictable. Employing Patrick - considered by less charitable souls to be unemployable - was a typically philanthropic Ritchie move, but his faith was to be well rewarded. Patrick might have been a bit morose with others, but he stayed loyal to Brompton Bicycle, brazing frames for the next twenty years, and becoming a slightly irregular fixture in three different factories.

Andrew needed a brazer as tough as Patrick at the Powerhouse. The winter of 1981-82 included the coldest December of the 20th century, with three weeks of bitter cold and snow. The workshop at the Powerhouse was on the ground floor, and rather poorly insulated. The ensuing Dickensian scenes made an impression on Steve Grosvenor:

"During that period Andrew hired Patrick. I remember one day when it was snowing and blowing a gale. Patrick was downstairs next to the big iron doors, wrapped up in scarves and a woolly hat, standing in a snowdrift which had come under the door, brazing up frames."

Grosvenor, obviously impressed, added "I've never known anyone with as much determination as Andrew Ritchie". Tim Reeve was less complimentary, but equally impressed with Andrew's drive and abilities: "I tried hard to persuade him to stop wasting his time on the bloody bicycle! I thought, 'this is a really clever engineer and this obsession is damaging his career.' "

Andrew recalled the Powerhouse days with a mixture of affection and frustration:

"The snow came in under the doors at the Powerhouse and lay three feet deep in the brazing area. We got cracking and made batches of a hundred. Patrick was brazing, but he turned up fairly irregularly, and I was rushing around dealing with customers, organizing suppliers, and trying to find painters who wouldn't fill the thing with shot-blast grit. If it wasn't that, it was too much chrome on the cranks, wrongly bent tube or whatever. Plenty of problems, and endless grinding and trimming. I toiled away listening to Radio 4, but I could have done without the repeats..."

Short-lived Boom

Despite the apparent chaos, bikes were being shipped out, and they were rather good. The Brompton cost £207 in 1982 (about £715 at 2016 prices) for a basic 3-speed hub-geared model, with options of a rather chunky dynamo lighting set for an extra £12.65, a front luggage carrier for £11.50 and a cover for £23. The luggage carrier was a simple platform, not Brompton's trademark luggage system, which was still some way off.

At this stage, Brompton received its first serious press coverage, with a favourable article in the *London Evening Standard*, and a major spread in the *Financial Times* by Nico Colchester. Then Foreign Editor of the FT, Colchester was the first of many opinion formers to be attracted to the Brompton, and his favourable 3/4-page article in the Saturday 'How to Spend' column proved to be a turning point for Brompton Bicycle. From selling by word of mouth to friends of friends, the bikes were actually being sought out by an eager public. Brompton even persuaded Fulham Cycles on the Fulham Road to act as a retail outlet, at the relatively low mark-up of 20%. This arrangement was something of a coup, giving Brompton a local showroom and at least a veneer of respectability. The outlet accounted for nearly a quarter of those early sales.

In May 1982, Andrew got back in touch with Raleigh, explaining that the Brompton was much improved and in limited production. His letter to Michael Boughton, the chairman of parent company Tube Investments, brought a polite reply to the effect that the information and enclosures (including copies of the *Evening Standard* and *FT* articles) would be forwarded to Raleigh in Nottingham.

Whether the Raleigh executives simply filed it under 'P' for potty, or gave serious thought to the much improved design and favourable reviews, we shall never know, but when Mr Boughton wrote back in June, the tone was cold and final. Raleigh considered the Brompton 'most ingenious', but once again, the stumbling block was cost and limited sales potential. "In the circumstances", concluded Boughton, " I feel it right... to decline your offer to discuss this with us further."

Whether Raleigh could have made a success of the Brompton then or now, is an interesting question. In 1982 the company was in the throes of a major reorganization. It had lost its Nigerian and Iranian markets and had recently been the subject of a Monopolies & Mergers Commission report that criticised certain anti-competitive practices. The company was also setting out on the long and painful road away from manufacturing that would soon result in its frames, then whole bicycles, being made in the Far East. The Brompton was a complex and sophisticated bicycle that would have required a great deal of input from the engineers and designers that Raleigh was in the process of shedding. Then there was the spectre of Moulton...The company didn't want the Brompton, and it's hard to imagine the relationship working out if it had taken it on. Andrew Ritchie was later to buy components through Raleigh's Parts & Accessories division, but the 1982 rebuff was to be his last communication with the manufacturing side of the company.

With little capital available for tooling, many parts were being crafted by hand, including the plastic handles and other small items. One of the few exceptions were the folding pedal cranks, which were sub-contracted out after Andrew had painstakingly cut the first 100 on a semi-automatic lathe. No matter how buoyant the demand, mass manufacture without capital is something of a Catch 22 situation: without tooling, unit costs remain high and volumes low, leaving little profit to buy tooling to reduce costs and increase output. Without an injection of serious capital, Brompton was unable to escape from the trap.

The final crunch came when the supply of hinge forgings dried up. Andrew had replaced the complex eccentric device (hand-crafted onto the pre-production machines) with a neater, simpler hinge similar to the system used on the junior version of the Dawes Kingpin. This used a pair of forged plates, one brazed to each tube, joined together by a hinge pin, with a simple C-shaped plate to pull the two forgings - and thus the frame halves - together. It was cheap to make, relatively foolproof, and self-adjusting to a degree, even eliminating play in the hinge pin as it was tightened, but each hinge required two forgings, so four were needed per bike. As Patrick and Andrew started work on the fourth batch of 100 bikes, the French supplier of the hinge forgings announced that production had ceased. With Brompton unable to fund the considerable set-up costs to produce its own, further progress was out of the question.

If conditions had been difficult before the hinge forgings ran out, production of the last hundred bikes was to turn into a nightmare, with Andrew sitting at a milling machine for three months, cutting hinge plates from blocks of solid steel. "I couldn't see any other way to do it", he said later.

Ironically, word was getting out that the Brompton was an excellent product, and further favourable press coverage, including a piece in *Design* magazine, was generating a steady stream of sales. The bikes (unofficially referred to since as Mark 1s) were almost identical to the modern Brompton, but identifiable by a sharper dog-leg curve in the mainframe tube, because Ritchie had been forced to use a standard pipe bending tool, as the company couldn't afford the custom tooling to produce a smoother curve.

At 14.1kg, the bikes were much heavier than today's machines, but not outrageously heavy for the time. The foldability and riding characteristics were widely praised, but reviews in those early days were not universally favourable. In early 1983 *Cycle* magazine tested the Brompton against the Airframe (still under development at that time), the long established Bickerton, and the by now long-in-the-tooth Dawes Stowaway. Summing up, *Cycle* - which presumably put more emphasis on weight than foldability or rideability - ruled out the Brompton as being too heavy (although acknowledging its sturdiness), whilst praising the Bickerton. This might seem odd, but cyclists can be a conservative bunch. The Bickerton might have been a wobbly horror, but it was a known quantity and easy and cheap to repair when things fell off. At the time, the Bickerton was grudgingly accepted as the default public transport machine. Both bikes cost a shade under £200, more or less twice as much as the conventional fold-in-half models from Raleigh and Dawes.

By the time this test was published in February 1983, production had already halted. In late 1982, after 18 months of production, Andrew reluctantly paid Patrick off and brought the brief run to a halt. Six months later, the last hand-made hinge plate had been fitted and the last machine sold.

The failure to find a licensee or sufficient funding to continue production seemed a major blow at the time, but with the benefit of hindsight, Andrew Ritchie feels it was another stroke of good fortune, allowing a breathing space to perfect the design. The steel handlebars had been welded to the stem, resulting in a potential failure point (although none seem to have broken in practice), but some of the frames actually did break:

"Those bikes were not right, and I had to repair maybe 60 of them. There were no real safety issues, but they developed a little crack around the seat clamp slot in the mainframe.

At the very worst, the saddle would have sagged a bit. The slot was very short and it went down at an angle of 45° and it was in tension, so it opened up. The plastic seat sleeve was made of old drainpipe, because I couldn't afford a mould. It had a little ridge cut into it to prevent it coming out of the frame, so every time I took these apart to braze the frame, I had to make another seat sleeve. The whole thing was wonderfully inefficient."

Mark 1 Bromptons ridden by Frances Grosvenor and Caroline Gibbs (later Caroline Reekie).

Brompton Mark 1s in action. The example to the left boasts the front luggage rack, later dropped in favour of an unobtrusive mounting block.

Mark 1s show a number of tell-tale design features - the shopping trolley rear rollers on a black tubular rack, folding left-hand crank arm, steel handlebars, hefty hinges, chrome headlight and perhaps most distinctive of all, the sharp bend in the 'mainframe' which was smoothed out on subsequent Marks.

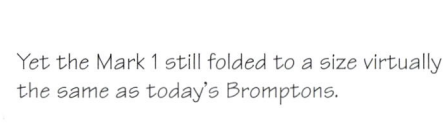

Yet the Mark 1 still folded to a size virtually the same as today's Bromptons.

Repairing 60 bikes was a nuisance, but a product recall involving 600 or 6,000 would have been a disaster. It might not have seemed it at the time, but the limited production run of 400 bikes was an ideal number for sorting out the practical difficulties that inevitably arose as a design was translated from hand-manufacture to the mass market.

Although production had ceased, Brompton Bicycle was by no means moribund. Andrew was busy redrawing certain bits, and the company continued to take out patents to cover key territories, to prevent earlier applications from lapsing. A US patent had followed close on the heels of the UK application in January 1980, with Japan being granted in May 1983, and Europe the following year. Despite the detail changes in the intervening years, these patents were all identical to the original one filed in the mid-1970s.

In 1983, Andrew Ritchie had no clear idea if or when his bicycle would go back into production, but he now knew that he had perfected an attractive, saleable, and easily manufactured bicycle and the innovative parts of the design were now well covered, should anyone try to pirate it. This was fortunate, because it would be five long years before another Brompton was made.

Left: Caroline Gibbs (later Caroline Reekie) would play a crucial role by introducing Julian Vereker to the Brompton.

Below: Andrew Ritchie and Frances Grosvenor demonstrating the Mark 1 Brompton, this time outside Kew Gardens railway station. The Mark 1 bike was in a class of its own, riding better than most of its contemporaries, yet folding into a package little bigger than its wheels.

Mark 2 Bikes In the early days, the Brompton fascinated people wherever it went. In 1996, this Mark 2 caught the attention of the guard on the Southwest Chief at a stop somewhere between Chicago and Los Angeles. This same bike would later be stripped and rebuilt as a lightweight special, then be reborn later still as the Junior Brompton (page 217), proving that old Bromptons never die!

Mark 2 Bikes
1984-1993

"The point is that it is a machine that will sell to non-cyclists and thus expand the market."
NEIL MURRAY

Julian Vereker's Influence

One of the most enthusiastic early advocates of the Brompton was businessman Julian Vereker. Vereker was in some ways the antithesis of Andrew Ritchie, but in other ways, their aims and achievements were strikingly similar. Something else they shared in common were tenuous aristocratic links, Vereker being the great-great grandson of the third Viscount Gort, patriarch of a distinguished Anglo-Irish family, whose title came to a rather confused end following the creation of the Irish Free State in 1922. The English arm of the family included Lord Gort, the sixth viscount, who won the Victoria Cross in the First World War, later leading the British Expeditionary Force into France in 1939, and saving his reputation by leading most of them safely home again a few months later. He rose to become Chief of the Imperial General Staff - effectively the head of the army - and was widely liked and respected.

The son of Charles Vereker, a professor of Political Theory at Durham University, young Julian seems to have been something of a rebel, leaving school with few academic qualifications, but like Andrew Ritchie, a love of, and instinctive empathy for, engineering. For a while, he became well known in the car tuning world, with particularly close links to the Austin Mini, racing minis (cars with Moulton-designed suspension of course!) with some success towards the end of the 1960s. For lesser intellects, this might have been career enough, but Julian Vereker sparkled with a restless energy, and by 1969 he had moved into electronics, designing an industrial sound-to-light unit, which was hired out to film companies.

Vereker went on to develop all sorts of entrepreneurial ideas over the years, but his primary interest was to be audio amplifiers, and Naim Audio, the company he established in 1973, is today a global business with a £25 million annual turnover. He had a fine ear for music, but couldn't play himself, something that might have been a frustration, but Julian turned to recording live music for friends. In echoes of Andrew Ritchie and the folding bike, he was appalled by the quality of commercial amplifiers, and in time-honoured tradition set about making something better. This quest to reproduce music with the utmost fidelity was to be the driving force behind Naim Audio, then and now.

At a time when the Japanese electronics giants were cutting a swathe through the global audio industry, Naim was (and remains) a remarkable enigma. A small British company, with headquarters in Salisbury, Wiltshire, Naim was able to compete with the big global players through the sheer quality of its products. Julian Vereker went on to add a classical music label, again applying the very highest standards to the genre.

A successful businessman by the age of 40, he had no need to get involved in new projects, and could have sat back to enjoy his growing wealth. But Julian was a born salesman, and he was also a perfectionist. That desire to champion the best product in its class made him a natural Brompton ally, and just what the company needed in the mid-1980s. Vereker also had a passion for sailing, commissioning and designing several yachts, and it was whilst cruising in northern France in 1982 that he first came across the Brompton.

Like many yachtsmen, Julian kept a couple of cheap folding bikes on board. The marine market has always been a valuable one for folding bike manufacturers, as yachtsmen are liable to find themselves with no practical means of onward transportation. Land at a remote harbour in western France or the Mediterranean, and the local eatery might be five miles up the road. That's a long walk under a hot sun, but easy with a bike, especially one that can be carried part way by taxi or public transport. Yachtsmen, realizing that a folding bike could open up the hinterland beyond the marina in a magical way, had always been enthusiastic users.

Moored alongside another yacht at a harbour on the Cherbourg peninsula, Julian Vereker got talking with a pretty girl on board. The girl was Caroline Gibbs, an old friend of Andrew's, who had appeared in the early brochure with Steve Grosvenor's wife, Frances, so she knew the bike well. When the subject turned to the inadequacies of folding bikes, Caroline told Vereker that her friend made much better bikes - why not give him a ring? Many would have forgotten the conversation, but Vereker was a man of his word. He was also a self-taught engineer, well aware of the failings of the cheap bikes he kept on deck, and something of a perfectionist in matters mechanical. As soon as the opportunity arose, he phoned Ritchie, visited the factory, and bought a pair of bikes on the spot.

Vereker went on to develop a real passion for the Brompton. It was neater and cleverer than anything he had seen before, and it rode better too. Ever the salesman, he cajoled friends and acquaintances into buying the bikes, and his enthusiasm had soon produced around a dozen sales.

The yachting community was to prove vital to Brompton.

Meanwhile, Andrew was winding down production, and renewed attempts to find new finance were failing. In three years, several venture capitalists had paid a visit and inspected the bike (and, more importantly, the business plan), but none had taken the bait. Despite the production of 400 Mark 1 Bromptons, and clear interest from press and public, the answer was always the same:

"There was the same level of interest. All these people arrived and loved the Brompton, but when it came to actually signing a cheque and putting their shareholders' money into a risky business, they backed away. They would obviously have been putting other people's money into it. Everyone says the banks are mean, but they're actually looking after your dosh!"

A couple of leads seemed to be going somewhere, but they were all destined to fall by the wayside. An approach from an engineering company in Redditch looked promising, as the company had contacts in China, but the deal fell through. In 1984, the Brompton project was still ticking along, but Andrew was working for Grosvenor-Reeve with increasing regularity.

At about this time, Julian Vereker rang up to order some more bikes and was surprised to hear that production was at an end. He must have made an impression, because Andrew Ritchie rang him back, the pair agreed to meet, and with characteristic enthusiasm, Julian offered to get involved. In September 1985, when all avenues seemed to be exhausted, Andrew wrote asking for help, and Julian was soon on board. The plan was to forget the licensing option, and go it alone, but with a third party subcontracted to manufacture the frame.

Andrew Ritchie and Julian Vereker became business partners and good friends, with Vereker purchasing a significant 20% shareholding in Brompton Bicycle. He was an ambitious man, but he was shrewd, realizing that the company would only flourish if Andrew retained control, while he gently guided from behind the scenes. The two met regularly to discuss prospects over a meal, often at La Pappardella on Brompton Road.

After exploring the venture capital option and discounting a fresh but derisory offer from 3Is (later described by Vereker as 'financial theft') the pair came up with a workable financial package that would enable them to go it alone. Using all his undoubted charm and selling techniques, Julian Vereker helped Andrew persuade other shareholders to come on board, from both the Vereker and Ritchie camps. Crucially, he also personally guaranteed a £40,000 overdraft with his bank.

These initiatives yielded only 60% of the capital Andrew Ritchie felt the company needed, but it was enough to fund modest premises, tooling and stock, including that elusive order for frame hinge forgings. "It was", said Vereker, "the most amazing joint venture - a lot of chance and some friends with money". Incredible it might have been, but it worked. Brompton now had two directors, 40 shareholders, modest funding, and a proven, patented product.

A New Lease of Life

Andrew wasted no time in stockpiling tools and equipment at the Powerhouse, foraging around London in one of the life-expired London House Plants Morris Minors, which even hauled back a sturdy old flypress, one of several historic - but very effective - machines still in use today, albeit under constant threat from Health & Safety legislation. By late 1986, he had resumed full-time work on the project.

Brompton was creeping towards full-scale manufacture, but even at this late stage, the directors were hoping to outsource the frame manufacture to Haden Brothers, a Midlands engineering company. This would have much simplified the London operation, removing the heavier engineering - the tube work, jigging and brazing - at a stroke. Haden's went on to become one of many suppliers to Brompton, but in the end, Andrew decided not to go ahead with the subcontracting deal. It had only been considered because the Brompton shareholders didn't have the faith that a small workshop in West London could build the frames with sufficient quality. The arrangement ultimately fell through because Andrew didn't have the faith to entrust the work to anyone else. The frames were complex assemblies that required very precise jigging to work:

Andrew Ritchie was always a hands on boss! This is one of several flypresses salvaged by Andrew in the 1980s.

"I didn't really trust Haden's in the organization of frame making: the jigging, the alignment, making sure the material was up to the right strength, and all the massive engineering to make the thing work. But the failure to reach an agreement with Haden's turned out to be a stroke of good luck, because if I had had subcontractors building the frames, they might have been wrong, and we would have had three bike assembly men standing around with nothing to do, or we would have taken what they'd done and it would have broken."

It was the third crucial stroke of luck that would set Brompton on the road to mass-production, but the last minute change of plan meant producing the tooling, including substantial brazing jigs, setting the project back 18 months. But it was certainly the right thing to do. When Brompton did start building bikes it was able to respond quickly and decisively to quality control issues in a way that would have been impossible had the frames been built by a subcontractor in Birmingham, or indeed China.

While the production was delayed, Julian - ever the marketing man - recommended launching the Brompton at the annual Cyclex trade show in April 1987. At that time, production was still some way off, but Andrew stripped and rebuilt a couple of the pre-production machines to produce bikes representative of the new design. The principal changes were those custom-made hinge forgings, aluminium handlebars, a new chain tensioner, and of course, the elimination of the sharply kinked mainframe tube.

The Brompton won the Best Product award, although it was indicative of the conservatism prevalent in the bike world at the time that the judges were split, one complaining that it was a sad sign of the times when the top prize had to go to a machine which 'you fold up and chuck in a car boot'. Such grumbles did nothing to dampen the spirit of the two Brompton directors who had gambled everything, and won this prestigious award at their first attempt. One wonders how the win went down on the Raleigh stand, where it must have reawoken echoes of the Moulton's spectacular success twenty years before.

According to Neil Murray, one of the Cyclex judges, the front runners were the Peugeot Comete, a traditional lightweight racing machine, and the Brompton:

"The point is that it is a machine that will sell to non-cyclists and thus expand the market. In a nutshell, there are other machines in the mould of the Comete which, if you stripped off the graphics, resemble it. There's nothing like the Brompton, so the Brompton won."

Cyclex was a turning point. Cycle shops weary of impractical, gangly, even dangerous folding bikes were forced to look again. It would be more than a decade before the shops were actually hammering at Brompton's door, but several key outlets signed up at Cyclex, the first being York Cycleworks, followed by Bicycle Doctor in Manchester, and a further four in London: Cyclecare Olympia, Condor Cycles, Ealing Cycles and Simpsons in Kentish Town. It was a very modest dealer network, and the handful of shops would have to wait a while for their bikes, but as the directors shook hands at the end of the show, they knew they had the nucleus of a dealer network up and running.

Winning Best Product award at Cyclex in 1987 was a great step towards acceptance of the Brompton by a wary cycle trade. At the time it ranked as one of Julian Vereker's and Andrew Ritchie's proudest joint achievements.

What they didn't have were bikes or even a factory, but both problems were soon to be remedied. In November 1987 a truck arrived at the Powerhouse to take away the big equipment, carrying it a few miles north to a former railway arch in Brentford. The railway had been part of a Great Western freight line to wharves on the river Thames, cut back a few years before, leaving four arches isolated beside a branch of the Grand Union canal, next to London Road, Brentford.

Two of the arches were being used by a car trader, Bird Autos, while the other two were let to 'Charlie' who dealt in Volkswagen Beetles. Finding himself behind on the rent, Charlie had been evicted from one of the arches, leaving behind a tangle of VW spares, and it was in this 1,000 square feet of leaky, insalubrious workspace that Brompton found its first home. The rent was a bit high for what it was, but the arch was perfect for a small manufacturing operation.

For Andrew Ritchie, the prospect of setting up the factory brought mixed emotions. As he later recalled, it was 'dead frightening', but they were exciting days too, and he set to work with enthusiasm. Once the arch had been tidied up, the ancient machinery was wheeled in with some difficulty and bolted to the floor, a rudimentary office established above, and Brompton Bicycle was ready for business:

"There was all this new tooling to prove, and I just started making bits. There were hundreds of new tools... which ones would work? Most of them did, which was extraordinary."

In March 1988 the first Brompton was delivered to York Cycleworks, the very first dealer, signed up at Cyclex almost a year before. Production of this 'Mark 2' machine ramped up gradually from a trickle to 60 a month, which wasn't bad going for a factory then employing only three staff. Andrew had brought in Sonny, a full-time brazer, and had been persuaded to employ a salesman, Charles 'Chuck' Shepherd. In the early days, Shepherd helped around the factory, but once he had bikes to demonstrate, he was sent out on the road to tackle unwilling bike shops. This small team were soon joined by an office girl, Esther Chubb, but she somehow never quite gelled into the team and didn't stay long.

Generally speaking, the relationship between Julian Vereker and Andrew Ritchie was harmonious in those early days, but there were occasional tensions that exposed the sharp differences in their underlying philosophies.

One element of Brompton manufacture that has barely changed is brazing. Here Sonny is turning out a rear frame at the Arches. Note the line up of main frames and rear frames in the foreground.

Mark 2 Bikes 1984-1993

The Mark 2 bikes had a new, smoother frame curve and were produced in red with black extremities, or all-over black, both options being available in 3- or 5-speed form, although 3-speed bikes were usually red. There were two models, the 'L', or lightweight (above) and the 'T' or touring model (below), which came with a steel rack (upgraded to aluminium by the time this photo was taken) and dynamo lights. Note that the 'T' type is fitted with the front carrier block, while the 'L' is not, but it has a fitting to accept the block which was optional at the time.

Andrew expected customers to come to him, and he saw no reason why he shouldn't produce bikes in a single colour: red with black extremities for the Mark 1, but with the addition of an all-black option for the Mark 2, initially only on the more expensive models. If customers wanted a folding bike, he reasoned, they would seek out a dealer, and once they had ridden the Brompton and found it to be the best available, they would buy one. It was a charmingly low-key approach, and the product was good enough for it to work by and large, but it was quite at odds with Julian Vereker's more flamboyant marketing philosophy.

Julian knew that many more people would buy the bike if they were educated in Brompton theory and practice. True, a handful of early adopters knew exactly what they wanted, but the majority of potential customers didn't yet know they wanted a Brompton. They hadn't yet discovered that a Brompton could change their lives for the better!

Both men were right in a way of course, and Brompton's subsequent development was to take a middle path between these two extremes, the company growing at a steady, but unspectacular rate, largely without advertising or pressure from sales reps. Back in 1988, Andrew wasn't happy with the principle of employing a sales rep, and Chuck Shepherd's time with the company would be relatively short. There wouldn't be another.

Meanwhile, Julian was working out his sales addiction by publicizing the Brompton at shows and exhibitions, particularly boat shows, where his slick, hard-sell routine always drew a crowd. As a yachtsman, Julian could talk to sailors in their own language. He knew the harbours of the English Channel and he knew from personal experience that - for example - a Brompton could carry a crate of wine back from an interesting vineyard, just out of reach for the average yachtsman. At caravan and camping shows, Vereker sometimes struggled, but with yachtsmen and pilots he excelled, helping to establish a niche market that Brompton has profited from ever since.

His early efforts resulted in a steady stream of sales for the growing band of dealers, whose proprietors were delighted to have had the hard work done for them. The bike trade often argued that the margins were poor on the Brompton, but the bikes soon gained a reputation for working straight out of the box, and Brompton made a point of never undermining the dealers with anything as vulgar as direct sales.

The company rapidly developed a slightly superior image that went down a storm with the yachtsmen and middle-class commuters who were the primary customers in those early days. The only real competition at this time was from the Taiwanese Dahon, sold rather half-heartedly through a motorcycle dealership in Ruislip, and never quite able to match the Brompton's effortlessly classy appeal.

Luggage & Gearing Develops

When Ritchie and Vereker launched the Brompton at Cyclex in 1987, dealers were told that the bike would cost from £210, but in an era of high inflation, this estimate was bound to rise. The increases were modest at first: the early machines seem to have sold for £220, but by May 1989 the price had edged up to £235.75 (£529 at 2016 prices), an increase of 15%, or 3% above inflation. But for the next two years, the basic price of the Brompton rocketed, hitting £270 in 1990 and £320.78 (£621 at 2016 prices) the following year; a whacking 36% increase in two years, twice the rate of inflation. To Raleigh, it must have looked as though its caution had been vindicated, but prices never increased as sharply again, and the revolutionary Brompton continued to find eager buyers.

These were basic prices, but the spec was still relatively simple, with 3-speed or 5-speed Sturmey-Archer hub gears, the two colour options, and a steel rear rack. On the Mark 1 machine, the rack had been integral to the rear frame, but it was now a chromed steel option, resulting in two models, the basic red 'L' or Lightweight without a rack, and the black 'T' or Touring model. This was exactly the same, but fitted with the steel rear rack and dynamo lights at a premium of about £50.

Either of the bikes could be fitted with Brompton's superb front pannier system. This involved a plastic block that bolted to the frame, making good use of the dead space where a 26-inch wheel would normally go. The 'T' type in particular was quite a prodigious load carrier, rather after the style of the Moulton, and with the rack and pannier bag mounted so low, it was also a very stable load platform.

At first there were three custom bag options: a steel frame that could be bolted to the rider's briefcase, another frame that could be bolted to a standard Spencer wire basket, and a Carradice pannier bag. All could be clipped on and off the mounting block on the bicycle headtube. It looked as though the load moved with the steering, but it was actually rigidly attached to the frame, and thus had little adverse effect on handling.

The briefcase frame was not a success and was soon dropped, and the wire basket was later replaced by a clever folding basket aimed at the same shopping and leisure market. This stayed in production, but it wasn't a spectacular success either, accounting for only 20% of bag sales over the years. On the other hand, the cloth pannier - although expensive at nearly £70 - went on to become something of a sales phenomenon, and an iconic badge of ownership, bringing together early-adopter Brompton owners. In the early 1990s, if you were carrying a Brompton pannier, you were clearly a clubbable sort of chap, and thus might find yourself in conversation with captains of industry, celebrities, or even MPs, whilst waiting at the traffic lights.

The Carradice bag went on to become something of a sales phenomenon, surviving almost unchanged until 2009. The folding basket (bottom left) succeeded the wire basket (top left). Neither of these options was a big success but the folding basket is still available today. The briefcase frame (centre left) and wire basket were soon dropped.

Feedback from the press and public continued to be positive, but there were one or two grumbles. The steel wheel rims were a bit heavy, and the chromed steel finish resulted in the braking effect more or less evaporating in wet weather. The brakes were poor anyway, and some riders felt the front of the bike was a bit flexible. All these issues would be dealt with, but the complaints about high gearing were not to be addressed for some years.

At this time Andrew Ritchie was riding into the factory on a Brompton most mornings. This sort of hands-on daily commuting was a logical move for a bicycle designer trying to iron out minor problems, and in some ways the key to the bike's success, but it could result in the machine being rather tailored to the terrain the designer was familiar with. Andrew had specified a 50-tooth chainring and 13-tooth rear sprocket, giving gears of 46", 62" and 82" with the 3-speed hub. Gearing is always a compromise, and as compromises go, this was spot on for West London, but a bit ambitious for hillier regions.

The 5-speed machine used the Sturmey-Archer 5-Star hub. This gave more gears and a bigger overall gear range than the 3-speed, but it was a rather odd device utilizing two gear levers. One lever gave three distinct gears like any other Sturmey 3-speed gear lever, while the other effectively switched between close ratios and wide ones. In practice, this lowered first gear and raised top gear, but left the direct-drive middle gear unchanged. Difficult enough to explain, it was tricky to adjust, and even more difficult to use effectively, and it's probably fair to say that many owners never fully grasped the concept.

The gear steps of -33%, -21%, direct, +25% and +50% seemed a useful bonus over the 3-speed model, but as there was some extra internal resistance in the more extreme gears, it wasn't much better at climbing hills. Nevertheless, the 5-speed was soon well established, appealing as much to those who naturally gravitated to the most expensive variant as those living in hilly areas.

Magazine testers and customers continued to grumble about the high gearing for years, but the standard ratios remained stubbornly unchanged. Eventually, a smaller chainring was offered as an option, but this cost more, and you needed to know that you wanted it before making the purchase. Somehow, these departures from Andrew's chosen script were always offered a

5-speed models were fitted with early Sturmey-Archer 5-speed hubs, controlled by two shifters via twin cables - a heavy and rather complex solution. The first Mark 2s were fitted with the S5/2, but this was soon replaced by the very similar 5-Star, which lasted until the single-cable Sprinter arrived in 1994.

bit grudgingly. It was the sort of 'nanny knows best' attitude to marketing that often had Julian Vereker jumping up and down with frustration, but it did nothing to upset sales, which continued to grow steadily. By the end of 1988, the little factory was producing 90 bikes a month, and when Charlie was finally given the boot from the adjoining arch in 1991, Brompton was quick to absorb the extra space, doubling the size of the factory. Staff levels gradually increased, and the following year, Andrew's original employee Patrick - who had found gainful employment as a security guard in the intervening years - answered an advertisement, and was soon back on the team.

The 5-speed certainly proved profitable for Brompton, selling for £368.95 in early 1991, against £320.78 for the 3-speed. These 'to the penny' prices were an Andrew Ritchie idiosyncrasy, and for a few years were to become as much a feature of the bikes as the neat fold and limited colour range. With luck, the price might come out at a low-sounding £499.83, but a Brompton might just as easily be priced at £501.01, which didn't sound half as good.

Some dealers were perplexed by this deliberately 'non-marketing' approach. Others jokingly displayed the exact price, while a few - even more tongue in cheek - made a big show of discounting the bike by 78 pence or whatever the surplus might be. Brompton, incidentally, always took a hard line on discounting or profiteering by dealers. It was all part of Andrew's sales philosophy that the bike was being sold at a fair price and dealers and customers could take it or leave it; and although Andrew Ritchie would never admit it, this strict adherence to pricing had a vaguely socialist ring to it. The enforced level playing field helped the small shops selling a Brompton or two a month to compete with the big ones turning over half a dozen a week. The big shops were angling hard for a superior discount to match their more aggressively successful sales, but Ritchie always resisted this too, staying loyal to the small shops that had shown confidence by placing orders at Cyclex 1987 and soon after. Brompton's refusal to allow discounting was later referred to the Office of Fair Trading by a disgruntled dealer in Yorkshire. The OFT subsequently found against Brompton, forcing it to make a humiliating apology to the cycle trade in press advertisements, but Ritchie still had the last word. Thereafter, the fledgling sales team would simply inform discounters very sweetly that the order book was full...

Getting dealers on board had been critical to the Brompton's early success, and the first shops had soon been joined by a handful of others: Avon Valley in Bath, Peddlers in Worcester, Drakes in Cambridge, Spa in Harrogate and Warlands in Oxford. These were quite small shops in the main, but they were mostly situated in cycling areas, which perhaps gave a little more leeway to experiment than those in less bike-friendly towns and cities.

Resistance to folding bikes was understandable. Older traders had witnessed the Moulton's spectacular rise and fall, while others had been scared off by the Bickerton. Production of the Bickerton had nearly ceased by this time, but many shops had been left with unsaleable stock, vowing never to touch 'portables' again. In practiced hands, the Bickerton wasn't at all bad, but it needed an engineer's delicate touch to perform well, and the dealers were consequently having a hard time with warranty claims.

It was against this backdrop that Andrew Ritchie - and for a limited period, salesman Chuck Shepherd - sometimes had difficulty getting a foot in the door, let alone demonstrating the bike. Resistance to the Brompton was strongest in working class and depressed areas, and even after sales had taken off in the south it would be some years before the bike fought its way out from a couple of strongholds in the North, and the single dealer covering the whole of Scotland.

Rapid Expansion

By 1991, Brompton had an impressive 56 outlets in the UK (18 in London alone), and was starting to make big inroads into Europe. The most important markets were Germany, where the bikes were distributed by Hans Voss, a specialist cycle manufacturer and distributor, and The Low Countries, which were handled by a slightly eccentric bicycle enthusiast called Simon Korn. Eccentricity has never been a significant stumbling block in the Brompton orbit of course, and Korn went on to do extremely well. Within a year of the Brompton's launch, half the output was being exported, mainly to The Netherlands and Germany, and by year two, exports were accounting for two-thirds of production, and have remained more or less at that level ever since. Exports brought extra complications in terms of lights and reflectors to satisfy local legislation, and this together with a steady stream of orders from the British shops, meant the little office in the upper storey of the Arches was close to being overwhelmed.

Brompton had been started by an inventive engineer, who had been joined by a marketing guru, but what the tiny company now needed was a steady hand to bring order to its administrative affairs. Almost exclusively masculine up to this time, it also needed a woman's touch, and so it was that a third key character entered the story.

Nicola McGregor was the daughter of a Scottish doctor. Born in Africa, her early years were largely spent in the Middle East, where her father was employed by an oil company. Nicola went on to graduate from St Andrew's University with a 2:1 in Zoology, and to start a PhD in microbiology at Oxford. But temperamentally unsuited to research, she left before acquiring any further academic qualifications. Following a short stint with the National Enterprise Board, through luck and a sense of adventure, she found herself back in the Middle East, now in the banking sector, enjoying the prosperity and ostentatiousness of the 1980s boom years.

This was brought to an end by Saddam Hussein's invasion of Kuwait, and Nicola, by now a product manager with an international financial information company, was moved back to the London office, but not before she had fallen for a US marine. By early 1991 the war was over, but with the Middle Eastern financial markets shattered, Nicola followed her marine back to the US. The relationship soon foundered and she returned to her parents' house in Scotland, effectively back to square one. It was in this somewhat downcast state that she contacted Penny Naylor, an old Oxford University acquaintance, now married to a Brompton shareholder. During the conversation it emerged that Esther Chubb was leaving, and Andrew was seeking a 'Girl Friday' to help bring the administration under control.

After a call to Andrew (who with typical financial caution, agreed to a meeting if she was willing to travel down from Dundee at her own expense!), Nicola made the long journey south and was soon on board, initially lodging with friends in Barnes, a comfortable cycle ride from the Brentford factory. Nicola fitted the Brompton mould to perfection: like Ritchie and Vereker she had a considerable intellect allied to a streak of non-conformity.

Another interesting and rather far-sighted element to Andrew Ritchie's management philosophy was that everyone who worked for Brompton must first learn to build the bike. This was fair enough while he was taking on engineers and brazers, but a slightly tall order for young Miss McGregor, whose CV had been varied, but always some distance from engineering. Nevertheless, after some initial trials, she had soon built her own bike, and as Andrew hoped, the experience gave her enough expertise to hold her own with the cycle shops, and ultimately gain the respect of hardened engineers on the shop floor.

But when Nicola sat down on her first day, she surveyed the cramped office with a mixture of dismay and a growing sense of excitement at the challenge ahead:

"It was really an organisational problem - letting shops have the bikes they wanted when they wanted them. It didn't require any extraordinary talents, but it needed someone who was independent and logical."

The office was packed with secondhand filing cabinets, the unisex toilet (which the 'Girl Friday' had to clean!) was a lean-to in the yard, the bin was a cardboard box in the corner, and rats and foxes were occasional visitors, but gradually Nicola took the administration in hand.

In the early days, each bike had been given a job card, four cards being laboriously cut from sheets of A4 paper with a Stanley knife on a block of wood. Gradually the systems were improved, and matters like the payroll and tax paperwork were brought in-house and computerized (often with a programme and/or programmer from Julian's long list of friends and associates).

Always keen to enhance the marketing side of the company, Julian suggested that Nicola be given a marketing role, but such was the rate of growth in the company, this never formally happened, although she did effectively oversee Brompton's low-key and rather gentlemanly 'marketing department' for many years.

The mid-90s were a period of rapid expansion for Brompton, and the company found it difficult to keep up with demand. Marketing may have played a role: Julian Vereker always enjoyed demonstrating the bike at shows, here testing a Brompton-mounted trailer!

'Girl Friday' Nicola McGregor also played a pivotal role in marketing. After several fruitless attempts to engage the railway companies, Brompton was finally permitted to position a small stand at Marylebone station, by Chiltern Trains, one of the most forward-looking of the new rail franchisees. This stand, designed and made by Andrew Ritchie was a folding design and could be carried in the panniers of the display bikes!

As Brompton found its feet in the late 1990s, the company began to undertake some tentative marketing. Here the Brompton is identified with another London icon, the red bus, an association that has stuck ever since.

Meanwhile, Andrew was busy refining the bike, introducing a number of key innovations in the first few years of production, mostly aimed at reducing the weight and enhancing the bike's rigidity. The steel wheels were replaced by aluminium in 1991, saving a few grams and improving wet-weather braking. In late 1992, the chain tensioner was strengthened, and at about the same time a cast alloy rack replaced the tubular steel rack on 'T' models. This was one of many small improvements made possible by the increased output. The steel rack had been expensively brazed together by hand, whereas the alloy rack was cast in one piece by a sub-contractor. It was lighter, and cheaper to make, but only possible once the factory was in a position to place the large orders that made casting cost-effective.

Later that year, the diameter of the handlebar stem was increased, and the headset enlarged from 1 inch to $1 1/8$ inch, a move that added little or no weight, but greatly beefed up the front end, improving the feel of the bike on the road.

There would be many, many changes in the years to come, but this machine, on sale from the spring of 1992 was the definitive Brompton. In a short, frenetic period, the bike had been brought to production and refined until most of the early criticisms had been overcome.

It was still on the heavy side compared to the Bickerton, but it was much lighter than the Raleigh, Dawes and cheap Far Eastern fold-in halves, and apart from a degree of small-wheel twitchiness, it rode superbly. Andrew Ritchie's slightly gawky brainwave had outshone its peers. It wasn't just a folding bicycle, it was a timeless classic, and although market penetration remained patchy, sales were starting to take off.

The Taiwanese Brompton

Soon, the two arches were bulging at the seams, but it looked as though salvation had already arrived in the shape of a call from the Far East. Out of the blue, late in 1991, Andrew had taken a call from Peter Wang of Eurotai in Taiwan. The Brompton had come to their notice and they wanted to build it under licence:

"Peter Wang said 'I think you've got the best folding bike there is, and I'd love to build it under licence'. I told him to piss off, but he came back several times and really seemed to mean business, and after talking it over with Julian, we said, 'OK, let's talk', and struck a deal with him."

The deal was for Eurotai to build machines destined for the Far East, particularly the large Japanese market, while the Brentford factory would continue to supply Europe and America. A licensing deal where the other party promises to build machines, market them, and pay you a healthy royalty sounds like a licence to print money, but these sort of arrangements can be expensive and potentially risky ventures. Brompton's confidence wasn't improved by a call from David Hon, the founder of Dahon, warning that Eurotai might not be a suitable partner. Dahon, of course, was Brompton's competitor, so hardly an unbiased source, but the warning set alarm bells ringing.

On the other hand, there were several strong arguments for going ahead: there was a real risk that Eurotai, if rebuffed, might start pirating the design anyway. Brompton also needed a breathing space to catch up with its overflowing order book, and the Taiwan link promised to provide a secondary source of components. It looked risky, but it was understandably a tempting deal at the time.

Training the Taiwanese engineers was a slow process, and involved a lot of effort and expense. First, the Eurotai engineers were brought over to Brentford for a week or two, before Andrew flew to the Far East to help design jigs, and train the engineers to build the complex and precisely-engineered frames. There followed a long period during which drawings and information were exchanged, at a time when Andrew was already in great demand improving and mass-producing the bike at home. The early Taiwanese prototypes were disastrous, as Ritchie later recalled:

"They were really taking short cuts. The wall thickness of the tube wasn't what it should be, and the material for the folding pedal was the wrong stuff. Everything was wrong and they'd just taken short cuts all over the place. Each bike - and they sent about six samples - was wrong. I wasted hours late into the evenings looking at these things, utterly pissed off with the way they were setting about it. Eventually I threw my hands up in despair and decided it was sort of near enough, but to this day I don't know how many of their bikes have broken. I gave them the go-ahead, and of course they then had the right to use the name Brompton. They did their best, but their best was crap. The jigging was appalling, the tooling was appalling, and it was all really badly made."

Eurotai had set up a new company, Neobike, to produce the Brompton. The promise was that Neobike would build and pay royalties on 50,000 bikes a year, but the actual figures were impossible to verify and Eurotai's irregular royalty payments left a lingering impression that it wasn't being entirely honest about the sales figures. Once the design had effectively been pirated, Neobike set about building as many bikes as it could and marketing them with mini-skirted models, playing vaguely on the bike's perceived value as a leisure machine. It was all too much for Andrew Ritchie, who had worked hard to convince the world that the Brompton was a serious commuting tool. To make matters worse, the Neobike bicycles carried large Union Jacks, whereas the British bikes made do with the tiny legend: 'Made in England. Patents Worldwide'.

Neobike played shamelessly on the Brompton's British associations, mixing images of London with sexy models (and bizarrely throwing in a New York icon in this example!).

Mark 2 Bikes 1984-1993

Associating the bikes with a brand like Rolls-Royce was quite absurd when the Taiwanese machines were so poorly made.

One of Neobike's key targets was Japan, a wealthy country with a strong bicycle heritage, and no cultural problems with small wheeled bicycles! In 1996, Neobike approached Mac Nakane of Mitsubishi and demonstrated the Taiwanese Brompton. At this time, Mitsubishi was selling a number of bicycle brands, including Mizutani, a family-run Japanese business producing racing bikes and run by Toshi Mizutani. Faced with increasing competition from China and other low-wage economies, Toshi was in the process of winding down racing bike manufacture to concentrate on distributing other bikes, principally folders.

Early in 1996, he had signed a deal to distribute the Birdy, which was being made for Riese & Muller by Pacific of Taiwan. Unfortunately, the Birdy name had been registered by Suzuki, so the Mizutani Birdies were labelled B-D1. At about the same time, Toshi spotted the Brompton in a European catalogue but was unable to secure the brand. However, soon afterwards, while chatting with his friend Mac Nakane at Mitsubishi, Toshi couldn't believe his luck when Mac produced a Taiwanese Brompton, and said Neobike was willing to talk terms.

For a while, Mizutani had problems registering the Brompton brand name in Japan, but with hindsight the delay was a bonus, because in 1996 the build quality of the Neobike machines was still very poor. But by the following year the brand name was safely registered and the quality problems largely resolved. The Taiwanese Bromptons were cheap enough for sales to take off in quite a big way, and by the end of 1997, Mizutani had distributed around 1,000. Japanese sales continued to grow in the next few years, averaging 1,500 to 2,000 a year. Mizutani was selling twice as many B-D1's, but the Brompton soon became a good solid part of the company's range.

Very little of this had got back to London, of course. Neobike went on to cause problems by selling into Turkey (claiming that it was an Asian rather than a European country), and its bikes also began to turn up in the USA, which was potentially a much more serious issue. Andrew had had enough:

"The whole thing was a bloody waste of time, just a mess. I could have closed the agreement earlier than I did, because they were not honouring it, but was it worth litigating? We let it run for the ten years of the first stage until they had to renew, which they forgot to do anyway. But if they hadn't, I would have said 'sorry mate, this is the end of it'."

Unfortunately it wasn't the end of it. Neobike returned some nominal drawings and tooling, but kept a great deal, including the essential know-how. The company was subsequently sold on to a Taiwanese businessman, after which all prospects of controlling pirate manufacture were lost. In the years that followed Brompton clones continued to slip out of Taiwan destined for Europe, the USA and elsewhere. For Brompton, this would be an ongoing headache, necessitating legal action to impound the counterfeits. The most galling thing for Andrew Ritchie was that these poorly made copies were being produced using his own expertise and drawings, expensively shipped out to Taiwan in 1992.

With hindsight, it seems odd that Brompton didn't simply go with the flow, sort out the quality problems and buy the Taiwanese bikes themselves. After all, by the mid-1990s, British manufacturing companies had virtually abandoned metal-bashing in favour of cheap Chinese manufacture. Why could Brompton not simply do the same? According to Andrew Ritchie, this had certainly been investigated, and several prominent shareholders were keen on the concept of outsourcing, but there remained serious issues with quality, and the cost advantages weren't quite what they appeared:

"We did entertain the idea of getting Neobike to build bikes for us, but the marginal cost of buying from the Far East was a big problem, let alone the quality issues… Let us say it costs us a hundred quid to make one here in Chiswick. When we came round to it, the Neobike machine was going to cost £110 by the time it had landed. OK, we have overheads on top, so the true

cost of building a bike here might be £140, making theirs slightly cheaper, but it wasn't miles cheaper. So for the hassle, for a sub-brand, it just wasn't worth it."
In the event, Brompton did source a few components from Neobike's suppliers in the 1990s, including, for a while, some rather unsatisfactory handlebars, but even this modest venture was later to turn sour, as we shall see.

The Asian approach to marketing was hardly subtle. A long way from the British Brompton's refined, often exclusive image - much to the dismay of Brompton UK!

And a Taiwanese Rival

With the Taiwanese adventure going horribly wrong, and customers and dealers crying out for bikes, a move to a bigger factory became essential, and in December 1993 Brompton moved two miles east, leasing what appeared at the time to be an enormous factory in Chiswick, opposite Chiswick Park tube station.

The move was a fairly fraught affair. Machinery movers were brought in to shift the lathes, brazing benches and flypresses, and in those simpler days before Health & Safety legislation went completely mad, the 15 or so staff simply downed tools and mucked in, dragging Dexion shelving, boxes of spare parts and other equipment to waiting removal vans.

The new factory (a 'cathedral' according to Andrew Ritchie) seemed big after the Arches, but with more staff arriving all the time, it soon filled up. After a pause, output began to ramp up and had soon reached 100 a week.

What had become of the competition? After Harry Bickerton's retirement in 1987, the Bickerton had begun to fade from the scene, a slow death that was hastened by the rebirth of the Brompton the following year. The Airframe had been designed back in 1978, but despite a great deal of promise, had never really entered into volume production and had disappeared by the late 1980s.

The Strida was an interesting machine. It had been designed by Mark Sanders, a young British industrial design student, as a means of overcoming his own walk to the railway station.

The Strida went into production in 1987, just before the reborn Brompton. Unlike most designs, it was a simple but elegant 'stick' folder - not the easiest thing to ride, but admirably fulfilling its design brief. The bike burst onto the market in a blaze of publicity, winning Best Bike at Cyclex in 1988, the year after Brompton. Sales at home were always disappointing, but the bike became a favourite in the Far East and by 1992 some 25,000 had been made. Unfortunately, the British manufacturer then went bust (after expanding into baby buggies, oddly enough), reportedly leaving some 15,000 unfulfilled Japanese orders. The Strida disappeared, but as with many folding bikes, this was not to be the end of the story...

British designer Mark Sanders produced the Strida in the late 1980s. It sold fitfully in Europe, but became a runaway success in the Far East, turning Mark into a delighted, if slightly bemused, folk hero.

The only real threat to Brompton's dominance at this time was from the Dahon, which was still being sold by HGB Motorcycles of Ruislip, but since 1986 it had also been 'badge- engineered', selling through Bickerton-Rowlinson as the Bickerton Dahon. The arrangement between Mark Bickerton and David Hon seems to have been mutually beneficial, because it was set to continue with the Bickerton Californian in 1988, the Taiwanese bikes being listed in the Bickerton catalogue alongside the home-produced models.

Within a few years, Dahon would be a real force to be reckoned with, but these early 16-inch (305mm) bicycles were crude, heavy and rather laughable. The Bickerton Californian was considerably cheaper than the Brompton, costing £260 in late 1993 (£480 today), against £345.45-£477.05 for the Brompton (£635-£876 today), but it only really appealed to those who felt they couldn't justify the cost of the real thing, a point made by several road tests of the day. The Dahon might have been cheap, but in Britain's rather class-conscious society, there was something faintly oikish about the Stars and Stripes flag (they were actually made in Taiwan) and go-faster colours and finishes. The Dahon was to become an established favourite with the caravan towing classes, habitually dominating tests in that sort of magazine, but for more serious travellers, the Brompton was already in a class of its own. All these factors, plus HGB's rather half-hearted and downmarket advertising, meant the Dahon - for the time being - remained little more than a minor irritant.

With quality imports like the Birdy and Bike Friday still some way off, the Brompton had a near monopoly, a good product, a smart new factory and a dedicated management team. The only immediate obstacle was the company's inability to supply bikes fast enough.

Architect Graham Herbert with his Airframe folding bike. The Airframe was a much cleverer design than the Bickerton and would have sold in big numbers had it not been for the Brompton.

Competition Hots Up - the Mark 3s
The bike looked almost identical to its predecessor, but nearly every component was different beneath the skin.

Competition Hots Up - the Mark 3s
1994-2000

At Chiswick Park

For Andrew Ritchie, Julian Vereker, Nicola McGregor and the growing band of shop floor staff, the Chiswick Park days were probably their happiest. After the Stygian gloom of the Arches, the factory was light, airy and convenient. Although only a few short miles east of Brentford, Chiswick is London proper, and Chiswick High Street, just five minutes walk from the factory, included some of the best shops and eateries in the capital.

For staff and the increasing number of visitors from home and overseas, this was all very convenient. Encouraged by Julian, Andrew continued to take on employees, keeping the growth in bike output more or less steady at around 10% a year. Unusually for a manufacturing company, this steady growth was achieved from sales rather than borrowings, this meticulous financial husbandry being something in which Andrew Ritchie was to take special pride.

Julian Vereker was always keen to point out at shows that this was a genuinely British bike. After Raleigh stopped building its own frames in 1999, almost every bicycle frame sold in the UK would be produced in the Far East, and within a few years, complete bicycles would be arriving the same way, reducing once proud British companies like Raleigh and Dawes to mere marketing shells. By the late 1990s only two companies were building bikes by hand in any number: Pashley, which held the Post Office bike contract, and Brompton.

Hand assembly meant exactly that. Brompton's increased buying power had made it possible for many mouldings and castings to be subcontracted out, but the bikes were put together in much the same way Andrew and Patrick had built the first 400. The frame parts and other steel components were cut and bent to shape, then inserted into complex jigs and brazed together. Once complete, the bare frames and other components were packed into special pallets and sent out to be painted.

Like many modern bicycles, the Brompton was actually 'powder-coated' rather than painted. In essence, the steel frames were cleaned, galvanized, and sprayed with a fine plastic powder, then placed in an oven, where the powder would melt and form a tough, seamless plastic coat. Clearly a rather complex process, the powder-coating was always done by outside sub-contractors, initially a few miles down the road, but later in South Wales, necessitating quite a trek out and back.

It was the complexity of the powder-coating supply chain that encouraged Andrew to stick with black for the extremities, and red or black for the frames, because with the small number of machines then being made, a range of colours would have added a disproportionate amount of complication and cost. The process was also a quality control nightmare, with a relatively high number of rejects, which had to be sent back to the sub-contractor, stripped back to bare metal and reprocessed.

The powder-coating shipments had to be built around another company's work schedule and holiday arrangements and timed to arrive back for final assembly to take place. Any mistakes in timing, or losses (one lorryload of frames - useless to anyone else - was stolen en route), and the factory could be in trouble.

Assembly was done at work stations equipped with all the small parts and accessories and a rotatable bike stand on which the bike would be built, each one taking anything up to 60 minutes or so, depending on the specification (the more complex 'T' type took a little longer). Once built, the bike would be sent to the quality control bench (as the years passed, more benches were added) for final inspection and rectification, and only then would the familiar 'Brompton' frame decals be added. Generally speaking, bikes were built to order, but common models could also be produced for stock, if orders were thin on the ground, and the parts available.

This sort of labour-intensive construction is time-consuming and expensive, each bike occupying around seven man-hours to build, but it was the only practical way to make such a complicated machine in relatively small numbers. Assembly staff were quite easy to train, and as in the early days, everyone from senior manager to the most junior clerk, was expected to learn the ropes by building a few bikes.

The real production bottleneck was the frame brazing, a specialist trade, and an area where poor workmanship could be expensive and potentially dangerous. Brompton faced a constant battle to find and keep enough brazers, and hold-ups often occurred in this area too, resulting in a shortage of finished frames for the assembly people, who would have to be found other roles at short notice.

In the early days these problems would all be dealt with by Andrew Ritchie. To the uninitiated he neither looked nor sounded like a natural personnel officer - he had a quick temper and didn't suffer fools, but he also had a ready smile and could communicate with anyone, from captains of industry to shop-floor trainees.

But managing these day-to-day purchasing, production and despatch problems inevitably took Andrew away from his core task of designing improvements into the bikes, so the management team began to grow, with new staff being brought in to specialize in particular fields - production, engineering, purchasing and so on. "I started taking on more brainy employees", says Andrew Ritchie, "all of whom wanted to be paid more than I was paying myself!" But there were to be no design staff at this stage, as it was an area he jealously guarded. For more than ten years he'd been working incredibly hard at it, sitting at his drawing board for long hours, often late into the evening after the last of the staff had gone home, and the rest of the factory was in darkness. In later years, the design work was transferred to computer, but the iconic drawing board was to survive into the modern era, although seeing much less use than hitherto.

Once the dust had settled from the factory move, the incremental improvements came back on stream. Some were of a technical nature, like offset cranks, and a shorter crank axle, but in June 1994, the old Sturmey-Archer 2-lever 5-Star hub was replaced by the latest design, which utilized a single cable

The very skilled job of brazing continued to be a production bottleneck for Brompton. Each bike took around 7 man-hours to build.

and rotary thumb shifter control. At the same time, the rear frame rollers were deliberately weakened. Bikes were usually packed in cardboard boxes and despatched by courier, and inevitably some of the boxes were dropped en route. If dropped the right way up, there was a risk that the extensions on the rear frame that carried the rollers would be bent, necessitating a return to the factory for a new rear frame. This was not only expensive and troublesome, but it was a particular menace when bikes were in short supply, as they often were, leaving the shopkeeper without profit and the customer without a bike. The new weaker rollers tended to break first, taking stress off the frame. They cost pennies to replace, and it was an easy job for the shops to do themselves.

Late in 1994, Brompton made an attempt to improve the brakes, which could be quite weak on early bikes, but the change from Sachs to Saccon calipers had little effect, and it was to be several more years before the braking performance reached a satisfactory level.

Meanwhile, Julian Vereker had been doing his stuff, generating publicity by nominating Brompton for a Queen's Award for Export Achievement. In early 1995, the award was confirmed, and although the subsequent publicity seems to have made little impact overseas, at home, the cachet of carrying the royal crest on company paperwork was a very tangible benefit, suggesting as it did that members of the royal family had somehow given the little bike a stamp of approval. Owners certainly included the great and the good of the day, but there is no evidence that members of the royal household were customers!

In the mid-1990s Brompton decided to introduce a new basic single-speed model, purchasing a batch of light and apparently serviceable rear hubs from Taiwan. Unfortunately, there were found to be problems with the freewheels during testing, and with demand for the 3- and 5-speed bikes rising all the time, the single-speed project was put on hold. It even appeared in the price lists in 1996 and 1997 as the C1 (Companion, single-speed) but was never actually made.

The gentle evolution continued in 1995, and again, some changes - like a lighter cartridge bottom bracket assembly, and lighter, stronger chrome-molybdenum front forks - were deliberate, while others were forced on the bike, as manufacturers and suppliers came and went.

The dynamo changed three or four times in this era, and continued to suffer from issues that were never really satisfactorily resolved. Dynamo seizures were relatively common, an issue eventually traced to the Brompton's folding action - in use, the dynamo bearing was shielded from rain and dust just as it would be on any other bike, but when the rear wheel was folded under the frame, water on the dynamo casing would run down into the bearing. Like most bicycle components, they were not designed to spend part of their lives upside down...

The handlebars were changed at this time too. For the first 18 months of production, Brompton had fitted bars produced by Chambers Churchill of Worcester. These had proved a bit frail and been replaced by larger diameter $15/16$" bars made by GB Cycles.

Unusually in the folding bike world, Andrew was diligent about rig testing equipment to British Standards, which laid down that components of this kind must withstand a certain number of flexures at a given loading, something that was easy to reproduce on a test rig running 24 hours a day to induce failure as rapidly as possible. The GB bars had passed the tests, but there had been a few failures since their introduction, so Andrew decided to test the Neobike bars. These were lighter, cheaper and stronger, and after passing British Standards, they were fitted to all bikes from mid-1995. It seemed to be a rare bonus from the collaboration with the Taiwanese, but history was to prove otherwise.

More Rivals Arrive

By late 1995, the price of the bikes had edged up to £378.35 - £534.63 (£753 - £1066 in 2024), but the Brompton continued to sell well in an increasingly competitive market. This was a boom time for folding bikes, and the market was expanding rapidly, with nearly 60 individual machines on sale from 15 manufacturers. Some of these, like the Bickerton range, were the last stocks of time-expired designs, but there was much that was new.

At the top end of the market, the Birdy from Germany and Bike Friday from the USA were making quite an impact. The Bike Friday, produced by GreenGear in Oregon, was designed for a rather different world. The company produced 20-inch wheel custom-made touring bikes (mostly fitted with 406mm wheels, but with a few 451mm) designed specifically for the US leisure market. Most Bike Fridays could, at a pinch, be 'quick folded' and carried by train, but they were really designed to be painstakingly dismantled and squeezed into a hardcase for carriage by air. These delightful racing bikes cost upwards of £1,000, and although Bike Friday also produced the 'budget' £695 Metro aimed more directly at rail and bus users, this didn't really hit the spot for European commuters. It was too cumbersome for regular folding, yet it lacked the custom fit and quality equipment that had become a Bike Friday trademark. In folding terms, the Birdy was a much more interesting prospect, and potentially a serious

Whilst the Bike Friday was undoubtedly a quality machine, it was designed primarily for long distance air travellers, and could even be purchased with its own hardcase/trailer, into which it could be squeezed at the airport.

Competition Hots Up - the Mark 3s 1994-2000

The Birdy appeared to be quite a threat to the Brompton, particularly the cheapest 'Red' variant shown here. However, cost was a big drawback, and although the bikes could be folded very fast in skilled hands, some people found them difficult to deal with on a daily basis.

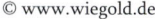
© www.wiegold.de

competitor. Developed in 1991 by Heiko Muller and Marcus Riese, two young German engineering students, the bikes had 18-inch (355mm) wheels, and folded in an asymmetrical manner. Rather than folding directly under the central frame tube, like the Brompton, the rear wheel came up alongside. The leading link front suspension then broke apart, allowing the front wheel to swing right around and pop up on the other side of the frame, rather like the early sketches for the Brompton.

This arrangement gave several advantages: with no mainframe hinge, the bike had a more rigid feel than the Brompton, it also had front and rear suspension, and most models came with derailleur gears, giving a wider gear range, and a slight efficiency advantage over the hub gears that were the norm on small wheelers.

When launched in 1995, the Birdy looked 'techy' and youthful, in contrast to the Brompton - which had not seen fundamental change for eight years and was beginning to look a bit middle-aged.

Unfortunately for Riese & Muller, there were problems. To keep the price down, the bike was built in Taiwan, but this Far Eastern manufacture meant compromises, particularly with weight, which emerged broadly similar to the Brompton, despite the use of aluminium alloy and some high-tech componentry.

In theory, 18-inch tyres were more efficient than the 16-inch (349mm) fitted to the Brompton, but the Brompton's tyres were nearer 17 inches in diameter in practice, and the range of tyres available in the (nominally larger) 18-inch size were pretty poor in the early days. Riese & Muller had designed the prototype around Dr. Moulton's excellent 17-inch tyre, which - rather confusingly - was a 369mm, so noticeably bigger than the 18-inch! They had only turned to the smaller 18-inch (355mm) tyres because the 369mm was made by just one manufacturer at the time, and was hard to find in Europe. With 369mm tyres it would have been a good bike, but it was to be some years before there were any really good tyres in the 355mm size and the Birdy was to be bugged by rapid tyre wear, poor handling and high rolling resistance. This was particularly unfortunate as it was a much sportier machine than the Brompton.

At this time, Brompton was still fitting the slothful (and historic) 55psi Raleigh Record tyre, inflated to 70psi to reduce rolling resistance to manageable levels! These too, occasionally failed, but by the mid-1990s lighter, freer-rolling tyres like the Primo Comet were being developed in the 349mm size, principally for the recumbent market, and these were just starting to arrive in the UK, giving the Brompton a real advantage for those willing to experiment.

The Birdy's derailleur gears gave problems too. If you didn't settle the bike into the right gear before folding it, the chain would come messily off as the rear wheel moved sideways. This didn't matter then or now to the dedicated enthusiasts, willing to take some care with folding, and often carrying a rubber glove for oily emergencies, but for everyday commuters, the finicky fold, reduced luggage options and lack of mudguards or fitted lights, made the Birdy less convenient.

Of course, for a younger, sportier market, such things as panniers, mudguards, hub gears and lights are positively negative attributes. The Birdy has always enjoyed a niche with this sort of user, but with prices ranging from £749 - £1,249 at the launch in 1995 (£1,299 - £2,170 at 2016 prices) it was never to gain widespread appeal.

At the cheaper end of the market, the Cresswell Micro and Fold-it looked quite a threat to Brompton for a brief period. These simple, straightforward machines were based on folding bikes designed by British engineer Peter Radnall in the 1970s. Both folded in half, the Micro around 16-inch wheels, and the Fold-it, which was originally designed to win the Post Office contract, around 20-inch wheels. Neither was successful in their original form, but in 1995, at the height of the folder boom, they were brought back into production by Richard Cresswell of Cresswell Cycles in Birmingham.

The Micro was a bit frail (shades of Bickerton here), but it was quite light, weighing only 9.5kg in basic single-speed trim. Both Cresswell bikes offered good value for money, the Micro being priced from £236 for the single-speed, to £299 for a 5-speed, while the larger Fold-it cost from £299 for a 3-speed to £378 for a SRAM 7-speed model - that's £409-£518 for the Micro and £518-£655 for the Fold-it at 2016 prices. This might not sound especially good value, but 'budget' folders in those days cost rather more than they do today.

Brompton, of course, had intended to respond to these cheaper bikes with the basic C1 model, which was to have been fitted with the single-speed hub and produced without mudguards as a cut-price leisure machine. Without the C-type, the cheapest Brompton was the L3, which now cost £378. For that price you could buy a Fold-it equipped with bigger wheels, a quality 7-speed hub gearbox, and drum brakes front and rear, but consumers weren't impressed.

The Micro sold in modest numbers to those looking for a cheap and cheerful occasional machine, but the Fold-it was a commercial failure. The bikes looked good on paper, and Richard Cresswell was an innovative hands-on engineer, but the Cresswell workshop was a chaotic place, and the bikes were relatively crude. Despite being a wobbly ride, and a bit frail, the Micro offered real advantages in certain markets, being much lighter than the Brompton, and folding almost as well. The Fold-it, on the other hand, was a big, clumsy beast. The ride was quite good, but the folded package was too cumbersome and heavy for regular commuting. It looked better value than the Brompton, but it was never a serious threat in practice.

Despite being given a thumbs down by the public, the Fold-it continued to be favourably reviewed, receiving the Gold Award for Best Cycle at the 1996 National Cycle Show. A few years later Cresswell Engineering was absorbed into the Pashley empire, and the Fold-it, and later the Micro, were dropped.

Other manufacturers would try to tackle the Brompton's effortless dominance by going smaller - in some cases, much smaller. The MicroBike was a Swedish design, patented in 1986, with a clever hinge mechanism allowing it to fold into a narrow, if rather long package, the narrow width being helped by small 12½" (203mm) wheels. It was a light, intelligent design, but undergeared, and a bit unstable.

In 1996 the Fold-it won Best Bike at the National Cycle Show. Designer Richard Cresswell with the Fold-it (on lower stand) and Two's Company tandem (upper stand). The Fold-it offered value for money, but was never a great success.

The Micro sold in much bigger numbers. It was rather spindly and wobbly, but significantly cheaper and lighter than the Brompton.
This 3-speed model (right) is ridden by enthusiastic owner Dr. Graham Cooke.

Twenty years later, in 2006, it was the turn of the French, with the Mobiky Genius. This used similar 12½" wheels, but folded concertina-style, with a double-reduction gear and 3-speed hub to give reasonably conventional gearing. It looked smart and effective, and it rode surprisingly well, but the figures just couldn't stack up against the Brompton: the Mobiky produced a bigger folded package, it was heavier, slower on the road, and more expensive.

Meanwhile, Sir Clive Sinclair had become obsessed with the folding bike problem, but his fixation with ultra-small wheels was to be his downfall. Working with Mark Sanders of Strida fame, Sir Clive produced a prototype X-bike in 1990, with 8-inch wheels and a simple frame that hinged like a pair of scissors from an 'X' shape to a long thin package. This machine failed to make it into production, but 16 years later Sir Clive did launch the A-bike - an 'A' shaped bicycle that concertinaed rather like the Mobiky. The A-bike was strikingly compact (less than half the volume of the Brompton) and light (more or less half the weight), but there were some fatal flaws. The 6-inch tyres, wobbly frame and single 41-inch gear made it almost unrideable on normal roads. The wheel size was later increased to 8-inches, which improved the rideability a little, but made the folded package bigger. A reasonable number seem to have been sold, but mainly to enthusiasts and collectors of folding ephemera. Increasingly, the real challenge was coming from Dahon, now starting to find its feet in the UK under Mark Bickerton's guidance. Dahon bikes were still a bit cheap and cheerful, starting with some rather basic 16-inch (305mm) machines in the £200-£300 region. But Dr. Hon was beginning to realise that Brompton had this compact market pretty well sewn up, and Dahon gradually extended its range to include 20-inch and 26-inch bikes, the 20-inch models in particular selling well. One of the best from this era was the Dahon Tailwind. It wasn't particularly compact or light, but it rode well, undercut the Brompton by £20 and ticked most of the purchasing boxes for most people.

Increasingly wily at marketing folding bikes, Dahon found that it could prolong the life of long-in-the-tooth models by 'badge-engineering' them. In 1996, Dahon was still only experimenting with this policy, but within a few years, half the folding bikes on sale in the world would be either Dahons, Dahon clones, or outdated variants badged as something else. When Dahon had finished with it, the Tailwind went on to bear a Ridgeback label, and was replaced in 2000 by a whole range of new Dahon 20-inch bikes, including the £299 Boardwalk, another serious Brompton competitor.

Clive Sinclair's A-bike was highly transportable when folded (above right) but with tiny wheels that proved an Achilles' heel when faced with the reality of uneven roads and potholes (above left).

Competition Hots Up - the Mark 3s 1994-2000

Sir Clive Sinclair had become obsessed with folding bikes, producing the A-bike in 2006. It was light and compact but almost unrideable, and thus little more than a curiosity as a transport machine.

Change at the Top

But the 20-inch-wheeled Dahon revolution was still some years off. In 1996, most of the competition was heavy, difficult to ride or both, and even the bikes that undercut the Brompton didn't do so by very much. There was plenty of competition, but none of it was especially good, and for long periods at this time, Brompton's Chiswick Park factory was swamped under a torrent of orders. During these all too frequent production famines, when waiting lists grew too long, output of bikes was rationed. Output had recovered rapidly after the move to the Chiswick factory, climbing to 3,363 in 1995-96, and 5,196 in 1996-97, but for various reasons it then stalled. Brompton now had more than 80 dealers in the UK alone, and as panic grew about waiting lists and shortages, customers were ringing around looking for a bike - any bike - as long as it was a Brompton.

This panic buying caused a lot of trouble for Nicola McGregor's small sales team, still under instructions to look after the dealers which had shown faith when the Brompton was an unknown quantity, but under daily assault from bigger dealers and chainstores, a handful of whom could have taken the entire factory output, and they knew it.

The export market alone could have absorbed most of the factory's output at this time. In 1997, the ADFC (the Allgemeiner Deutscher Fahrrad-Club, similar to the British Cyclists Touring Club) gave the Brompton its Bike of the Year Award. It was, of course, a great honour, but the award put yet more upward pressure on sales at a difficult time.

Just five years earlier, Andrew Ritchie had likened the Chiswick factory to an empty cathedral. Now it was full and overflowing, and the only easy way to increase production was to move again, to bigger premises. In October 1998, Brompton moved back west, to an anonymous factory in Brentford beside the elevated section of the M4 motorway. With the Neobike affair still ongoing, the factory move finally brought an end to discussions about overseas assembly. In the short-term, the move caused considerable disruption, and annual production was to languish in the 6,000 to 7,000 region until the latter half of 2000, when output began to climb again, only to be knocked back by outside events.

Despite selling every bike it could produce, Brompton was starting to lose the technological race. In some ways the company had been the victim of its own success. The factory had been running to catch up for so many years that changes in the market had passed it by. In some ways the company had been the victim of its own success. The factory had been running to catch up for so many years that changes in the market seemed to have passed it by.

Enthusiasts had been fitting better quality brakes and tyres for several years, and the general feeling was that the factory neither knew nor cared about developing the product. This sort of talk was anathema to Julian Vereker, the instinctive marketing man, who had overseen the company's growth from the sidelines to a position of real strength, and was now pressing Andrew to pass at least some control to a younger management team.

Very gradually, the harmonious relationship between Ritchie and Vereker began to fracture, and Julian - who had always preferred fresh challenges to old arguments - began to spend more time developing his other businesses. He had supported Andrew Ritchie through all sorts of difficulties, and had backed him at crucial, and often lively, shareholder meetings. Now he was frustrated that the company was not developing as it might, and as a minority shareholder, he had no power to influence events, other than by persuasion.

During 1998 he was also becoming increasingly ill. When finally he was diagnosed with terminal cancer, Julian calmly decided to put his remaining energy into his core business, rearranging Naim Audio's affairs, to ensure that his widow would be secure, and the jobs of his employees safe, after his death.

Competition Hots Up - the Mark 3s 1994-2000

With quite a large sum tied up in Brompton, and no further interest in playing a role, Julian asked Andrew to buy him out in May 1999, a request that would involve some complicated financial juggling. Under the circumstances, it's perhaps not surprising that the relationship between the two men was put under some strain, with Vereker refusing to return Andrew's calls at one stage.

As so often in the Brompton story, the answer lay in choosing the right person, and Andrew did exactly that, calling his old friend Tim Guinness. Since politely refusing the offer to invest in Brompton 23 years before, Guinness had gone on to do very well for himself in the financial world. In 18 years, his asset management business had grown from 20 employees to 350. Originally a subsidiary of a small merchant bank, the business had just been sold to Investec, a South African bank, and although he was still busy tidying up loose ends, Guinness was already looking for a new challenge. Initially, he had no intention of getting closely involved with Brompton, but he agreed to help out his friend by overseeing the delicate negotiations over Julian's departure. With a legal requirement for two directors, he also agreed to take Julian's place, but with no plans to make this a long-term commitment.

Tim Guinness was the perfect man for the job. He had a light, breezy manner that belied an incisive financial mind, and he quickly agreed terms on which Brompton would buy back Julian's 14,000 shares (an 18% shareholding) for £301,000. It was a considerable sum, reducing the company's assets by a quarter, but the company could now afford it, and it served to reduce the number of shares in circulation, to the benefit of the remaining shareholders.

By the turn of the millennium, everything was in place, and in November 1999, Andrew sent a memo to the shareholders:

"Following Julian's departure, I will be seeking the appointment of new directors, ideally with the skills needed to develop the business. Tim Guinness is assisting with this and he has agreed to join the board, with the main aim of assembling this team, and possibly remaining long-term himself. I will be able to outline progress in more detail at the AGM."

All went smoothly at the shareholder's meeting, the arrival of Tim Guinness clearly being seen as something of a coup for a small West London engineering works, and Tim Guinness duly joined Andrew Ritchie as a director. Andrew then asked Tim to become chairman. Initially, he refused, suggesting instead Christopher Stewart-Smith, a businessman involved in the computer software industry. In the event, Stewart-Smith joined the board, but in an unusual reverse coup, agreed with Andrew that Tim Guinness was the best man for the chairmanship!

In January 2000, Julian Vereker died. He had not neglected his yacht business, and the computer-aided Wind-Express 48 was launched the same day. Vereker will be remembered by a great many people for a great many things, but his financial know-how and steady managerial hand had been essential elements in the Brompton story.

Brompton Mark 3

Despite pressure from Julian Vereker and a few shareholders, Ritchie had refused to relax his control of Brompton in the late 1990s, but this wasn't entirely a matter of stubbornness. As an engineer, he knew what needed to be done, and with the company settled in the bigger premises, and a competent management team keeping the lid on day-to-day decisions, he embarked on the biggest redesign of the Brompton since the launch of the Mark 2 in 1988.

The Mark 3, rolled out from March 2000, was a tremendous advance, and it effectively silenced the critics. Behind the scenes, the factory had looked closely at every element of the bike. The Mark 3 looked almost identical to its predecessor, but nearly every component was different beneath the skin (see the summary on page 77). With surplus capacity at last, the 'C' type was resurrected, partly as a way of using up stocks of Mark 2 components. For the time being at least, the C-type would only be sold as the C3, fitted with the 3-speed Sturmey-Archer hub gear, for £353, almost £100 less than the much improved L3.

The Mark 3 had its own Brompton-branded tyre, based on the Primo racing technology that owners had been fitting for several years. Andrew Ritchie had never designed a tyre, but with a mixture of engineering guile and dead reckoning, he seems to have done an excellent job. It rolled markedly better than the Raleigh Record, lasted for a considerable mileage, and it was lighter. The tyre was, however, criticised for a degree of waywardness on white lines and drain covers, particularly in the wet, although most owners were delighted with the easier pedalling, and it soon became one of the most popular retro-fit accessories, finding its way onto Moultons and Micros too. From being close to death, the 37-349mm tyre now seemed to be guaranteed a bright future, and in the years that followed, other manufacturers released tyres in this size, although to date none has quite matched the Brompton tyre's broad appeal.

Some of the changes, like a rear mudflap, might seem insignificant, but they were important. For years, owners had grumbled about the 'Brompton stripe' - a thin stain of mud thrown onto the rider's back by the rear tyre. Because of the way the bike folded, it wasn't possible to fit a conventional mudflap, but the Mark 3 had a small, tough flap that worked almost as well. Other changes were cosmetic, such as stainless steel spokes and fittings, but they were things the public had been requesting for years.

Like the tyres, braking had long been an issue, and again, the factory adapted the aftermarket accessories that had become popular with enthusiasts, settling on a much more powerful dual-pivot caliper design, again reworked especially for the bike, and matched with new shorter brake levers.

Elsewhere, the front end had been beefed up yet again, this time with stronger German-made handlebars, and the folding left-hand pedal - formerly an accessory - had become a standard fitting. The list of components went on and on. New suede-effect handlebar grips were lighter and more comfortable, and there was an improved pump that actually worked when you needed it. Lighting had been completely reworked, with halogen front lamp and Basta LED rear light on the 'T' type, and a similar battery-operated rear light on the 'L' allied to a rather dubious battery front lamp. Not perfect, but as there had previously been no battery lamp option, it was a huge advance.

Most of the changes added a little weight, but the Primo-style tyres were lighter, making the machines slightly lighter overall. The feeling was of a much stiffer, livelier bike, faster in a straight line, and - thanks to the lighter wheels - quicker to respond in fast turns as well.

Just to demonstrate that Andrew Ritchie had finally relaxed his autocratic style and taken on board the desires of his customers, the gearing on the 5-speed had been reduced, keeping a practical top gear, but giving better hill climbing. And the colour range had finally been extended too. Green had been a popular option for some time, but it now became a standard colour, and

Competition Hots Up - the Mark 3s 1994-2000

NEW FOR THE MARK 3

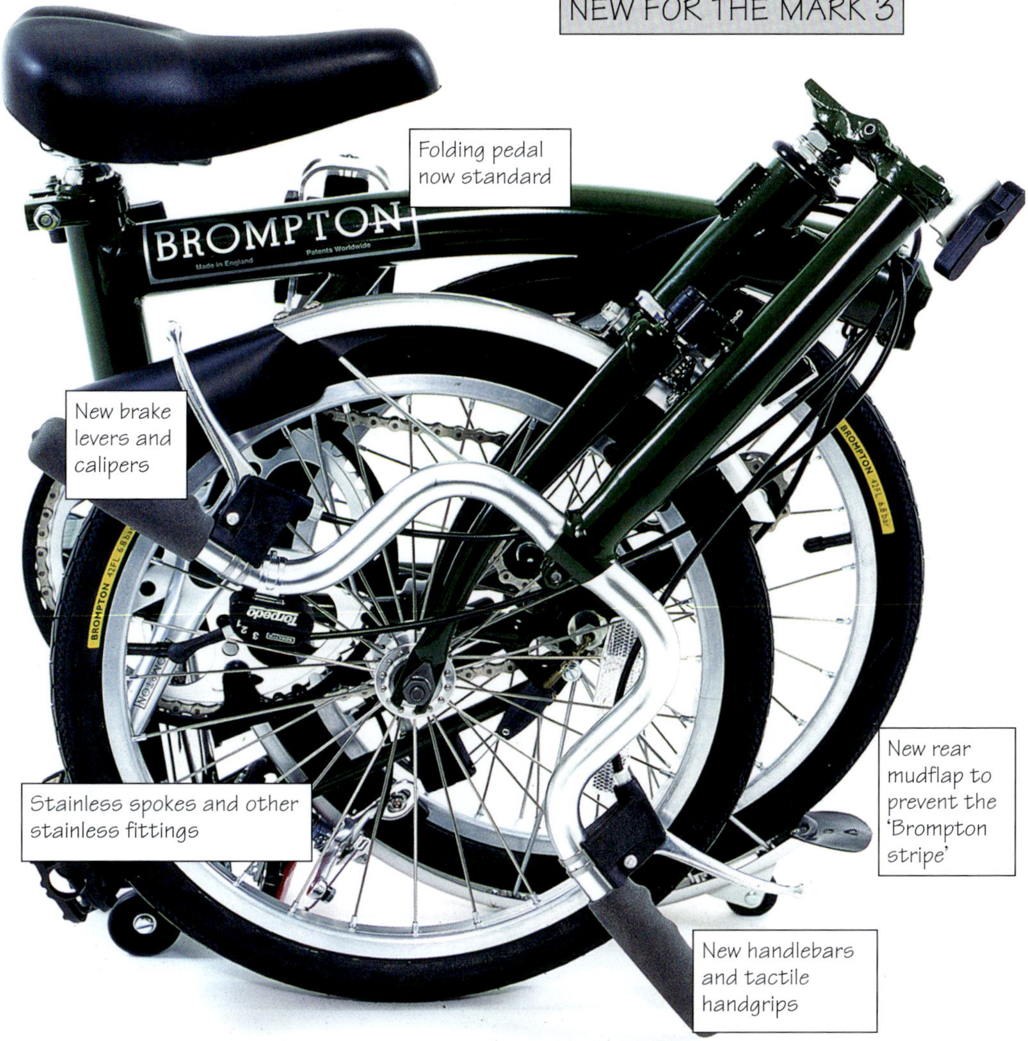

Folding pedal now standard

New brake levers and calipers

New rear mudflap to prevent the 'Brompton stripe'

Stainless spokes and other stainless fittings

New handlebars and tactile handgrips

Brompton own-brand tyres. Designed by Andrew Ritchie. A yellow band means 'normal' and a green band means kevlar puncture proofing.

The Mark 3 looked similar to the Mark 2, but was completely revised. A year later, Brompton was forced to drop the Sturmey-Archer 3- and 5- speed hub gears. This very typical green L3 is fitted with the post April 2001 SRAM 3-speed hub and gear shifter (left).

The bikes were also fitted with an improved pump, and at long last there was a battery lighting option for the 'L' type.

77

the other recent options of yellow, ivory and blue had been extended to include aquamarine, and reduced in price. For an extra £30, you could have a rather flash silver.

In the greater scheme of things, the Mark 3 Brompton was a relatively insignificant engineering project, but it was big news in the folding bike world. Ritchie had demonstrated that his engineer-led management style could respond to customer demand in a positive and technology-led manner. In this respect, it was a considerable tour de force.

Brompton's bulging order book and relative lack of development had resulted in a flurry of investment by other folding bike companies. The Cambridge based Airnimal - a sporty long distance tourer designed to compete with the Bike Friday rather than the Brompton's speedier, easier fold - had a low key launch in 1998, but by 2000 was gaining popularity with good reviews, especially from 'serious' road riders.

By 2000 the Cambridge-based Airnimal was gaining popularity with good reviews. As a 'suitcase' folder it never competed head on with the Brompton.

Also in 2000, the Airframe was back on the road to production, the Strida 2 had already been on sale for a year or so, Birdy and Bike Friday were making top-end inroads, and Dahon was expanding in all directions. If Brompton had not introduced the Mark 3 when it did, the bike would have drifted into a genteel middle-age, appealing to a diminishing pool of older enthusiasts. The unexpected revamp knocked the opposition right off its feet, and re-established the Brompton brand at the top of the pile.

Despite this success, there were boardroom battles over marketing. Sooner or later Andrew Ritchie was going to retire, and before this could happen a satisfactory succession would have to be arranged, both on the engineering and marketing side. Andrew Ritchie, with characteristic caution and thoroughness, wanted the right people in place, but this was proving difficult, especially on the marketing side. Tim Guinness had already concluded that the company needed a marketing manager, and an engineering / production manager, as a matter of urgency. One immediate change was the employment of Bubblegate, a design company based in Kent, to oversee Brompton's advertising and publicity material, its first rather thankless role being to produce a brochure for the Mark 3.

Ritchie had introduced a superior bike, agreed to compromise on colours, and even listened to his customers, but he continued to resist attempts to 'market' the bike with lifestyle images and trendy rather than truthful words and phrases. After a great deal of time, effort, and hair tearing by creatives, Bubblegate triumphantly unveiled a new brochure some months after the arrival of the bike. It contained a modest number of tasteful images of young, and young-at-heart users, plus a good meaty technical section. Once again, a compromise had been reached.

Competition Hots Up - the Mark 3s 1994-2000

Another 21st century folder was the Skoot (left and below). Designed and built in Britain in 2001, it cost £1,000, weighed 15.8kg and had a single 55-inch gear. Folded volume was about the same as the Brompton, but in every other respect it was comprehensively outclassed. Within a year it had gone.

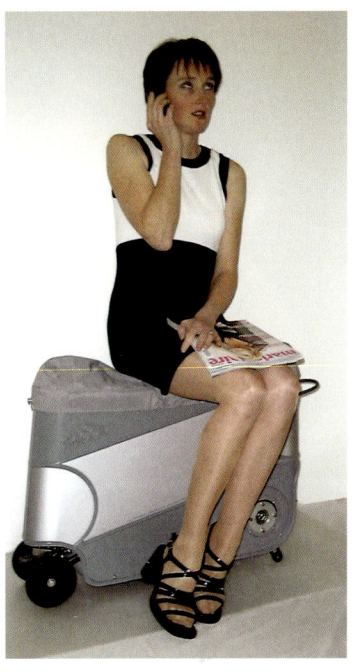

Against the Skoot, the Brompton Mark 3 looked pretty conservative, but where the Skoot failed, the Brompton continued to sell in even greater numbers.
It might have looked conservative, but the Mark 3 had incorporated lots of new technology, keeping it ahead in terms of ride quality and foldability.

The Modern Era The Mark 4 bikes were a triumph of lightweight engineering, and marketing too.

Into the New Millennium
2000-2011

"So far we don't know whether the marketing is successful, because the bike's selling itself. We can't produce enough." TIM GUINNESS

"The message is that we've taken a decision to grow and become a competitive global player. We're proud to be a British company, and determined to remain independent."
WILL BUTLER-ADAMS

Handlebar Problems Sorted

The road to mass production can be long, hard and strewn with unexpected obstacles. In 2000, Brompton seemed to be safely established, with a new factory, big enough to accommodate foreseeable growth, a new chairman, and a highly respected and reasonably profitable product, recently revamped in Mark 3 form to good reviews. But during the following two years, Brompton was to be rocked by a couple of serious incidents. Neither put the company in jeopardy - it was now much too well established for that - but such incidents demonstrate the importance of double and quadruple checking the supply chain and reliability of third party components.

The first problem came out of the blue. We've already seen how Brompton had found it necessary to change handlebars several times. The handlebars - and particularly the point where the bars meet the stem - are a highly stressed and vulnerable area. And failure can have serious, and potentially fatal, consequences.

Most cycle manufacturers have had some sort of trouble with handlebars, and it's no surprise. If they're made of steel and clamped to the stem, there's not much that can go wrong, but steel is heavy, so handlebars are usually made of lighter, but more vulnerable, aluminium. Whatever the material, welds or brazing in this area will tend to weaken the bars (this was the weakness with the early steel Brompton handlebars), and if clamped to the stem, aluminium in particular has a tendency to scoring and scratching inside the clamp, especially if the bars are twisted. A scratch here is invisible but under constant stress, and if it fails, the bars can simply fall into two halves. Even without stress gatherers like scratches and welds, all handlebars have a finite fatigue life, and the trick for a manufacturer is to use enough material to give a reasonable life without adding too much weight or price - a very tricky equation when there is so much at stake.

Andrew Ritchie had used steel bars on the prototypes, but these were replaced with aluminium for the production bikes. The first aluminium bars were replaced by a stronger design from GB Cycles after about 18 months, and these in turn had been replaced by the Neobike bars in mid-1995. There had been only a handful of failures with the earlier designs, but the upgrades had seemed worthwhile. In the late 1990s, a small number of Neobike bars began to fail, and it was decided to cure the problem once and for all by upgrading to a thicker, heavier and better quality handlebar produced by Humpert of Germany. This was introduced in September 1999 and brought an end to the problem. But what of the tens of thousands of older bikes in service?

On top of the low background failure rate of the older bars, it gradually became clear that an increasing number of the Neobike bars were failing, and the company started to watch the statistics with growing unease. It looked as though the handlebars - superficially well up to British Standards - were failing early through fatigue. But would this problem affect every single bar, or was it just a small batch? Were there geographical or chronological factors involved? There didn't seem to be, but the failures kept increasing.

In 2000, the rate of failures reached 0.4%, high enough to trigger action. Rather than recall every bike for the dealer to fit new bars (and possibly cause more damage in the process), it was decided to manufacture a brace and distribute these free to distributors and dealers and thus to owners worldwide. The brace clamped around the vertical parts of the handlebars, which had the effect of reducing the bending stress at the root of the bar, and in the event of a failure, keeping the two halves in place, enabling the bike to be brought to a stop safely.

It was a classically meticulously engineered little device, and once the bracing kits had been publicised and several thousand distributed and fitted, the rate of failures dropped dramatically, proving that the brace was a very effective remedy. It was also made available for £8.75 to owners of newer bikes who expected to ride hard.

The affair highlighted a growing problem for the Brompton. Designed as a commuting tool, the bike had proved able to perform all sorts of niche functions for which it wasn't intended, such as surveying, loaded touring and many other high-stress applications. Under the circumstances, Brompton seem to have got off quite lightly with the failure of a handful of frames and a larger number of handlebars. The crossbar braces have found all sorts of uses since, principally as a handhold when carrying children, another activity for which the Brompton really wasn't designed!

The Brompton has been used for many expeditions including map surveying in the Himalayas, accompanying scientists to the South Pole (see inside back cover) and for trips through underdeveloped countries. Above left: Ishmahil Blagrove riding a Brompton through Cambodia in the mid-1990s. Above right: Adam Hart-Davis took his Brompton to various exotic locations in the 1990s, including the top of Mount Etna. Despite such varied and exacting use the handlebar issue has been the only significant concern over the bike's construction and safety. See page 204 for a photo of the brace issued to remedy the problem.

Dodgy Dealings

The other big problem started to develop at about the same time, and although it didn't involve safety issues, it very nearly stopped production of the Brompton altogether. Sturmey-Archer geared hubs had been manufactured in Nottingham for almost a hundred years and the hub was an integral component in the Brompton design. There were two other manufacturers of 3-speed hubs in the world - SRAM (formerly Sachs) in Germany, and Shimano in Japan - but neither was ideal for the Brompton. The SRAM was heavier and more expensive, while Shimano's

Nexus hub was too wide, and fitted with a roller brake. This could be resolved, given time, but re-engineering the Brompton to accept either hub wasn't an easy option. And both involved the complication and expense of importing heavy components, whereas stock from Nottingham could be brought down the M1 in a few hours.

With the 5-speed hub, there really was no alternative source of supply. SRAM produced the only other 5-speed, but it was significantly wider and, like its 3-speed counterpart, heavier and more expensive than the Sturmey hub.

None of this seemed to matter in late 1999, because it was inconceivable that Sturmey would fail. The company wasn't very profitable, but it was part of the much larger Raleigh Group, which itself was backed by the giant Derby Cycle Corporation, a multinational based in the USA. Sturmey enjoyed a niche market, and after some uncertain decades as hub gears declined in popularity, sales had stabilized, and were now particularly strong in the large and reliable Netherlands market. The company had a full order book, and a healthy turnover in 1999 of some £12 million.

As late as September 1999 Sturmey had introduced a new variant of the 5-speed hub, the 'ball-locking' system, and Brompton, like many other end users, had no reason to imagine that supply problems were even on the horizon. But Derby Cycles was engaging in one of those periodic navel-gazing exercises which multinationals tend to perform once in a while, and a rather inexperienced US management team had reached the conclusion that Sturmey-Archer's eclectic output of hub gears, spokes, leather saddles (under the Brooks brand), and small components for the automotive industry didn't fit well with its global ambitions.

Consequently, the Sturmey-Archer and Raleigh factory sites were sold for a reported £4 million to the University of Nottingham, the aim being to relocate and downsize the bicycle business and sell Sturmey-Archer. Raleigh was primarily an assembly operation by this time, so relocation would be easy.

Sturmey-Archer was another matter. At first the Sturmey management was optimistic. The company would be sold, and a new owner would mean a new factory, new equipment, and hopefully the capital to invest in new products. It had several multi-speed designs on the drawing board at the time, and a considerable amount of engineering expertise, plus patents and drawings dating back over many decades. As a major customer, Brompton was kept informed, but had been assured that the change of ownership and subsequent factory move would have little or no effect on hub production.

On 30th June 2000 Sturmey-Archer was sold for a reported £3 million to a hitherto unknown investment group called Lenark, but the deal was not quite what it seemed. Quite how and why a respectable company like Derby - that relied on Sturmey-Archer's parts to support its other brands - had allowed one of its subsidiaries to be sold to an insalubrious, almost penniless outfit, then only two years old, is a great unanswered question.

It later transpired that one of Lenark's principals, one Simon Allso, was a recently discharged bankrupt with a criminal record for fraud. Derby had actually been paid the princely sum of £30 (about the price of a 3-speed hub!) for Sturmey-Archer after Lenark agreed to take responsibility for a redundancy bill of nearly £3 million.

In fact, Lenark was no more than a shell. Despite protestations to the contrary, the company had no intention of paying redundancies, building bicycle hubs, or anything else, other than getting its hands on Sturmey-Archer's assets, which amounted to some £300,000 in cash at the time of the transfer. Matters came to a head on 11th September 2000 when the Sturmey MD Colin Bateman presented the Lenark directors with a £75,000 bill to cover the early stages of moving the factory and purchasing new machinery, and the Lenark people subsequently went to ground, Lenark director Clive Walton allegedly making a clandestine exit from the building via the fire escape.

In the next few days, the scale of the financial collapse became apparent - Sturmey-Archer was effectively bankrupt. On 15th September, Bateman brought together his 260 staff and told them that not only had their jobs evaporated overnight, but production was at an end, and there was no prospect of even paying the current wages bill, let alone redundancy payments. Lenark continued to drain the company's reserves until the bank accounts were frozen a few days later, but despite attempts to sell the factory, and an undertaking by Nottingham City Council to underwrite the cost of the move, no buyer was subsequently found for the business. Brompton actually gave serious thought to buying Sturmey-Archer itself, but for such a small company the financial and logistical nightmare of finding premises, and re-establishing a much bigger company some 200 miles north of its London base, proved just too big a risk.

While the receivers continued to search for a buyer, a skeleton staff of volunteers were winding down production at Sturmey-Archer. One morning, Andrew Ritchie received a call from Nick Sanders of Sturmey: if he could get up to Nottingham quickly with a van, he could 'liberate' stock before the whole operation collapsed. Brompton always kept a good stock of hubs to cover production irregularities, but an extra van load was a priceless offer. Ritchie headed north, and came away with 1,100 hubs, mostly 3-speed, and delivered them to Mike Hesson, Brompton's long-term wheel-builder in nearby Wolverhampton:

"It was a really helpful gesture on Nick's part. The van was well overloaded with all that weight, but we now had an extra six weeks supply, and enough hubs to keep production going for just over six months."

It wasn't much, but it gave a vital breathing space to negotiate a price for a slightly customized hub gear from SRAM and re-engineer the Brompton to accept the SRAM 3-speed. But there was no chance of replacing the 5-speed, and when stocks of hubs were exhausted, the model was deleted, never - as it transpired - to return.

In April 2001, the first consignment of SRAM hubs arrived, but it had been a damn close run thing: the factory had only two days' supply of Sturmey hubs left in stock. Any further delay would have meant redundancies at Brompton.

The only positive fall-out from the Sturmey-Archer affair was that Andrew had also 'liberated' Steve Rickels, Sturmey's chief designer, to help share the design workload at Brompton. Rickels' first role was to assist in the design of a very Bromptonesque replacement for the 5-speed.

The Six-speed Emerges

Ritchie and his team had decided to put a 2-speed derailleur on the nose of a 3-speed hub, producing a 6-speed bike, and this was one reason SRAM had been asked to produce a custom hub.

This arrangement would have several advantages and several disadvantages. The gear range (the difference between the lowest and highest gears) would be a little narrower than the former 5-speed hub, but without the inherent inefficiency of the 5-speed's wide-ratio gears, this wouldn't be a great issue. Perhaps more of a problem was that there would now be two gear triggers, something that users had found so confusing on the original 5-speed. There would be a slight weight penalty too, but some intriguing prospects for saving weight on certain models, because the 2-speed derailleur could be fitted without a hub gear to a future lightweight version of the bike. This was uncharted territory for Brompton. The company would have to design a complex and unique derailleur assembly, plus a new derailleur trigger, again quite unlike anything else, and the systems would have to be prototyped, tested and put into production as soon as possible, because the lack of a multi-gear bike was losing customers and hitting the profitability of the bikes that were being sold.

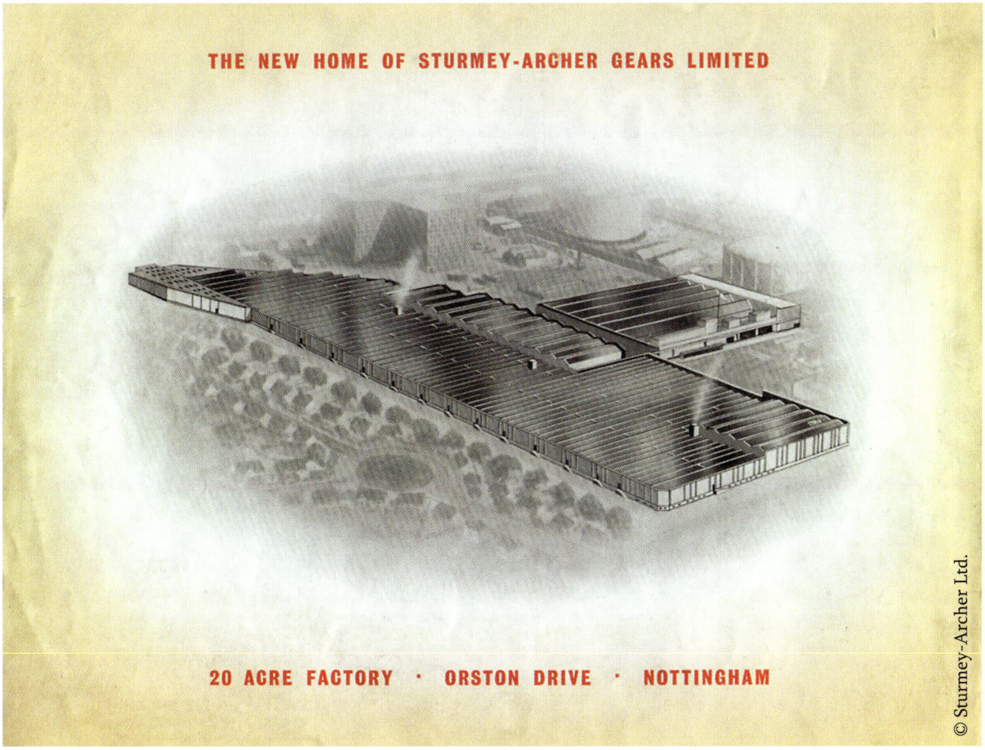

Into the New Millenium 2000-2011

THE NEW HOME OF STURMEY-ARCHER GEARS LIMITED

20 ACRE FACTORY · ORSTON DRIVE · NOTTINGHAM

© Sturmey-Archer Ltd.

Raleigh's Nottingham factory and its Sturmey-Archer sister plant, pictured here when it opened in 1954, once employed thousands. All this came to an end in 2001, when a planned move to a new Nottingham site was fatally mishandled. Production subsequently moved to Taiwan, but the affair was very nearly disastrous for Brompton.
The shot below was taken in 2003 and shows all that was left of the once-mighty Raleigh works.

© Paul Lenton

85

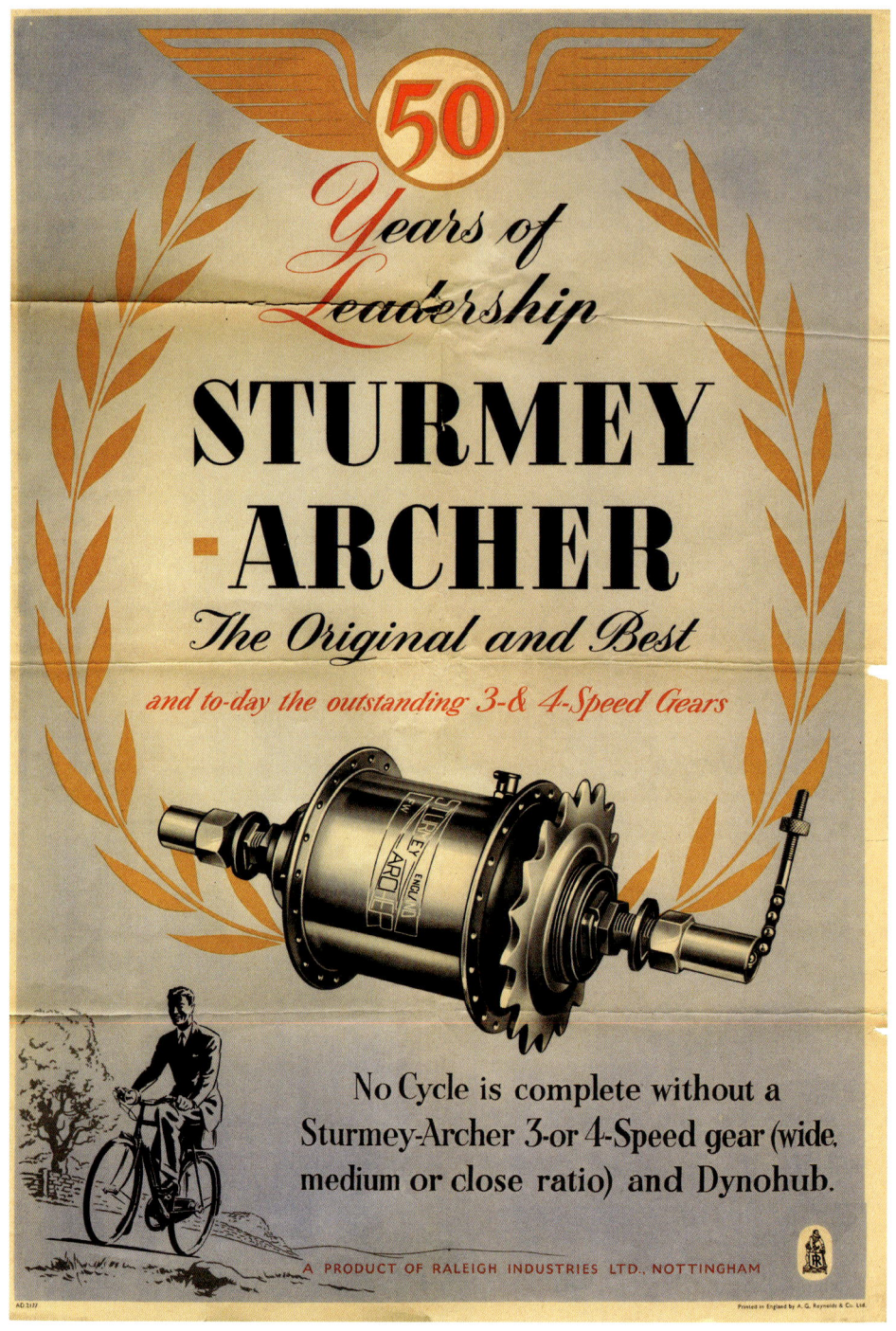

At the height of its success in the early 1950s Sturmey-Archer hub production reached over 2 million units a year. As this 50th anniversary poster from 1952 states, hubs came not only in 3- and 4- speed variants, but in a variety of gear ranges. More than half a century later, in 2009, Sturmey would collaborate with Brompton to produce an ultra-wide ratio hub, the Brompton Wide Ratio (BWR).

Design and testing of the 6-speed Brompton took exactly a year, and in April 2002, the new system was introduced. As always, it was carefully thought through and meticulously engineered. The Brompton had always been fitted with a chain tensioner to take up the slack in the chain when the bike was folded, effectively packing the chain away when out of use. In a bit of classic Andrew Ritchie ingenuity, the tensioner now performed a second role, keeping the chain correctly tensioned as the rider changed between the two derailleur gears.

Technically, it was quite interesting. The derailleur idler wheels were allowed to 'float' on their mounting bolts to align with either of the two sprockets fixed to the input 'driver' of the hub gear. Derailleur changes were accomplished with a little shifter that pushed the chain one way or the other, and was controlled by a second lever on the handlebars.

With only two sprockets to worry about, the usual derailleur adjustment and indexing problems did not apply. The lever was cleverly spring-loaded in both directions, with enough spare movement to allow for cable stretch and wear. This two-way spring-loading meant that the shifter could be moved without damage when the bike was stationary, just like a hub gear shifter (important because the other lever still did control a hub gearbox) and once set up, the device was pretty tolerant to wear and tear, enabling it to keep working for some time before requiring adjustment.

Testing and early production threw up a few technical issues. Situated low down next to the rear wheel, the shifter was rather vulnerable to mud and water, causing the tiny ball bearing inside to seize. It was soon replaced by a cruder and less delicate plain bearing, and in most other respects the system worked well. The gear range wasn't very wide, but it was adequate, and in marketing terms, it gave Brompton back its top end model.

When introduced in April 2002, the 6-speed sold for £524 in basic 'L' form, or £626 as a 'T' type; a premium of £65 over the 3-speed models, something of a bargain considering that two years before, the less sophisticated 5-speed had sold for a premium of £74 over the 3-speed. Despite some 6% inflation over those two years, the new bikes were only £10 or so more expensive than their 5-speed predecessors, a distinct cut in real terms that helped to get sales moving again after the long hiatus.

Sturmey-Archer had not actually died back

The new 6-speed was technically clever - the chain tensioner, already fitted to the bike, doubled as a derailleur, the idler wheels floating on their mounting bolts, allowing the chain to move between two rear sprockets. Like all early 6-speeds, this example is fitted to a SRAM hub.

in the autumn of 2000. The Brooks saddle business had been bought by its own management before being sold to Selle Royal of Italy, and in December 2000, just as the Sturmey assets were about to be liquidated, it was announced that the hub gear business had been bought for £750,000 by Sunrace of Taiwan. Consequently some twenty container-loads of equipment were shipped to Taiwan, together with three former employees. Alan Clarke, a Sturmey-Archer manager of 31 years standing, became general manager of the European arm, Sunrace Sturmey-Archer Europe BV, based in its core market, the Netherlands.

Production in Taiwan took much longer to build up than had been hoped, and it was not until June 2001 that the first 3-speed hubs reached Europe. Ironically enough the order was destined for Raleigh, arriving just as the Sturmey factory was finally being demolished!

By this time, Gary Matthews, the Derby chief executive who instigated the Sturmey-Archer debacle had gone, and within a few months, Derby itself had imploded, although most of the bicycle manufacturing businesses survived intact.

For Brompton, the resumption of Sturmey output from Taiwan brought a sigh of relief. At long last Brompton had two potential suppliers, and although the company did not immediately revert to using Sturmey hubs, the rear frames were adapted to enable either hub to be fitted.

Evolution and the Mark 4

The Sturmey affair had caused two years of uncertainty, and more or less stalled other engineering developments at Brompton. Almost unnoticed back in June 2000, the handlebar stem hinge had changed in shape. This change meant little to the average purchaser, but to Brompton it was a very big deal indeed. The change, from a forged to cast hinge assembly, was the first step in a scheme to automate some of the frame brazing. This programme had been held up during the Sturmey problems, but would soon be back on track.

Several minor changes were introduced during 2002 and 2003 - a new moulded nylon hook to 'catch' the front wheel when the bike was folded, a new seat pillar frame bush, and a thinner chainring to suit the two different widths of chain used on the derailleur and non-derailleur models. Later, the dynamo was replaced yet again, with a better Axa design, and a new handlebar catch introduced, finally laying to rest one of the longest-running grumbles from users that the bars would occasionally fly out from the folded package. A new, lighter front bag carrier frame was also introduced.

One of the technical difficulties unique to the Brompton was water ingress into the brake cables. Like the dynamos, these were affected by rain. Both brake cables pointed upwards when the bike was being ridden, and ingress of water was made worse because the small wheels put the brake calipers much closer to the ground than would normally be the case. The rear cable also had to contend with being flipped over and coiled when folded. Regular commuters rode home in the rain, folded their bikes, and left them in a warm hallway where the water would work its way down inside the cable, causing premature seizure, reducing the already weak brake performance. This was solved by fitting little rubber gaiters between the cable and caliper.

In 2002, Tim Guinness introduced two characters to the Brompton story who were to play key roles in the evolution of the bike in the modern era. First to arrive was a young engineer named Will Butler-Adams, who - for the time being - slotted quietly into the engineering team. The other was Edward Donald, a young marketing man who had worked for some of the big brands and seemed to offer a very clear vision of the way he wanted to carry Brompton forward. One of his first decisions was to put time and resources into the American market. Since 1995 sales in America had been handled in a gentlemanly and relaxed style by Channell Wasson, a laconic real estate agent, working out of Palo Alto, California.

Ed Donald decided to shift US sales up a gear by exhibiting the Brompton at the annual Interbike show in Las Vegas and building up a country-wide dealer network. At first, the US bike shop owners were bemused by the little European bike, but the policy gradually paid off, and sales began to build.

Meanwhile, Donald turned his attention to Japan. Japanese company Mizutani had been selling the Neobike Brompton for several years, but supplies had been cut off in 2001 when the agreement between Brompton and Neobike was wound up. From 2002 Mizutani had been forced to place orders for the British bikes, which travelled via Mitsubishi London and Mitsubishi Tokyo, a tortuous and expensive route. The price had rocketed overnight, causing sales to slump by 90% to 200 a year. This could all be sorted, of course, and Japan remained a territory ripe for exploitation, but with bikes in short supply there was little point in investing time and money in streamlining deliveries, cutting costs and increasing sales, in Japan or anywhere else. For Edward Donald, marketing the Brompton was proving a frustrating process. He could see numerous opportunities, but limitations on the production side made them impossible to exploit. When he had arrived, in July 2002, the company had been selling 8,000 bikes a year, but with the clearing of the Sturmey log-jam, and launch of the 6-speed, demand began to outstrip supply, despite record growth in output.

The following year (2004) saw a small change that heralded a major revision that would culminate in the Mark 4 Brompton the following year. As part of the ongoing project to automate some of the frame brazing, the mainframe hinge had received the same treatment as the handlebar stem two years before. But this time, some subtle juggling of the geometry had resulted in a 3cm longer mainframe. An increase in the wheelbase from 102cm to 105cm sounded pretty minor stuff, but it resulted in a surprising amount of extra room for taller riders, and gave the bike a noticeably more 'grown-up' look, all for no penalty in terms of folded size. When it arrived in early 2005, the Mark 4 effectively brought the bike into the modern era, and although there were many innovations, the revamp was also interesting for the increased emphasis on marketing, suggesting that Andrew Ritchie was at last loosening the reins and passing control to his younger team. The new brochure was relatively short on technical information, but full of big, colourful lifestyle shots of pretty young things fooling about on a Mediterranean photoshoot. The overall feel was slick and smart, and once again in tune with the times. Rather than the take-it-or-leave-it Stalinist output of the early factory, the customer was now in charge, and free to order from an impressive range of accessories, specs and colours, including a vaguely grungy 'raw lacquer' finish - basically a coating of clear powder rather than pigment, that exposed the underlying brazes and cosmetic tube imperfections. The list of options was now so large that Brompton was able to boast that each bike was effectively custom-built, something that could never be emulated by the likes of Dahon, building millions of identical bikes 5,000 miles away.

The Mark 4 bikes saw a new emphasis on presentation as well as engineering, typified by the raw laquer finish that showed off Brompton's trademark frame brazing. The finish has gone on to become a Brompton classic.

From 2005, the long-standing model designations - T, L or C, followed by the number of gears - changed to a more complex system. The first letter now denoted the type of handlebars, of which there were three designs: 'M' for the traditional 'violin case' bars, 'S' for a new lower straight bar, and 'P' for an extraordinary touring bar, designed to give a choice of riding positions. The only exception to the handlebar nomenclature was the 'C' type, which had become the C3E.

As before, the number related to the number of gears, but the last letter now denoted the model type: 'E' (Excluding mudguards) being the basically equipped 'C' type, 'L' still meant Lightweight, and the former 'T' had become a more logical 'R', denoting a machine with a rack.

For older and more conservative customers looking for basic models, little had changed apart from the model numbers, and a few pounds here or there on or off the price. The C3 had become the C3E at £380, the L3 the M3L at £480 and the T6 the M6R-PLUS at £635. But thereafter, the range of bikes, options and accessories was almost unrecognizable.

New parts were relatively few. New reach-adjustable brake levers, a lightweight fi'zi:k saddle, and a clever Pentaclip saddle adjuster designed by Steve Rickels and Andrew Ritchie. All these parts were introduced on the more expensive models, but the Pentaclip was later to migrate across the range.

The most obvious change was that the Sturmey-Archer 3-speed hub was back, and with Steve Rickels on board, and the bigger buying power that comes from increased sales, Brompton was able to work with Sturmey to produce a Brompton-specific 3-speed hub - the BSR, or Brompton Standard Ratio. For the time being, the SRAM hub continued to be fitted to the 6-speed models, but the new rear frame meant that either hub could be used.

After the false start in 1996, Brompton had finally designed its own single-speed hub, and this could also be fitted with the derailleur from the 6-speed to give a 2-speed option, both these derivatives being light and cheap for the yachting and leisure markets.

But the real changes were reserved for the top end, where a number of titanium parts had been introduced. Having learnt a hard lesson with the Sturmey debacle, this time Brompton took care to source the titanium from two completely different factories - one in Russia and the other in China!

A titanium frame had been suggested many years before by shareholder Richard Goode, who had links to the Russian aeronautical industry, but for various reasons the project hadn't progressed at the time. Producing the hinges in titanium raised all sorts of engineering challenges, so when titanium was finally introduced, its use was restricted to the seat pillar, the rear frame and the front forks, plus mudguard stays and the folding pedal centre bolt.

Into the New Millenium 2000-2011

The Mark 4s are available in three broad ranges (above), classified by handlebar type - S, M and P from left to right above.

Also new were the Pentaclip (far left), for stepless seat angle adjustment, and Eazy-Roll rack wheels (left) for those taking the folded bike over rougher ground. To the left of the wheels is a seat pillar bung, allowing storage of small items in the seat pillar.

New for the Mark 4 was a weight-saving titanium rear frame (opposite page). Smaller weight saving measures included a new lightweight fi'zi:k saddle (right),

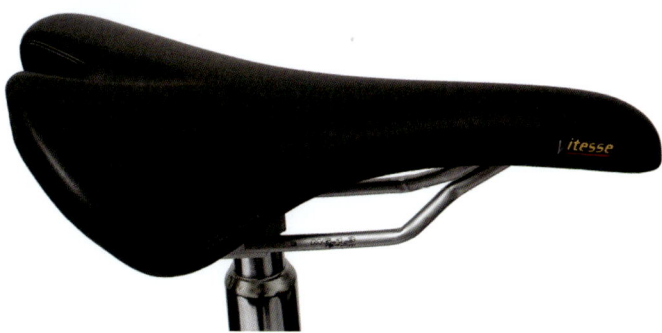

Rather than run out of steam at £600-£700, the Brompton range was now finally able to confront its upmarket rivals. The purchaser could specify virtually any combination of parts, but in as much as standard models existed, the S2L-X at £965 and P6R-XDL (£1,225) stand out. The S2L-X was a real delight, becoming an overnight classic. It was light, yet even with two gears, it was fast enough in a flat city like London to undertake serious daily commuting. The P6R-XDL was completely the opposite: seemingly bigger, it actually occupied the same folded volume as the 'S' type, but it was heavier, despite the full titanium kit. However, fitted with the rear rack, dual-position bars and a special narrow SON hub dynamo, it was the package serious leisure riders had been asking for. These machines were introduced to satisfy the perceived needs of Brompton owners, but they also helped Brompton to do battle with the 'go faster' folders, the Birdy, Bike Friday and Airnimal. Although edging up into four-figure price territory, the titanium Brompton variants were still far and away the cheapest of the 'super-folders', and much more compact, although limited gear range remained an issue, even with the 6-speed hub/derailleur system.

One option, taken up by enthusiastic owners over the years, was to fit an aftermarket chainwheel gear known as the Mountain (or Speed) Drive. This Swiss-made device doubled the number of gear ratios, giving a mountain bike gear range, but it was expensive, heavy and inefficient. Another alternative was to fit wider range sprockets to the 2-speed derailleur, and a kit was produced by Highpath Engineering for a while. This gave Mountain Drive results, without the upfront cost, inefficiency and weight, but the sprockets had quite a short life. Most users found these options too complicated and expensive, but it would be some time before Brompton finally cracked the gear issue in-house.

The P6R-XDL offered full touring features at a little over 12kg - rack, dynamo lights and mudguards included! This was largely due to the extensive use of titanium parts extending from the rear frame through to many smaller parts such as mudguard stays and pedal axle bolts.

Into the New Millenium 2000-2011

The new Mark 4 bikes of 2005 were built to customers' specifications, but of the many spec packages two became instant classics - the S2L-X (above) has become unbeatable as a fast, lightweight commuter (9.7kg) with two gears and many titanium parts - for example forks as inset.
The P6R-XDL (12.1kg) was designed for longer leisure or touring rides, its bars ideal for altering hand position to stop wrist fatigue and its beautifully engineered and ultra-reliable SON hub dynamo giving superb lighting.

Brompton Bicycle

> Note: For an updated graphic explanation of the Brompton naming system see Appendix III on pages 234-235

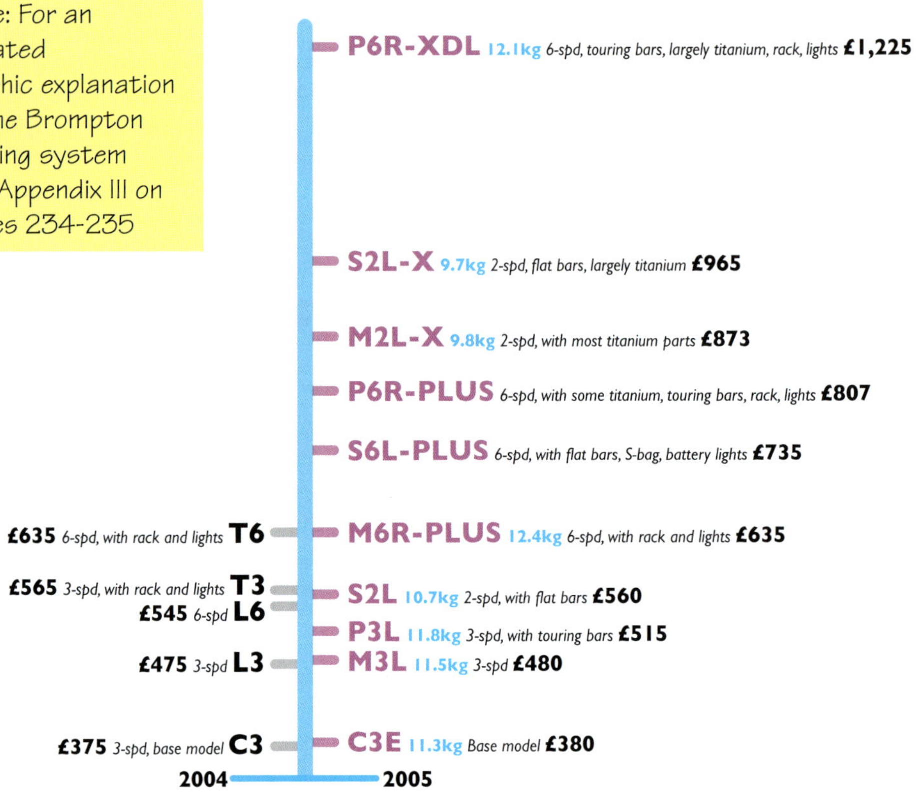

P6R-XDL 12.1kg 6-spd, touring bars, largely titanium, rack, lights **£1,225**

S2L-X 9.7kg 2-spd, flat bars, largely titanium **£965**

M2L-X 9.8kg 2-spd, with most titanium parts **£873**

P6R-PLUS 6-spd, with some titanium, touring bars, rack, lights **£807**

S6L-PLUS 6-spd, with flat bars, S-bag, battery lights **£735**

£635 6-spd, with rack and lights **T6** — **M6R-PLUS** 12.4kg 6-spd, with rack and lights **£635**

£565 3-spd, with rack and lights **T3**
£545 6-spd **L6** — **S2L** 10.7kg 2-spd, with flat bars **£560**

P3L 11.8kg 3-spd, with touring bars **£515**

£475 3-spd **L3** — **M3L** 11.5kg 3-spd **£480**

£375 3-spd, base model **C3** — **C3E** 11.3kg Base model **£380**

2004 — **2005**

The Mark 4s spanned a bewildering range of specs and prices - but the budget C3 was still there as the C3E (below). The C-type has since been deleted, but using Brompton's 'B-Spoke' ordering system, the customer can order an M3E with very similar spec.

Into the New Millenium 2000-2011

Available in a previously unthinkable range of styles and colours, the Mark 4 Bromptons have become style icons with young and old alike.

© Andrew Stevenson

The Opposition Regroups

The launch of the Mark 4 had resulted in a big increase in demand for the Brompton, while production continued to rise at a relatively steady 10% a year. Edward Donald had arrived too late to influence events, but he felt that under the circumstances the engineering effort put into the lightweight bikes and other upgrades would have been better spent on increasing production.

Factory output had been hit by the Sturmey debacle, hovering just below 8,000 in 2001-02, and the arrival of the 6-speed had created demand that the factory just couldn't satisfy, output rising to 9,563 in 2002-03, but stalling at 9,888 in 2003-04. By the time the Mark 4 was launched, the waiting list had reached six weeks, with the number of pre-orders from desperate dealers allegedly reaching 19,000 bikes for a while. Demoralized by the company's inability to supply this growing demand, Donald left in October 2005. Ironically, production was just starting to pick up, which was fortunate because his early marketing work was bearing fruit. Output rose 15.6% to 11,432 in 2004-05 and a further 19.1% to 13,620 in 2005-06. Brompton was back on track with a vengeance.

In March 2004, Tim Guinness had flown out to Japan and arranged for the paperwork trail to be streamlined. After prolonged negotiations, Mitsubishi agreed to bow out and a direct sales line was established with Mizutani, where former Mitsubishi manager Mac Nakane had now become the International Manager. Gradually Japanese Brompton sales improved, until by 2008 they had reached 1,800 a year. America too, was starting to see increased activity.

The waiting list for Bromptons had not gone unnoticed by its competitors, and 2005 was to see an explosion of relaunched and newly designed folding bikes. The most interesting, and in many ways the first serious competitor to the Brompton, was the Mezzo. Designed by Jon Whyte of ATB Sales, this was an interesting attempt to capitalize on Brompton's failure to engage with the more fashion-conscious end of the market.

The Mezzo got off to a flying start with younger males, as Whyte had done design work in Formula One, as well as producing high-end MTBs. Like the Brompton, it featured 349mm 16-inch tyres, but with its gunmetal grey colour scheme, and chunky, techy looks, it was a world apart.

By rights, the Mezzo should have done a roaring trade, but there were a couple of self-imposed weaknesses. The first i4 bikes were fitted with Shimano's rather uninspiring 4-speed Nexus hub gear and the later i9 with the much better Shimano Capreo derailleur. But the gear ratios were laughably low, top gear in both cases being much lower than top on the Brompton 3-speed, and lower even than the 2-speed. This was all compounded by sluggish and outdated tyres that made pedalling hard work.

The Mezzo was a reasonable, if rather heavy, folder, but despite its youthful, sporty good looks, it was (literally) streets behind the Brompton in terms of rideability, because of this poor choice of componentry. It's hard to image a designer of the calibre of Jon Whyte designing a mountain bike around dubious tyres and gears, and one is left with the distinct impression that he simply hadn't taken the folding bike format as seriously as he should.

Mezzo insisted for a while that market research indicated a desire for low gearing in the folding bike sector. It might have been true in the sub-£200 sector, but left the £600 Mezzo looking a bit sad. Three years later, the tyres were improved and the gearing quietly sorted, but by then it was much too late. The Mezzo was something of a wasted opportunity.

Increasingly, the real competition was coming from Dahon. UK importation and distribution had long been in the hands of Mark Bickerton's Cyclemotion, but in early 2004 Fisher Outdoor Leisure was appointed UK distributor, and this bigger, more aggressive company soon became the importer too.

Within a short space of time, the size of the dealer network, and UK sales, had exploded, many dealers taking Dahon because of Brompton's hub problems and continuing difficulty in meeting demand, even for 3-speed bikes.

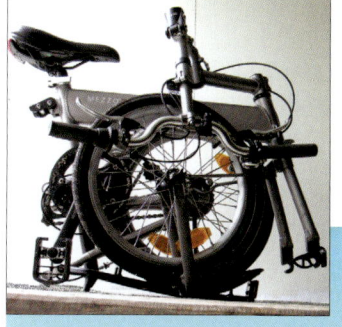

The Mezzo looked sporty and had an ingeniously designed and compact fold - one of the few attempts to really try and rival the folded package of the Brompton.
Unfortunately it was let down by unsuitable components, out of keeping with its fast and futuristic appearance.

In 2004 Dahon was selling 28 different own-brand machines (not all available in the UK), of which 20 were core 20-inch bikes of various kinds. Two years later, the company was producing 33 distinct models, most of the growth being in larger conventional machines, but with a continued presence at the compact end of the market. Dahon prices had gradually crept up too, until by 2006 the mean price of £745 was slightly higher than the £741 mean of the Brompton range.

Considering that ten years before Dahon had been regarded as a purveyor of cheap and cheerful Chinese tat, this was a remarkable turnaround. The Dahon bikes covered a huge price range (£350-£1,730), and at the bottom end - where Dahon no longer bothered to look for sales - Dahon badge-engineered bikes filled the gaps down to £100 or even less. Sitting in the middle of this vast range of folding bicycles, Brompton looked vulnerable, and in truth, it had only really survived through the sheer quality and originality of its design, helped by the regular, well-timed upgrades.

But Brompton had survived and it was looking stronger and more self-assured than ever. As the Mark 4 settled down, the company entered a period of relative stability, concentrating on increasing output and quality. Some dealers covered themselves by selling both brands, but most - a fickle lot bike dealers - simply swapped back to Brompton, citing Dahon's poor spares back up, and a range that was too big to handle.

Meanwhile, two bikes from the past were making a comeback. The Airframe had been brought back to life in 2002 by Silkmead, an engineering company based in Dunstable. Despite a lack of torsional stiffness, it was a decent bike, but set against the titanic Brompton/Dahon battle, it struggled to make serious inroads into the market. In 2004 an improved 'Super 8' version was launched equipped with the Sturmey-Archer 8-speed hub, which had originally been conceived by Brompton's Steve Rickels whilst an employee of Sturmey-Archer. But despite a competitive weight, price and gear range, it failed to make any serious headway, and production of the Airframe was later quietly wound down, although the bikes continued to be produced in small batches.

Mark Sanders' Strida had never sold well in the UK, but it had a big following in the Far East, particularly in Japan and Korea. It was relaunched in Mark 2 form by British company Roland Plastics in the late 1990s, but when this operation ran out of steam, it was passed to Steedman Bass, whose Midlands factory saw it through a Mark 2.5 version to a Mark 3. In 2005, the Strida was sold to Ming Cycles of Taiwan, which made a lot more sense, as the primary markets for the bike were in the Far East. The number 4 is considered unlucky in China, so under Ming Cycles control the series jumped to a Mark 5. The new machines are greatly improved: easier and safer to ride, making the Strida a

Dahon were behind a huge range of 'badge-engineered' folders - in this case a Kalkhoff.

cheap and practical leisure bike for those who can live with one, two, or more recently three gears. The Strida went on to become established as the top-selling folding bike in South Korea, spawning a whole family of models in two wheel sizes. Rather inexplicably, sales in the UK remain small, but it is recognised today as one of the most interesting and innovative folding bikes around.

In 2007, Bike Friday unexpectedly broke away from its traditional 20-inch sports market, launching the 16-inch Tikit. This was a really interesting design: comfortable and fast to ride, reasonably light, and with an extremely fast 'Hyperfold' folding mechanism, helped along by Bowden cables which allowed the stem to fold down automatically when the rear wheel was folded under the bike. It didn't fold very small, but was compact enough for regular rail or occasional bus use.

At £870, the Tikit was competitively priced for a quality American product, and right in the middle of the Brompton range. Interestingly the Bowden cables suffered from the same problems as the cables on the Brompton prototype, and were later made an option.

The Bike Friday Tikit was an innovative US design that rode well, was well-priced and folded very quickly. However, it failed to fold as small as the Brompton and didn't make serious inroads into the UK market.

For thirty years the accepted wisdom had been to outsource engineering production to the Far East, but in 2007-2009, this policy would be called into question. The global 'credit crunch' brought turmoil to world markets, with a period of volatile raw material and fuel prices, plus a collapse in the value of sterling. For home manufacturers, high fuel costs and a weak pound were less serious, the weak currency actually helping exports, but for importers, it was another matter. Brompton was, of course, still a British manufacturer, but in the decades the company had been building bikes in Britain, many of its home component suppliers had disappeared. By 2009, most of the components on the bike (including big items like hub gears) were imported, mainly from the Far East.

In both 2008 and 2009, Brompton managed to keep annual price increases down to 5%, markedly below those of its competitors, but the reliance on imports was taking its toll, and for 2010 the company was forced to increase prices by an average of 12.5%. Surprisingly, in such straitened economic circumstances, the biggest increases were aimed at the cheaper bikes, the humble M1E rising by 20%, and the mass-market M3L by 18%, while the pricey titanium machines rose by only 10%.

Its competitors - without exception importing complete bikes - did even worse. During the summer of 2009, Birdy prices fluctuated wildly, falling by 11% in August, and rising by 29% later in the year. Dahon prices had been similarly chaotic in 2009. In November, new distributor Zyro revealed that the number of models reaching the UK would almost double in 2010, from 16 to 28. Not all the bikes were comparable, but those that were had risen in price by an eye-watering 35% year-on-year. And with a general move upmarket, the average price of a Dahon had risen even more, from £582 at the end of 2009 to £955 in 2010. Even five years before, it would have been hard to imagine a typical Dahon costing almost as much as the most expensive Brompton variant. In the end it all proved to be too much, and in June 2011 Zyro dropped the brand, citing poor spares availability and an over-large and over-priced range. Back in Taiwan, Dahon also seemed to have over-extended itself, and it was announced that the parent company would split, with David Hon's wife Florence, and son Joshua leaving to set up a new folding bike company called Tern, and taking much of the management and overseas sales teams with them, including Mark Bickerton in the UK. In late 2011, with Joshua's father David threatening legal action, Dahon's UK distributorship in disarray, and the Tern range yet to be launched, the Hons were - temporarily at least - on the ropes. Tern went on to do more or less everything right, with subtle more youthful advertising, and a carefully chosen bike range. In the UK, Mark Bickerton's links with Tern were to result in a reborn Bickerton brand, albeit using badged Tern machines.

Dahon fell on its feet in the UK by landing a distributorship deal with Raleigh in 2012. By 2016, the two rival Hon companies had begun to occupy surprisingly similar territory, but with Tern at the slightly classier end of the market. Within a few years of the credit squeeze of 2008/09 prices had stabilised, and a measure of order had returned to global trading. All the major folding bike manufacturers had survived, but the ensuing 'Great Recession' had depressed output and sent a chill wind through the industry. Not at Brompton, where sales just rose and rose, far outstripping the modest 10% annual growth of the early years.

With precious little UK manufacturing available, and Brompton conveniently situated in west London, government ministers were tripping over each other to fly the manufacturing flag in Brentford. Just a decade after Sturmey-Archer had effectively been left to rot, British manufacturing was very much back on the agenda. For companies like Brompton, now heavily dependent on imports, a resurgence of British component manufacturing would be very welcome.

Into the New Millenium 2000-2011

A New Generation

In 2007, after some thirty years in the driving seat, Andrew Ritchie was preparing to hand over control of Brompton to a new younger team. The changeover was overseen by Brompton chairman Tim Guinness, who would later regard the smooth transfer of power as his most important contribution to the company.

Emerson Roberts had joined Brompton in January 2006 with a brief to lead a growing marketing department, but management of the company was to go to Will Butler-Adams, the young engineer who had arrived in 2002. Tim Guinness had met Butler-Adams - then maintenance manager of a petro-chemical factory on Teeside - back in 2001. Still in his '20s at the time, Butler-Adams had been raised in Yorkshire, leaving Newcastle University with a 1st class Honours degree in Mechanical Engineering. He was, in his own words, "madly passionate about all things mechanical. And mesmerised by Andrew Ritchie's invention."

Butler-Adams seemed ideal. He had already demonstrated leadership skills on expeditions to the Amazon and Argentinian Andes, and he had five solid years industrial experience behind him in Middlesbrough, but crucially he was an engineer. The various players in the Brompton story have denied that this was a prerequisite for leadership, and Butler-Adams himself makes it clear that he is a very different sort of engineer to Ritchie, "I'm not a designer, and I'm not good on the detailed stuff!" But there's no doubt that Andrew Ritchie was only persuaded to hand over because he knew the company would continue to be engineer-led.

Joining the engineering team early in 2002, Will Butler-Adams initially expected to stay for about five years, improve the operational efficiency of the factory, and move on, but he gradually worked his way up, becoming a director in 2006.

As he saw it, Brompton could follow one of two roads: it could remain as a small specialist manufacturer, rather like the Morgan car company, building perhaps 15,000 bikes a year, and generating modest profits for its group of long-standing shareholders. Brompton was growing at around 8% a year at the time, but the market was growing at 25%, so the company's market share was effectively slipping year on year. The other option was to rise to the challenges and grow with the market, with the aim of developing into a serious global player. If the company chose the first course, he would move on to face fresh challenges elsewhere, but if there was backing for growth, he was prepared to invest his own future by leading the company.

It was a convincing argument, and the young engineer found backing from chairman Tim Guinness, the majority of the shareholders, and finally and reluctantly, from Andrew Ritchie. After all the years of talk about the 'succession', Andrew was finally satisfied that he had found a potential leader who had empathy with the Brompton philosophy, and understood the bike. Will Butler-Adams was made of the right stuff, and he wasn't just a manager - he knew every component, and every stress and strain in the Brompton design.

The Butler-Adams deal, completed in 2008, was quite a complex affair. Just as Andrew Ritchie and Julian Vereker had done in 1988, Will Butler-Adams and a group of family and friends bought shares in Brompton, although this time they were buying existing shares from existing shareholders. Some of the original shareholders sold all their shares, but most - including Andrew Ritchie - sold half. For the first time, Andrew's personal holding fell below 51% - he had lost overall control.

The first stage of the plan was to invest in the Brentford factory, then three years into a 15-year lease. A total of £1 million was spent on enhancements, principally moving the offices to a new mezzanine floor above the engineering shop, giving vital extra production space below. The second stage involved increasing the manufacturing efficiency, with a significant investment in further auto-brazing equipment and other modern machines.

The luxury of success - a totally refurbished modern factory.

In November 2008, Brompton unveiled an intelligent solution to the gear ratio problem. The 2 x 3 derailleur/hub system introduced in 2002 had always been seen as a stop-gap measure, because although it was light and efficient, the gear range was simply too low. Several options presented themselves, but none quite fitted the bill. A pure derailleur system was out of the question for all sorts of reasons, leaving a multi-gear hub; an option that had its adherents. A hub like the Shimano Nexus 8-speed could be squeezed in without too much re-engineering, and a kit had been produced in Germany by Juliane Neuß for several years.

But it was a relatively expensive hub, and it weighed at least half a kilo more than the Sturmey 3-speed which Brompton was already using. Worse still, like most multi-speed hub gears, it worked through compound gears, so that the rider's leg power wound its way up and down through a series of cogwheels before it reached the rear wheel. This arrangement was relatively inefficient, and put together with the cost and weight of the hub, ruled out this option. Other hubs existed, some better than the Shimano Nexus, but all were big and heavy.

The answer, first discussed some years before, was to design a special wide-ratio version of the archetypal Sturmey-Archer AW 3-speed hub, the BWR (Brompton Wide Ratio), which would be made, like the BSR, in Sturmey's new Taiwanese factory. The BWR kept the light weight, low cost and reasonable efficiency of the hub, but extended the range, giving three very widely spaced gears. The new hub would work in tandem with the 2-speed derailleur already in production, but with revised sprockets, to give a total of six evenly spaced gears.

Into the New Millenium 2000-2011

In late 2008 Brompton went into the hub design business, introducing the BWR, or Brompton Wide Ratio hub - basically a 7-speed gear range in a 3-speed package.

This cutaway shows the simple, rugged construction and Shimano-pattern multi-spline output shaft, enabling the hub to work reliably with sprockets as small as 12-tooth. The BWR is manufactured for Brompton by Sturmey-Archer, now part of the Taiwanese Sunrace group.

In earlier days, such a task would have been beyond Brompton's capabilities, but it was now a bigger, more self-assured company, with enough engineering expertise to handle day-to-day problem solving, leaving former Sturmey-Archer engineer Steve Rickels to concentrate on the new designs.

The weakness of the new arrangement was the need to continue with dual changers, but otherwise it was all positives. Using modern design techniques, the BWR actually weighed some 60 grams less than the standard 3-speed, but increased the existing 177% gear range to a generous 245%. With the 2-speed derailleur mounted on the hub driver, the overall range increased to 302%, which was only a shade less than the heavier, less efficient 7- and 8-speed hubs produced by SRAM and Shimano. It was a typically clever Brompton solution, and it was the first major development engineered by a team, rather than Ritchie alone. Finally he had demonstrated enough confidence in the group to take a back seat, albeit remaining (in Andrew's words) "very closely involved"! He was not to know that it would be the last significant development for some years.

The new hub really was the final piece in the jigsaw, answering the last of the long-standing criticisms that had held it back. Gears had always been a weakness, and the Brompton now had a bigger gear range than most of its competitors.

How was the new regime bedding in? Speaking in the summer of 2009, Tim Guinness remained cautiously optimistic: "So far we don't know whether the marketing is successful, because the bike's selling itself. We can't produce enough..."

Brompton as Icon

By 2009, Brompton had become something of a national icon. For overseas visitors, the little bikes were now as much a part of the London scene as the red double-deckers and policemen's helmets. As if to confirm the bike's new status, a Brompton was used to represent London in the closing stages of the Beijing Olympic Games.

Down in Brentford, Andrew Ritchie would still sit at his drawing board once in a while, the relic taking pride of place amongst the smoked-glass, the PCs and modern engineering tools. He now worked part-time, still commuting to the factory from his flat in Brompton two or three days a week. For a while, it looked as though married life and semi-retirement in Oxford would take him away from the factory on a more permanent basis, but this turned out to be a step too far, and neither the marriage nor the retirement was to last very long. Although technically he was no longer in charge at Brompton, whenever there was a flurry of activity at the drawing board, the engineers got nervous. Either Andrew had had a new idea, or was looking again at something they had hoped to sign off. Part-time perhaps, but very much a guiding role.

Ritchie's real achievement had been to develop a 1970s design for three decades to the point where this young management team (few of whom were over 40) could take over and hopefully move the design on. Such longevity is not unique in the transport world, but it's extremely unusual, and testament to the clarity of vision behind the machine all those years ago and Ritchie's dogged persistence in honing and perfecting the design, often in the face of considerable opposition. And despite his rather donnish appearance and sometimes unconventional business methods, Andrew Ritchie had demonstrated an instinct for the realities of the commercial world, without which his company could never have survived.

Throughout the long evolution of the Brompton, Andrew Ritchie - and indeed the Brompton itself - had received surprisingly little official recognition, but in October 2009, against a formidable shortlist of the Great & the Good, he won the 2009 Prince Philip Designer's Prize 'for outstanding achievement in design'. For the engineer behind an intensely practical and 'non design' creation, it was a long overdue honour.

Cycle historian Tony Hadland is an authority on folding bikes, and he has no doubts about how and why the Brompton succeeded where so many others have failed: "The key to its success is that the bike rides reasonably well, is relatively light, well engineered, soundly constructed, and folds and unfolds quickly and easily. Any folding bike should do all these things but in practice, very few do. Most are deficient in at least one of these parameters, and some are deficient in all of them. With the Brompton, however, the original design compromises were exceptionally well balanced and over the years the detailing has become increasingly refined."

Andrew Ritchie with bike-builder Terence Franklin, one of several members of the Franklin family employed at the London factory.

Into the New Millenium 2000-2011

Brompton's iconic status became associated with business success in times of difficulties, and the factory saw several high profile visits from Conservative and Liberal politicians in 2011. Here Prime Minister and former London mayor Boris Johnson, himself synonymous with cycling in the capital, tries out an electric Nano-conversion whilst on a factory visit.

Brompton and the Future Could the Brompton Dock herald a revolution in personal transport? This internal shot of Brompton's public bike hire concept gives an idea of how space efficient the Docks are. In fact it can fit forty folded Bromptons into a single car space.

Brompton Electric and International Turmoil
2011 - 2020

"Describing our bike takes 30,000 to 40,000 drawings, but in describing the machines to make our bike there are maybe 300,000 - 400,000 drawings. So the cleverness is in the bike, yes, but there's far more cleverness in how to make the bike."
WILL BUTLER-ADAMS

The severe winter weather of 2010/11 should have been an opportunity for Brompton. Following a number of productivity improvements, the company had eliminated its long-standing waiting list, and was planning to use the slack winter season to initiate the long-awaited 'big bang': reconfiguration of the bike assembly area, from batch (i.e. one man building one bike at a static work station) to production-line manufacture. In the event, the hardware wasn't ready for the planned November 2010 changeover, and the company hit December with the old system still in place. The severe snow storms and prolonged freezing weather of that most unusual winter resulted in shortages of key components and a collapse in sales. Suddenly, Brompton was unable to build or sell bikes, something the company hadn't experienced for a very long time. Sales faltered badly, but true to recent form, turnover and profitability showed barely a ripple.

By June 2011 the production line system was finally on stream. Unlike the process that revolutionised car manufacture in the early 20th century, the Brompton bike builders were free to move up and down the line to help out where needed. There was also something of a high-tech efficiency drive at this time, with the introduction of computerised quality control of frames, new technology for testing hinge plates and further automation of the simpler brazing procedures.

Sales were soon back on track and Brompton was looking to the future again, but December 2010 had sent a chill wind through the company. Profitability had been more or less steady at 10% of turnover for nearly 20 years, but it dipped badly, and would remain depressed for a couple of years. Sales, however, resumed their meteoric rise, turnover doubling to £12 million in 2010-11, and almost doubling again to £21.3 million two years later. At long last the production log-jam had been cleared, allowing sales to bounce up to find their own level. It sounded just the medicine the company needed, but the drive to increase output inevitably came at the expense of engineering developments.

Titanium from Sheffield

The dash for sales would result in some engineering faux pas that one suspects would not - could not - have happened with Andrew Ritchie at the helm. The most serious involved the October 2010 change to a nickel-plated aluminium seat pillar to replace the titanium pillar on Superlight bikes. This was significantly lighter than the steel pillar, (307g against 387g) and only 22 grams heavier than titanium, but it was much cheaper, and was expected to replace steel on all Bromptons from 2012, but within weeks incidents began to arise of the nickel plating flaking and failing, resulting in a panic withdrawal in June 2011. As stocks of titanium pillars had been used up by this time, and the contractual arrangements with the manufacturers discontinued, Superlight bikes were quietly fitted with the everyday steel pillars thereafter. Embarrassingly, Brompfication, an aftermarket manufacturer in Hong Kong, stepped in with a neat titanium pillar with a stated weight of 300g. The company later ceased trading, but aftermarket manufacturers were on the case. They weren't allowed to copy the Brompton, but they could sell upgraded and/or discounted spares. In late 2016 New York's NYCeWheels began selling an H&H branded titanium pillar weighing a claimed 237g, but this - like most titanium components, from fastenings to whole frames - was actually sourced in the Far East.

In mid-2012, Brompton compounded the seat pillar issue by quietly withdrawing the lightweight front hubs fitted to 1- and 2-speed bikes after a few failures, but rather inexplicably failing to source an alternative. It also replaced the Superlight's titanium folding pedal axle bolt with a heavier steel item. It looked mean and penny-pinching, and the impression was of a company chasing the bottom line rather than developing the best components for the job. The flagship Superlight bikes were more expensive than their predecessors, but with significantly fewer titanium components. By 2016, a typical Superlight bike would cost around £1,600 and weigh the better part of 11kg. Comparisons with the £2,500 Hummingbird might be considered a bit unfair, because it's single speed with a carbon-fibre frame, but it weighs a corroborated 7.3kg, making it far and away the lightest British folding bike, and almost certainly the lightest production folder anywhere in the world. Tern's Verge X11 cost a similar £2,400, but it had 11 gears and was claimed to weigh 10.2kg. Brompton seemed to be walking off the field.

Another rather regrettable incident was the neat in-frame toolkit, developed by fashionable consultant Goodwin Hartshorn, but made in Taiwan. It was introduced in 2012, but rapidly withdrawn after breakages, and grumbles about the impracticality of some of the tools. The issues were eventually sorted, but the affair left the smell of a company losing its engineering focus.

This was all to change with a remarkable project launched in 2013, not in Brentford but in South Yorkshire.

Importing titanium components from Russia and China had worked reasonably well for eight years, but it involved long distance relationships with countries that - to be frank - might not always have the UK's best interests at heart. There was a very real prospect that trade sanctions or something more serious could cut off the supply of components overnight.

Brompton had always prided itself on building brazed steel frames in the UK, but fabricating titanium parts such as rear frames and front forks was just too specialist for the Brentford factory. The answer was to find a partner in the UK with the necessary skills, and Brompton's Specialist Products Design Manager, Paul Williams found just the company in C W Fletcher of Sheffield. Fletchers was a long established Sheffield steel maker, best known for its high quality 'flatware', primarily cutlery and kitchen utensils. This part of the business had been sold to US company James Robinson Inc in 2002, leaving C W Fletcher to concentrate on specialist materials including titanium, much of its output being jet engine parts for Rolls Royce and others. But aerospace is a rather cyclical business, and in 1999, after settling into a big new factory on a former coking works outside Sheffield, C W Fletcher was looking to diversify. Brompton was looking for expertise, and C W Fletcher was looking to build a consumer product in titanium. It was a near perfect match.

The two companies set up Brompton-Fletcher Ltd with the aim of going where British manufacturing hadn't really gone before, producing consumer-level titanium components at a price to compete with the Russians and the Chinese.

C W Fletcher provided a small self-contained working area in the heart of the Sheffield factory, and began recruiting and training staff. South Yorkshire - not unlike Brentford - had seen its industrial base decimated in 30 years, so there were grants for training and recruitment, and plenty of willing volunteers. Seven started the training - drawn from such unlikely employers as Sports Direct and Thorntons chocolates - and four saw the course through to join the payroll, with a fifth arriving in 2016. Bizarrely, one of the potential recruits picked by C W Fletcher had previously done time in the Brentford factory as a brazer before moving north to assemble frames for Mercian. Applicants were not told they would be making components for Brompton, and Fletchers didn't know about his background until he started work in October 2015.

By the summer of 2016 Brompton-Fletcher was turning out 200 rear frames a month, or around ten each working day. These were very small numbers for Brompton, which was building some 3,500 bikes a month at the time but, with the Russian rear frame contract cancelled, there was plenty of incentive to gradually increase output. The medium-term aim was to meet the existing demand of 400-500 lightweight rear frames a month, which would need a total staff of eight or nine. The number would expand a great deal further in the years to come.

When brazing steel components, the speed of manufacture is only really limited by the skill of the operative, but titanium oxidises very readily when heated, and it absorbs oil like a sponge. Oxygen and oil are the front runners for ruining welds, and there are plenty of other potential contaminants. No parts can be touched with an ungloved hand without constant cleaning, and welding has to take place in booths screened with thick red plastic curtains. This is partly to shield passers-by from the arc glare, but also to minimise draughts around the welding jig. To prevent contamination, the jig is bathed in inert argon gas, but if the tiniest puff of wind blows the gas clear of the weld before it has cooled, the weld will be ruined. After each operation, the welder has to sit completely still in the red booth, waiting for the heat to dissipate out of the weld.

Like so much else in the strange world of titanium mass-production, the exact length of the pause (a few seconds) has been found by trial and error. With each raw tube costing more than £5, scrapping even a sub-assembly can be annoying, but a momentary lack of concentration with a complete rear frame will ruin your day.

Titanium welding is a painstaking process. Here you see the eerie pink glow of the welding itself and also the thick orange screen - partly to protect the eyes of passers-by but also to prevent draughts diluting that essential pool of argon.

Argon is mighty expensive, and cost in excess of £7 per frame, so it isn't practical to swamp the work area in the stuff. The flow has to be carefully metered through the jig at each work station, bathing the exterior and interior of the tubes to keep the dreaded oxygen at bay. Once the argon is flowing and welding has commenced, the operative needs total concentration, sitting absolutely still for the required time, spinning the jig to do the next weld, and so on, until the rear frame is finished. After quality control, frames are checked for alignment and shot-blasted, then oiled to prevent finger marks marring the finish (on the principle that if it has absorbed its fill of oil, it can't absorb any more) and another frame is carefully placed in a plastic pouch in the despatch boxes. At the end of the week a large van leaves Brompton and makes the long journey up the M1, bringing back 18 to 20 of the filled boxes to the Brompton production line.

If the rear frame fits precisely in the quality control jig (above) it's time for the welders to relax before their concentration moves onto the next frame.
Individual numbers and welder's codes (left) show the pride the welders take in the finished product.
This frame was made in week 22 of 2016 and is the fourth one produced by operator F.

The intention was to mark each frame with the date and batch number, but the staff wanted the parts to be given an individual number and welder's code, something Paul Williams was happy to accede to. Lightweight Bromptons sold from late 2016 carry this code on the plate that bears against the rubber suspension unit. The first number is a week code, the second identifies the year, the third letter is the welder's personal code, and the fourth shows how many he had completed that week.

With a plant still getting into its stride, the future seemed a very long way away. By 2020 the Brompton-Fletcher assembly line was still a tiny venture to both companies, with output hitting a relatively modest 650-700 rear frames a month before the virus struck. Richard Phillips, Business Development Manager at C W Fletcher, accepts that it's a small venture, but it's one element in the process of diversification: 'If it turns over £300,000 a year, it will only be one-point-something percent of Fletcher's turnover, but it's helping the company diversify away from Rolls-Royce and the aerospace industry.'

Where too next? The obvious step was a whole bike. That seemed a long way off in 2016, but it would come. A completely titanium bike would mean redesigning the components one by one to suit the strengths and weaknesses of titanium, which is as tough as steel, but relatively elastic. Initially, the Chinese and Russian factories had just been given the drawings for the steel components and told to remake them in lighter stuff. To achieve the full weight-savings - allied to long life at reasonable cost - would mean a lot of fine-tuning, a process that turned out to be painstakingly slow.

The Electric Bike

Another 'post Ritchie' project that was destined to be an astonishing eight years in development, was the power-assisted bike. Ritchie had hinted at power-assist in his original patent application, but for the next twenty years the Brompton remained a pedal-only machine, until small-scale after-market conversions began to appear in the 2010s. The power-assisted 'Nano' is mentioned in the 'Brompton Specials' chapter, and the Electric Transport Shop in Cambridge, Freedom eBike of Israel, and NYCeWheels in New York, went on to produce similar machines, although most were flawed to a greater or lesser extent. In 2024, the best of this new crop is probably the British designed and manufactured Cytronex, of which more in the next chapter.

When introduced in 2007, the Nano-Brompton was fitted with a 100mm wide Tongxin motor in the front wheel - the smallest and lightest unit then available - later reduced to 80mm in width. The company went on to reduce weight even further with the option of small 36-volt battery packs designed for powering garden equipment. In terms of weight, the Nano-Brompton would be a hard act to follow. Brompton sensibly concentrated its attention on reducing the size and weight of the motor at first, aiming to produce a 2-speed power-assisted bike that was lighter than most non-assisted variants, but the design gradually became bogged down in unsuitable technology from unsuitable Far Eastern partners. The electric variant was expected to be shown for the first time at the Eurobike show in Friedrichshafen, Germany in September 2011. And with other folding bike companies busy developing power-assisted machines, the Brompton package needed to be as practical, light and user-friendly as the original Brompton. It was a very tall order.

The final product was expected to go on limited sale in Germany and the UK in early 2012, with a more general roll out later in the year, but the project foundered and the whole concept was quietly put to one side. It was, however, still simmering on a back burner, and in the early summer of 2015, Brompton surprised everyone by announcing that it was working with a new partner - Williams Advanced Engineering, the commercial arm of the Williams Formula One team. The project smacked rather of public relations, as it didn't look likely that the Formula One company's Kinetic Energy Recovery System would be of much practical use on a folding bike, but Williams had plenty of expertise in developing race-hardened electronics, and their input proved invaluable.

The long heralded Brompton Electric made two obvious visual additions to the non-electric version, the front hub motor and the battery pack mounted where the lugguge block sits on non-assisted versions. The battery pack removes at the push of a button to make two lighter packages for ease of carrying, though it can be left on the bike if the user doesn't mind a larger, heavier folded package.

With the launch set for 2017, the Brompton design began to crystallise. Despite the massive excitement on- and off-line for nearly a decade, the spec was relatively conventional: a motor in the front wheel with an over-run clutch, so no regenerative capability, a pedal torque-sensor in the bottom bracket and a battery bag that mounted on an especially-adapted front carrier block. Luggage capacity was still available, but only by purchasing a special pannier bag that fitted round the battery, so the bag could either be removed with the battery or on its own.

The Brompton Electric's larger battery bag (above) is an optional extra with 20 litres luggage capacity arranged around a centrally housed battery.
The battery itself also houses the control unit, meaning you need to bend over the handlebars to alter power level and LED light settings.

To avoid folding issues with switches and cables, the machine had no handlebar controls, the assistance buttons and lights, light switch and battery meter being built into the top of the battery - clearly visible, but difficult to operate while on the move. The battery was expected to have a capacity of about 300Wh, giving a reasonable weight/range compromise.

In the event, deadlines continued to be missed, and the very first bikes didn't even go out for review until late summer 2017, with fitful deliveries starting a few weeks later. Perhaps inevitably, early examples were riddled with development issues. Most of these were quickly sorted with software patches wired down the line to early adopters, but there were some more fundamental problems in the hardware too, and these were well beyond the scope of simple tweaks.

Far Eastern manufacturers have their strengths and weaknesses, and one of their real strengths is fine-tuning the design of apparently complex but conceptually straightforward machines, like wheel-mounted electric bike motors, and the Chinese are now rightly considered world leaders in producing the more straightforward type, with internal gearing and an over-run clutch.

If Brompton had been going for unique features, such as regenerative braking, or bus-wire or Bluetooth controls, the partnership with Williams would have made sense, but in the end, the only innovative part was trying to build a motor as light, quiet and efficient as something available in Shanghai for a few tens of dollars. This didn't go well, and the motors were heavier than best practice from the Far East and early examples were noisy, and liable to overheat on gradients. Much of this was sorted, or mitigated, in the months and years that followed, but the motor turned out to be just the tip of a mis-development iceberg. The bike wasn't a complete lemon by any means, but it smelt of development by a team that was somewhat out of its depth.

Whilst Brompton invested considerable time and money in producing their own brand motor in collaboration with Williams (above) it turned out to be quite an unwieldy beast compared to the latest Far Eastern technology. This is exemplified by the 3rd party motor used by the Cytronex retrofit kit (right) - more of which in the following chapter. A to B magazine calculated Cytronex's motor wheel was some 500g lighter than Brompton's.

Perhaps the most glaring weakness was the multi-way connector linking the battery bag to the rest of the bike. It was adequately protected for leisure use perhaps, but unable to deal with the dust, vibration, damp and salt-ingress of daily commuting. Testing seemed thorough enough, but the connector was a failure waiting to happen, and once in the hands of the public, they began to suffer from all manner of odd issues, from the occasional glitch to complete failure. Most of these could be sorted by wiping the contacts with a dry cloth or a squirt of contact cleaner, but the public didn't know this, and bicycle shops couldn't (or wouldn't) get to first base repairing electrical faults.

The multi-way connector between the battery bag and the motor system provides a slick, quick and convenient design but real world use would highlight its weaknesses.

Putting the control systems on the battery had seemed a good idea, but actually pressing any of the buttons whilst underway could be quite a fraught affair because the lights and buttons were so far from the rider and changes meant looking away from the road, and riding one-handed for longer than most people would find comfortable.

An even bigger issue for many potential users was the inability to retrofit the system to an existing bike or use a conventional bag on the Brompton Electric. Brompton had always been known for it's voluminous panniers, which were, incidentally, fully interchangeable until the lower S-type bars became an option (the low bars generally don't deal well with the biggest panniers). On the Electric, luggage capacity was seriously hampered. The standard 'Essential' bag could carry nothing but a slim purse, and the 20 litre, £130 optional City Bag was barely adequate, particularly considering the extra luggage-hauling power available from the Electric.

This would be less of an issue if the Electric variant was available as an option on all new bikes, but it was only produced in two-speed or six-speed form. The two-speed was fine in most respects, but six gears were completely unnecessary on an electric, serving only to add a lot of extra weight to an already heavy bike.

The torque-sensing bottom bracket had caused issues too. To save money, this only had a sensor on the left side, so it primarily picked up pedal torque from the rider's left leg, receiving only a weak signal from the right. And instead of indicating the torque applied with the right foot, this weak signal was largely showing the weight of the resting left leg being carried back up! These characteristics were barely noticed by most riders, but caused some strange effects for a sizeable minority, whose pedalling characteristics could result in unpredictable and faltering power delivery.

Torque sensors should provide smoother power assistance than their more budget cousins crank motion sensors, but Brompton chose a design that only sensed pedal pressure on the left pedal crank leading some riders to complain of unpredictable power delivery.

The effect was compounded by a safety delay that prevented power being delivered until a full pedal stroke had been detected. If you tended to start pedalling with the left foot, take-up could be very slick, but if you used the right, you could find yourself doing all the work for two or more pedal strokes - a particular problem on hills, which forced some users to walk. A series of clever software tweaks by Ellie Sherwen, Brompton's algorithm specialist, helped to amplify the 'blind' pedal stroke, but the sensor was never going to suit everyone.

On the positive side, the bikes were pretty efficient, achieving a mileage of 27 miles according to A to B magazine - quite a good figure from a modest 300 watt-hour battery. And there were some good details, such as the USB socket, integrated Busch & Muller sensor-controlled lights (useful with the switches so far away) and the bag removal button on the handlebars, but this too suffered from a fatal flaw. Stealing a Brompton pannier has always been fairly easy, but the button was fiddly to locate under the bag. In this case, though, the all-too-accessible button also removed the £450 battery... Interestingly, Brompton is adamant there will not be a power-assist upgrade kit, although there are no technical issues to fitting the bits to existing bikes. Finally, and perhaps most damningly, the bikes were pretty expensive at £2,595 - £2,755, depending on gear options. And at 17kg (again, varying slightly with gear options) it was hardly class-leading in the weight department. Adequate perhaps, but considering the development budget, a bit of a lump, and if we ignore the rather Heath Robinson Velospeeder, 2.2kg heavier than the Cytronex, the lightest kit to date.

The aim of the Electric project is to widen the scope of the bicycle, and increase its appeal to those who might not consider themselves regular or commuter cyclists, a huge and largely untapped market. Despite rising fuel prices and chronic traffic congestion, more than 60% of regular commuters still travel by car in the UK. Of the remainder, modest numbers walk or use public transport, but less than 3% cycle. Even encouraging a tiny percentage of car drivers to shift to a Brompton or car-Brompton commute would result in hundreds of thousands of sales, and a big increase in market share. One way to do this is to make the prospect of cycling less physically daunting.

Predicting future electric-assist sales is tricky, but it's worth noting that in 2019, in the cycle-friendly Netherlands, electric-assist bikes accounted for 42% by volume, or 420,000 units. Germany looks similarly potentially lucrative; by 2023 e-bike sales there had reached 2.1 million, or 53% of the entire market. Brompton was well placed to exploit the growth, having recruited a sales manager for the Germany, Switzerland and Austria region in 2020.

Alexander Henshaw on the Brompton Electric. This model is fitted with the City Bag which gives 20 litres of storage space in addition to the space occupied by the battery within the bag.

The difficult price-weight equation has kept electric folder sales very limited, but there will be rich pickings for the manufacturer that eventually gets it right. In the event, Brompton was able to rely on the great fund of goodwill for pretty well anything it produces, and sales were by no means catastrophic, reaching 2,500 after ten months, with a target of 6,000 in 2019/20, although this was to be firmly ruled out by the Coronavirus epidemic. An online report from 2022 quotes Butler-Adams as saying Brompton was on track to produce 15,000-20,000 electric bikes that year and that ultimately he envisaged them accounting for 30-40% of annual unit sales but around half of its revenue.

Has the failure of so many other folding electric bikes (see pages 164-173) caused any nervousness? It seems not. Will Butler-Adams remains confident that power-assisted bikes will continue to take a substantial share of a growing cycle market, and the Brompton will take its place as the premier power-assisted folder: "The average distance to work is nine miles. The folding electric bike isn't the whole solution, but it has to be part of the solution."

Other Projects

With the titanium offshoot and the electric project starting to bear fruit, Brompton turned its attention to the rather confused mishmash of rider controls. The gear and brake levers had fallen into place at different times between 2002 and 2013, and a long-held ambition was finally realised to design matching 2- and 3-speed shifters, with integrated shifters and bell and improved brake levers.

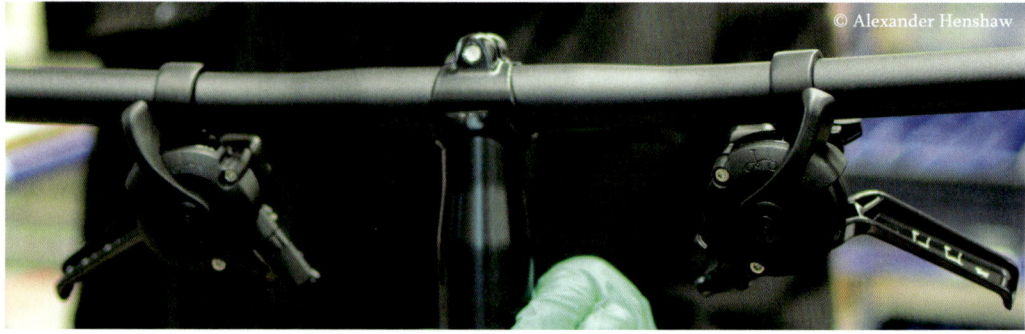

Integrated shifters, brake levers and bell became available in 2016

After a prolonged period of testing, the changeover to the new controls came in November 2016, together with new lockable handlebar grips. These controls were clever and very complex, but the integral bell was rather fragile and they relied heavily on 'lubrication-free' plastics, both in the housings and internal components. There were accolades at first, but in the long-run, they did not work well. Brompton had begun to look like a marketing, rather than an engineering-led company, and there certainly was a period when the roster of marketing managers overtook the engineers, with the main thrust of developments in such things as colour schemes, designer bags, option packages and an ever-growing range of clothing.

But with the success of the complex titanium venture and the redesign of the handlebar controls it seemed as though the momentum was swinging back towards the engineering team. "We've got to innovate", says Will Butler-Adams. "A company that isn't willing to innovate isn't going to be here in ten years."

Meanwhile, the marketing operation was inspired. The Brompton World Championship series, which evolved from some lighthearted entertainment arranged by the Spanish distributor, was adopted by Brompton itself in 2005, and turned into a world series, with a final in the UK each year, initially at Blenheim Palace in Oxfordshire, then rather less successfully at the Goodwood Motor Circuit

Rather than spend money on glossy advertising Brompton has chosen to rely on looking after existing customers and supporting the annual Brompton World Championships - illustrated by this classic poster image by Diana Powell (left).
The championships have also spawned their own sartorial style too! (above and top of page).

in West Sussex before settling on central London in 2015. In 2016 the series attracted a slightly reduced nine regional heats (there were 12 in 2013), from Europe and the USA to Japan and Korea, with heat winners travelling to London to join 500 British competitors for the final on the Mall in front of Buckingham Palace. For Brompton, the publicity works on several levels. The concept of racing folding bikes may have started as a bit of a joke, but it rapidly began to attract a top international field, and the races are now taken very seriously. The World Championships not only helped to engender a public impression that the bikes were race-proven, but the requirement for competitors to wear everyday clothing has helped to widen the appeal of cycling as a day-to-day activity - and more specifically, cycling by Brompton. If top athletes can win races on this little bike, Mr (and more particularly, Mrs) Joe Bloggs should be able to cycle to work on it. The car manufacturers use exactly the same techniques to associate their everyday products with achievement and success.

Brompton has engaged in numerous cycle promotion activities too, especially in London, where it has been a lead sponsor to the 'Love London, Go Dutch' campaign. It's hard to imagine a better placement for Brompton. Go Dutch is about moving the image of cycling from reflective clothing, helmets and Lycra, and empowering ordinary people to cycle in the capital. The campaign has been quite successful, persuading a rather half-hearted London Assembly to increase cycle funding. The city still has a long way to go, but Brompton has played a unique role in the campaign, both as a local manufacturer, and - in terms of commuter volumes - providing the raison d'être for better facilities. Legislators have belatedly realised that cycle facilities are not only a potent vote winner, but a simple and cost-effective means of improving the transport environment in London.

Sponsorship deals of this kind work both ways, of course. Many of the ordinary folk tentatively trying the new cycling experience will purchase the non-threatening, but subtly race-proven locally-built bike. So getting more ordinary Londoners cycling means increased sales for Brompton, and increased employment for what is now one of London's biggest manufacturing companies. Not surprisingly, ex-Mayor Johnson was a regular visitor to the factory, as Mayor Khan is today, part of a steady stream of local and national politicians, and every political visit brings the media in tow.

Brompton Dock

Perhaps the most daring project in recent years has been the Brompton Dock. This had nothing to do with the technology of the bike itself, but it promised a revolution in the way it was used.

The idea came to Will Butler-Adams after Brompton launched a bike hire project at Waterloo station. This early trial worked well, but only because South West Trains had agreed to store and hire the bikes from the fully staffed Lost Property Office at the station. To roll-out a network of hire centres nationally, and indeed internationally, the process would need to be automated - a Brompton dispenser in effect. To do this, Butler-Adams teamed up with a company called Street Associates that had developed an automatic storage system for bicycles called CycleDock: effectively a cycle shed accessible by text from a mobile phone. CycleDock was not a commercial success, primarily because it required a great deal of bulky hardware to store a handful of bicycles, but Butler-Adams had concluded that if the system could be reconfigured to suit the ultra-compact folded Brompton it stood a chance of being made commercially viable.

Brompton Dock was set up as a sister company to Brompton in April 2011, claiming to be the only bicycle hire scheme in the world to operate without grants or subsidies from government or transport authorities. The idea was that local government, transport operators, colleges and hospitals could buy the Dock and the bikes, and either join the national 'public' hire network, or establish their own 'Exclusive Network'. Either way, Brompton Dock would manage every aspect of the scheme, including bike repair (usually sub-contracted to a local Brompton dealer) and maintenance of the hardware and software of the Dock itself.

Specifically designed around the Brompton, the Docks are economical on space, even the largest 40-bike model taking up only a single car parking space. Manufacture had been kept in the UK, the Docks currently being made by Birmingham electronic engineering manufacturers CHH CoNeX.

The first fully automated 'B-Dock' opened at Guildford railway station in July 2011, after which there was a pause of almost a year while teething issues were settled, before the next two opened at Manchester Piccadilly and Stoke-on-Trent railway stations in partnership with Virgin Trains. These initial Docks were rapidly followed by another for Ealing Borough Council, close to Ealing Broadway rail and tube station, and two for First Great Western at Exeter St David's and Bristol Temple Meads railway stations in October 2012. Three Docks were also installed at the University of Greenwich.

An ambitious programme of openings was planned for early 2013, with the aim of getting the brand established in 25 towns by the spring of that year, but in practice things went rather slower than had been hoped. In March 2013, new public Docks opened at Peterborough and Oxford, bringing the total to ten, but growth thereafter was fitful, and concentrated on the southeast of England. Two years later there were still fewer than 40 Docks. In truth, the complex wireless technology and computer software had been so plagued by technical problems ('Every problem under the sun', says Will Butler-Adams), that Brompton had stopped seeking new sites, at least for the time being.

In June 2013, the Docks were rebranded by design consultancy Form, and in May 2015, the company was renamed Brompton Bike Hire Ltd. The reason for this ostensibly suicidal change was a very modern one - potential customers were using the search terms 'Brompton' and 'Hire'. The new name gave a clearer indication of its raison d'être, but was clumsier and less dynamic than the 'Dock' concept, although the actual hardware has kept the smart new Dock branding.

With partner organisations paying upfront for both the bikes and the Dock, it's difficult to see how the concept could lose money, but the losses continued to mount, and Brompton found itself supporting the bike hire arm for rather longer - and to a greater extent - than had been hoped. An initial capital injection of £200,000 in 2011-12 was followed by smaller sums in the next two years, and a massive £745,000 in 2014-15, when the operation should have been well into profit.

By June 2016, Brompton held shares with a nominal value of nearly £920,000, but the network seemed to have stalled at 45 sites and around 1,000 hire bikes. Inevitably, the early network was starting to centre on areas where the Brompton was already well known and well used - seven in London and five in Birmingham - but the docks remained thinly spread elsewhere.

The 'Catch 22' for Brompton Bicycle Hire is that take-up depends on a comprehensive network, and growth of the network depends on seed corn funding by willing partners or demand from an existing core of users. Hundreds more Docks, and tens of thousands of new members would be needed to create a viable international network.

With this relatively small network, users generally hired and returned bikes at the same place, but the much grander long-term vision was to integrate the scattered units, including the private schemes, allowing full interchangeability of both users and bikes. This has - at least partially - become a reality. Writing in 2024, there are more than 60 public docks nationwide. Registration and hire is simpler and bikes can be pre-booked by mobile app - a crucial element missing in the early 'smartcard' days. After a period of hire that might be anything from a few hours to several months, the bike can be returned to the original dock, or (in theory) to any other worldwide. But the concentration in the southeast remains a problem. Half are in the London area, another six in Birmingham, and the rest are scattered far and wide, mostly in cities, usually at railway stations. The international element has long since been abandoned, although the docks have reached as far north as Stornoway on the Hebridean Isle of Lewis, and south to Jersey.

If the scheme does survive - and in the post-Covid world survival is very much in the balance - the impact will be huge. For occasional Brompton users, actually owning a bike might no longer be necessary. Registered users would be able to access a folding bike wherever and whenever they need it. In the event of a failure - down to a simple puncture - the user simply swaps bikes at a convenient Dock. The system automatically reports the failure to the local service agent, and prevents it being hired until the repair has been completed. This concept of 'leasing' rather than buying a bicycle brings several advantages. The user has the freedom to pick up a bike when it will be most useful, and - more importantly - to get rid of it again when it would be a hindrance, as on a crowded train, and that has played well with the train operating companies.

Initially Brompton Dock offered two tariffs: frequent users paying £50 a year, plus £4 a day, and occasional 'leisure' users paying £10 a year, plus £8 a day. The tipping point between the two options was at 10 days a year, or just under one hire a month. This was rather more than the company had hoped to charge, and the high annual fees proved a stumbling block with such a new and innovative scheme. Later, the regular user charge was cut to £20, and the leisure charge to £1. It's now open for all comers, with hire at a round £5 a day. With most Brompton models costing well in excess of £1,000 to buy, leasing a bike on easy terms looked like a cost-effective option for occasional users, particularly as the cost included all maintenance and repair, but things would not go Brompton's way. In London there was stiff competition from the Santander 'Boris' bike scheme, which charged users in a slightly different way. There was no pre-registration, and you could simply turn up and go using a credit card, booking access for as little as £2 in any 24 hour period, made up of a free 30 minutes of hire, plus £2 per 30 minutes thereafter. The price has risen since, but the offer remains very tempting. The real issue with the 'Boris' scheme, and the many other regional alternatives springing up, is their sheer size and marketing muscle. The Brompton Dock was only ever going to be viable if it could reach critical mass in terms of size, but in London alone, it's up against 800 or so Santander docking stations.

Brompton is understandably tight-lipped about the viability of the dock scheme. The concept could yet fulfil its potential, but all the signs are that it's teetering on the edge of financial viability. In 2017/18 losses reached £182,209 on turnover of £459,066 and in 2018/19 the company lost an alarming £290,529 on turnover of £303,720. The Dock scheme appeared to hit rock bottom in 2019/20, posting a loss of £705,039 before bouncing back with a £67,891 loss in 2021 as turnover exceeded £1 million for the first time, reflecting the massive Covid-lead demand for bikes. More recent figures show Brompton Bike Hire Limited continuing to be dogged by losses - £117,658 and £67,771 for 2022 and 2023 respectively, with turnover static at £1.1 million.

Happily for Brompton, the Covid-inspired boom in hire revenue has not yet receded but the real drain on profitablility appears to be 'administrative expenses', with the last three years figures ranging between £672,339 and £876,041. The recent explosion in the popularity of 'dockless' bike schemes in London and to a lesser degree other parts of the UK, demonstrates a real demand for the convenience offered by short term bike hire but profitability is another matter entirely. When dockless bike behemoth Lime claimed to have turned a profit in 2022, it was said to be the first full year of profits in the entire micromobility industry! The Brompton Dock was, and remains, a hugely appealing idea, but the company was competing with big players with bottomless pockets.

It might still all come right. The thousand-odd hire bikes represent a mere pinprick on annual sales of almost 100,000, but the Docks are a good means of encouraging commuters to 'try before they buy', and the company now offers 'up to £150' (£250 on electric models) as a cash-back reward for Dock users who go on to buy a Brompton. As Brompton themselves admit, good marketing drives sales, but it's arguably just another nail in the coffin for the principle of long-term hire.

In some ways, the development of the Dock was an admission that the Brompton couldn't, at that time, realistically be made much smaller or lighter. This sounded like neat lateral thinking; if it doesn't need to be heaved into a car boot, or carried by train, the bulk and weight of the machine becomes less of an issue. But in a post-Corona world it looks more likely that the emphasis will return to small, light, low-key and *personal* transport.

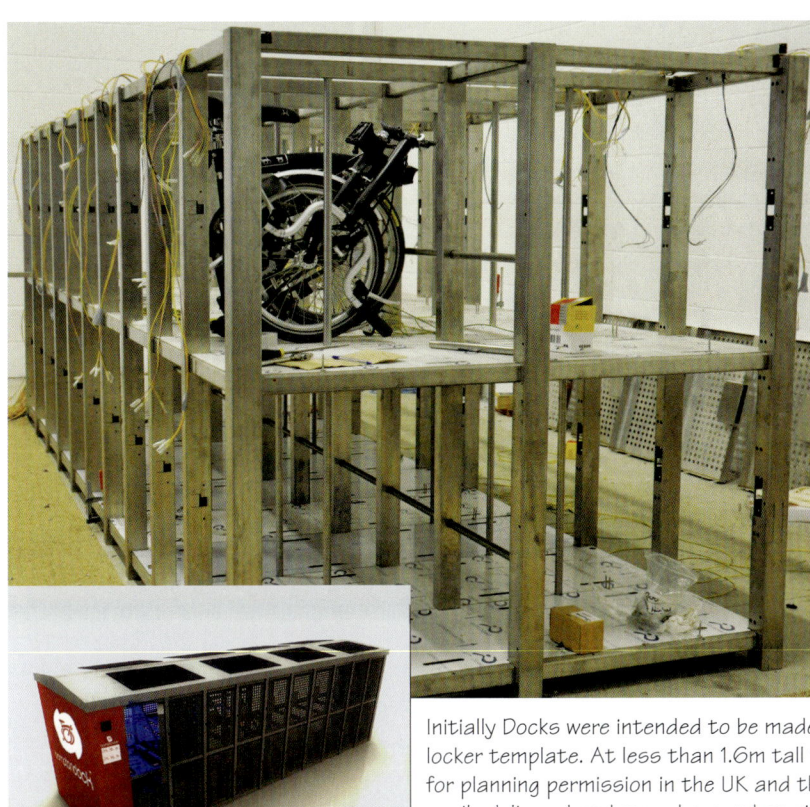

A Brompton Dock takes shape at Street Associates' factory. Not only do the Docks have to be storm, vandal and user proof, but the high-tech electronics required mean each locker has to be wired up as part of the construction process. The contract for manufacture has since been awarded to CHH CoNeX and docks are made at their sizeable Birmingham plant.

Initially Docks were intended to be made to the same forty locker template. At less than 1.6m tall there is no requirement for planning permission in the UK and they can be relatively easily delivered and moved around on site if required. Bespoke colouring (left) is also available to suit organisations running schemes.

The current Dock design is much sleeker than the original slightly industrial appearance, with some having the option of solar power providing the electricity for their running. This obviates the need for connecting to the mains supply, itself a process that can be problem fraught.

Moving House Again

In 2013-14, Brompton sales amounted to 44,755, of which 77% were exported, and turnover once again broke all records at £27.2 million, yielding record profits of £3.5 million. The following year, the seemingly inexorable growth stuttered for the first time since the Sturmey-Archer collapse of 2000. This was partly down to running-in a new Benelux distributor and issues in Japan, but the primary cause seems to have been overstocking by dealers and distributors in 2013-14, when output finally exceeded demand after another of the periodic famines. Sales fell to 42,941 bikes, turnover almost levelled off at £27.5 million, and profits plummeted to £2.2 million, and then £0.2 million the following year. Staff costs were on the rise too, and another big expense was starting to make itself felt, as the company began the move from the Brentford factory to bigger premises. Brompton had considered Wales, Northern Ireland, and even Eastern Europe, but eventually concluded that the theoretical advantages to the bottom line were far outweighed by the loss of that iconic 'Made in London' tag, so the search was refocussed closer to home.

In truth, the company had outgrown the Brentford factory some years before. Stock storage space had long been overwhelmed, and the company had leased a satellite site just off the Great West Road since April 2013. This was primarily used for storage, but had increasingly become a sub-assembly area too. Running back and forth between two factories, and sending more and more frames to Wales for painting was clearly expensive, inefficient and unsustainable. To achieve further growth - and Brompton was aiming to more than double output to 100,000 units a year - it was essential to bring everything back under one roof.

After a few fruitless leads, the company found a warehouse in Greenford, a few miles north of Brentford. In logistical terms it was ideal, sandwiched between Greenford's tube and railway stations, and the Paddington arm of the Grand Union canal, giving easy cycle access to central London, and - in the longer term - the proposed Old Oak Common HS2 station. In the more immediate future, the factory would be a couple of cycling miles from Ealing's Elizabeth Line station.

Formerly used by the H&M fashion chain, the warehouse offered some 84,000 square feet of factory and office space - four times as much as the Brentford factory. Brompton was growing fast at this time, and although the new unit seemed to provide a massive amount of room for expansion, by the time the move was complete, it was looking quite well filled.

Back in the 1990s, with a handful of staff and a few manually-operated machines, moving from the Arches to Chiswick had been no more than a temporary inconvenience, but with over 200 staff producing 100 bikes a day, it was a much bigger deal. The move alone cost over £2 million, with the extra rent and rates expected to add around £1 million to the annual outgoings. On the other hand, a great deal would be saved in reduced transport costs and tighter control over logistics through bringing everything in-house (except of course the Yorkshire titanium operation). Even in a worst-case scenario of zero growth the new factory was expected to pay for itself, although no-one could have guessed back in 2015 just how bad the worst case scenario would look.

The factory move was announced in August 2015, with the move and build-up of production at the new site being carefully phased to minimise disruption to production schedules. The new plant was substantially up to speed by early 2016, and officially opened by His Royal Highness the Duke of Edinburgh in November 2016.

Core of the new plant was the much bigger factory floor, including brazing stations, and two production lines. When the Brentford factory reached capacity, the single line had gone to a seven day week, operated by two teams - one working four days, and the other a three day weekend (at a time and a half rate - an expensive solution). In the new factory, the two lines worked conventional hours simultaneously, but of course the capacity was there to introduce two or even more shifts per line.

Workers conditions and pay have changed almost out of recognition. The days of piece work - when workers were encouraged to churn out as much as possible - are long gone, and Brompton now pays employees by their skill level, a change that has staff positively queueing up to pass out with new skills. The multi-skilled are especially prized for their ability to move on and off the various assembly jobs as required. Generally speaking, each line runs at full speed with 19 staff, reducing to half speed with eight or nine.

The brazing stations are essentially unchanged, but gas is now piped in rather than stored in bottles at each station. This eliminates the time-consuming, and sometimes back-breaking task of swapping bottles.

The bigger shop floor (above) could now accommodate two production lines like that below.

Frame brazing underway at the new Greenford factory. The aim was to increase quality and production in this critical area with the introduction of these bespoke built brazing bays, complete with gas piped directly to the station.

In place of that 'break' from work, brazers are encouraged to rest and exercise at intervals. Again, without the piece-work system, brazers are paid a set skilled rate, with build and quality-control targets. The accent is on a steady pace rather than periods of frenetic time-is-money activity. Efficiency is slightly up, despite starting with 35 brazing stations, slightly fewer than at Brentford. The last element to fall into place were the two major areas of outsourced production - painting (actually powder-coating, as it has been since Brompton's earliest days) and wheel-building. But the half million pound Greenford paint shop gradually took over the painting operations from the long-established subcontractor in South Wales, which had been given two years notice, to allow for an orderly transition.

The paint shop - a convoluted miracle of tightly coiled hanging conveyors - carries components through a dense spray of oxsilan primer/bonding agent, followed by a trip through a low-temperature drying oven, a visit to the main robotic spray booth, and a high temperature oven bake, which melts the powder, leaving a tough, durable finish. Early Bromptons were primed with gold-coloured zinc phosphate, which was later outlawed for its toxicity and replaced with less effective iron phosphate, recognisable by its black colour. Today's Oxsilan is nearly as effective as zinc, non-toxic, and its application uses less energy and water.

The spray plant has more than enough capacity to undertake subcontract work for other companies, and - although no-one will even hint at this openly - make it much easier for Brompton to introduce variants such as child-carriers in the future.

Wheel-building is a specialist craft that had long been subcontracted to two small factories in the West Midlands, but again, both suppliers were put on notice that this operation would gradually be brought in-house, which it eventually was. One was the very long-established Mike Hesson, by now somewhat past retirement age, who had been building wheels for Brompton from the earliest days.

The new factory is an airy, relaxed place. Fig trees grow from old handlebar boxes (an Andrew Ritchie-esque touch, but actually post Andrew), and staff are encouraged to relax in a Google-style mezzanine play area, complete with elderly, but serviceable piano, a pool table and a bar area, brazed, as you might expect, from reject rear frame tubes.

The paint shop has brought the operation in house allowing for extra capacity to take on work from other firms.

In the early days, Brompton was too small to develop an 'us and them' management-worker culture. Today it is big enough, but enlightened enough to avoid such industrial pitfalls. There are no remote 'suits' upstairs, and no awkward union reps on the shop floor.

Quality is the key word. For 15 minutes every morning workers from every area, both upstairs and downstairs, come together for a Quality Team meeting, Brompton's answer to the Japanese Kaizen (or continuous improvement) concept.

© Alexander Henshaw

© Alexander Henshaw

© Alexander Henshaw

Having painted frames more readily to hand (above) will increase efficiency at the new factory.

Indeed, the large new Greenford premises are a blend of the innovatively practical, such as the new 'rumbling machine' (left - for more on this see page 136) and a new management culture that encourages relaxation as one element in producing an efficient workforce (below left).

Brexit and The Bottom Line

Like many other young, vibrant British companies, Brompton saw itself as just another European manufacturer, albeit one with complex links to the USA and the Far East. And in common with most, it paid little attention to what became known as the 'Brexit' referendum over membership of the European Union announced in February 2016 by Prime Minister David Cameron. It was just the latest in a long series of attempts to force the strident anti-European camp to either put up or shut up, but it turned out to be a fatal miscalculation.

It seemed almost unimaginable that the British people - wealthier and enjoying near full-employment - would vote for an unpredictable future outside this comfortable family of nations, but in June 2016, that's exactly what happened. Beneath the surface, an undercurrent of deep resentment had been welling up for some time, and a majority of people really were prepared to swap comfort and wealth for the relative freedom and uncertainties of navigating an independent path in the world.

The initial effect was to deeply fracture the British establishment and cause three or four years of upheaval, with politicians falling like nine-pins on all sides, beginning with Cameron himself. Industry was told to plan for a worst case of no deal - a so-called 'hard' Brexit - and like many others that relied on imports, Brompton began stockpiling spares, renting a warehouse at Heathrow to house an estimated £1 million worth of stock in the event of import and export issues developing, either through the hard Brexit, or delays caused by customs issues. Writing in early 2024, tariff issues with Europe appear to have settled down but compensatory free-trade agreements with other large trading blocs have yet to materialise. They still might, but in an ironic silver lining, the warehouse would soon find another even more unexpected use.

In many ways, Brexit (to date of course) has been a bit of a phoney war for Brompton and other vulnerable manufacturers. The political storm raged back and forth, with first one side, then the other, getting the advantage. The pound suffered a bit, but Brompton saw its profits rise by 24% in the year to March 2018, which was very helpful after the triple whammy of moving to the big new factory, the ongoing drain of keeping the hire scheme afloat and developing the electric bike, which had yet to sell in any appreciable numbers.

In June that year, the Electric variant was officially launched, but the celebration was a bit of a damp squib, as early adopter enthusiasm had been more than satisfied by the soft launch, and the factory was too tied up with fighting the Electric's many reliability issues to lay down much champagne.

With other products, though, it was business as usual. It was all very profitable, but you couldn't help wondering where the beef had gone? Bags, jackets and trick paint schemes seemed to arrive monthly in a welter of good news PR, lapped up by well-onside social media influencers.

Typical was the rather cozy launch of the 'X-CHPT3', the small production run disappearing like the proverbial hot cakes, the price in 2019 being a seriously profitable £1,990 apiece, making it by far the most expensive bike to date, after the Electric. A new lightweight bike perhaps? Some sort of sparkling new technology? Any sort of technology? Well, no. It was yet another variant based on the existing theme, helpfully plugged by retired professional road cyclist David Millar, who had set up the CHPT3 brand, and apparently chosen the spec of the new Brompton. Just for the record, it had no luggage block, no mudguards, a rather odd paint scheme, and was furnished with the few remaining titanium components. The only genuinely new thing were the Schwalbe 'One' tyres, although these didn't arrive until demand for the CHPT3 had forced another short production run in February 2019. The sceptical could be forgiven for thinking that the whole affair was being carefully stage managed to follow the path of maximum PR guff with minimal genuine innovation.

The CHPT3 'limited edition' had the cachet of endorsement from retired pro racing cyclist David Millar, but beneath the marketing gloss the new Schwalbe One tyres were the only new element of the bike.

Tyre technology has been one of the few areas of technical development for Brompton in recent years, with the Greenspeed Scorcher (right) and the Schwalbe One (top right). The former came from Australian master of cycle design innovation Ian Sims (above).

The 349mm version of Schwalbe's existing One tyre was excellent. It was reminiscent of the Primo tyre that arrived in the 1990s, but even freer running, tougher and more comfortable. At first Brompton did a slightly grubby deal with Schwalbe for the tyre to be supplied as an exclusive fitment on the X-CHPT3, but such was demand, they were forced to relent and allow sales by third party suppliers, initially in the European Union, but later worldwide.

At about the same time, on the other side of the world, Ian Sims, CEO of Greenspeed, was moving as fast as he could to bring to production a similar high performance 37-349mm tyre for the Brompton - a narrower version of the well proven 40-349mm Scorcher, developed by Ian for his Greenspeed recumbent trikes. By early 2019, with a handful of samples doing well on test, Ian knew he was dying of liver cancer, and that he might not get the tyre into production in time.

He was right. The illness was made public in late January 2019, and by May this remarkable engineer was dead. Unfortunately, the tyre appeared to die with him. A year later, in February 2020, it was announced that Greenspeed had been acquired by WhizzWheelz of Grand Rapids, Michigan, USA, and rumours suggested that even the 40mm Scorcher might be discontinued.

At Brompton, the 'launches' continued with the 'Limited Edition' B75, a machine that appeared to defy logic in most respects. It was basically a basic M3, but it came with a strange variety of bits and pieces from the Brompton parts bin, yet you didn't get three of the most important day-to-day accessories - mudguards, folding pedal and carrier block. It was heavy, and rather impractical, and it appeared to be a means of disposing of surplus stock! One element that did make sense was the very competitive price of £745, although any purchaser hoping to upgrade as funds allowed would have found themselves paying well over the odds against starting out with a conventional M3. In subsequent years it was quietly withdrawn.

Whilst the B75 had an eye-catching price tag of £745 it seemed a developmental backward step in the form of a non-folding pedal and extended seatpost.

By contrast, the 'Explore', launched in August 2019, seems to have been an appallingly cynical marketing exercise, although it's hard to criticise the company for making money (quite a lot in this case) from public demand for just about anything carrying the Brompton of London logo, which served to show the breathtaking gullibility of some consumers. Launched in August 2019, it was basically £1,000-worth of M6E (mudguard-less, with M-type bars and six gears) dressed up as an all-terrain bike. The sales spiel is worth quoting for its sheer chutzpah, if not its grammatical accuracy: 'Informed by our design and product teams (sic) many long distance trips by Brompton, the Explore edition has been carefully spec'd and kitted out to make sure you're ready for the next long trip, or any slight diversion from the city'. For a bicycle once heralded as a work of technical brilliance every bit the equal in its humble way to the hovercraft, Land Rover and other icons of British industrial design, it was a sorry state of affairs. The Explore was the latest in a series of launches by Brompton's big and profitable marketing department. It featured no special all-terrain technology, because Brompton hadn't developed any. Indeed, it rode on ordinary Schwalbe Marathon Racer tyres, albeit with marginally reduced gearing courtesy of a 44-tooth chainring. Off-road, it would achieve little over a conventional Brompton, but at £1,525 a throw it was a tonic for the bottom line.

Coronavirus

A lot of this profitability came about through the company's ever expanding trading relationship with China, which represented both a source of components and a vast, nascent pool of consumers the company was just beginning to tap into. The Chinese were moving rapidly into higher-technology, but this vast sprawling workshop of a country still had plenty of small- and medium-sized businesses willing to produce more conventional engineering at knock-down prices. There were a few provisos over exchange rates and government interference over tariffs, so it wasn't quite the license to print money it might have seemed, but for Western engineering firms, some of the deals were very tempting. After more than 30 years, this comfortable relationship was about to be profoundly questioned.

There is still some debate about the exact origins of the virus, but it's agreed that the first handful of cases of a flu-like illness were reported in Wuhan, a city in the Chinese province of Hubei, as early as November 2019. At first, the authorities seem to have wasted valuable time by hushing up the affair, and most Western governments badly underestimated what the shattering impact of the virus would be when it did arrive. The Far East had experienced mild and more serious flu-like illnesses before, and none had resulted in serious outbreaks elsewhere. Even after the illness had spread with a frightening virulence through the area around Wuhan, and out into the wider population, little notice was taken in the West. It was just another localised rural Chinese issue surely?

This all changed when the virus exploded into Europe in late February, spreading rapidly through Italy, Spain and France, then into the UK in a matter of weeks. It was much more virulent than anyone had thought, and much more deadly, cruelly targeting the old and infirm.

Suddenly, the world had become a dangerous place, and a series of increasingly draconian panic measures were brought in to try and control rapid transmission of a disease that the UK had clearly misjudged. The principal control measure was to keep citizens at home, forcing the closure of most schools, colleges and work-places. But in the UK, there was no legislation to enforce blanket closure of private businesses, and in any event the government had declared bicycle businesses essential. Brompton - like many other small firms with a full order-book - kept trading after a fashion.

Demand for bicycles seems to have grown, primarily because exercising and shopping locally had become the normal pattern. Motorised travel wasn't banned, but it was frowned upon, and felt somehow unpatriotic, although in itself, driving around was pretty harmless. The danger came from mixing with strangers, and to reduce this to a minimum, government advice was towards walking and cycling in one's local area. With cheaper bicycle imports disrupted, the home-produced and now very

high-profile Brompton was in demand, but with very few shops open to sell it initially.
With most retail outlets (including Brompton's own shops) either wholly or partially closed, mail-order began to take on a new importance, as both Royal Mail and the primary couriers were still open for business, albeit with serious delays and disruption. In April 2020, Brompton set up a 'Direct-to-Home' service, offering free delivery in seven to ten days, 12 months interest-free credit and even a 28-day returns option. It was pretty generous, and a perfect response to the challenges of the era, when many other companies had simply chosen to turn out the lights and lock up for the duration.
Actually building bikes was more of a problem. Government rules stipulated that people should keep more than two metres apart from anyone outside their own designated household, and employers were obliged to make suitable arrangements. This rule had huge implications both in terms of running a production line, and providing rest rooms, toilets and canteens where people could move around en masse in safety. To some extent, for Brompton and other companies still trading, this issue resolved itself, because many employees were off work with the virus, others were choosing to keep away because they shared a household with a vulnerable relative, and some were working from home, so staff numbers fell quite naturally. By April, Brompton only had 160 out of around 450 employees still working in the factory, which more or less matched the 35-40% fall in sales.
Productivity was way down, profitability more or less a thing of the past, and with many suppliers closed or unable to produce parts because their own supply chains were disrupted, output was bound to be much reduced. Nevertheless, Brompton slogged bravely on, thanks at times to the Brexit spares stockpile at Heathrow, and outside funding: "…we have sought a £3 million overdraft from our bank," said Will Butler-Adams in April. "Hopefully, we won't need it, but it's there for an emergency…"

Wheels for Heroes free loan scheme was popular with NHS staff wanting to avoid public transport.

There were high spots though, and occasionally, the marketing department found a crumb of comfort to throw to a media desperate for a good news story in the gathering gloom. Public transport had been cut to a skeleton service for key workers when the pandemic struck, but doctors and nurses - many of whom had already lost colleagues to the disease - were keen to commute by bicycle in the worst affected areas such as London and Birmingham to avoid all contact with fellow citizens.
In April 2020, Brompton Bike Hire helped satisfy this demand and stir up a rash of positive headlines by launching Wheels for Heroes, a free loan scheme for NHS staff, offering bikes in NHS colours of pale blue and white. The first thoughts on a loan scheme had come from St Bartholomews Hospital a couple of weeks before, but within a very short space of time, the clamour for bikes had spread far and wide, and the scheme was extended to 1,000 bikes, covering all UK Health Service Trusts. Brompton was even able to take advantage of the near religious public veneration of NHS front-line staff, by crowd-funding the loan bikes, taking £40,000 in a few hours, and eventually receiving £345,000, primarily from a grateful public through Crowdfunder, but including £100,000 from a grateful government, and £20,000 from British Cycling and Barts Charity which had already agreed to fund the purchase of 20 Brompton Electrics for staff commuting longer distances, the aim being to eventually use the bikes to help with the rehabilitation of cardiac patients once the outbreak had been adequately suppressed.

By 1st June 2020, 2000 NHS staff had signed up to the scheme, and more than 500 free loan bikes had been distributed to health trusts, with a further 300 in production. It was quite an impressive affair, and it was hoped the association with the NHS would continue long after the pandemic had eventually been brought under control.

Inevitably, once the pandemic was under control, the public and NHS professionals just wanted to put it behind them. To make matters worse, doctors and other front-line staff began flexing their industrial muscles... perhaps they were ordinary mortals after all. 'Wheels for Heroes' faded very quickly, turning into a three month free trial, then effectively disappearing in a couple of years.

Backing Britain

Brompton has rarely advertised in the past, but spends a great deal on marketing today (the prize money at the launch race for the X-CHPT3 in 2018 was £10,000). Hopefully that sort of wasteful excess won't recur. The marketing budget, says Will Butler-Adams, is best spent on looking after existing customers. Experience has shown that happy customers are ambassadors for Brompton, enthusiastically demonstrating and selling the bike. The company will continue supporting events like the annual Brompton World Championships, helping it fulfill its aim of continued growth without advertorial, along with continuing dealer support, all in the best tradition of the Ritchie marketing philosophy that has worked so well for so long. So is the future an exciting place?

Will Butler-Adams: "The message is that we've taken a decision to grow and become a global player. We're proud to be a British company, and determined to remain independent. Hopefully, we'll still be here in another 25 years!"

For Will Butler-Adams, the future holds many challenges. In 2011/12, annual output reached 30,000 bikes, and in 2016-17, it hovered around the 40,000 region, and today it's hovering somewhere over the 90,000 mark. If the company can build 90,000 bikes profitably in Greenford, one might assume it could build 300,000 a year even more profitably in China. Is Brompton still committed to manufacturing in the UK? Fifteen years ago building bikes overseas might have been an option, but in post-Brexit, post-pandemic Britain, manufacturing is very much back on the political agenda, and with the pound at a historic low in late 2022 (it has bounced back since), the balance sheet has moved decisively towards the UK.

Brexit has been something of a mixed blessing for Brompton. The low pound is good news for the 80% of output that's exported, but bad news for imports, and - as we've seen - Brompton imports a lot of raw materials and parts. Nevertheless, the company has kept prices relatively stable in turbulent times, which can only be good news for sales.

It was hoped that leaving Europe would result in favourable trade deals with the Far East and the USA - both areas of huge growth for the company - but there is little sign of positive trade deals to date.

On the other hand the UK has joined Russia as a 'Dialogue Partner' with ASEAN, a grouping of ten Southeast Asian states. This political link could be hugely significant for Brompton, as it continues to find and exploit new markets in that part of the world.

Brompton's issues are broadly those of UK PLC. The company has always been dependent on links to Europe, but Europe now takes only 30% of output, and that proportion is shrinking. There's growth just about everywhere else, from the USA to China, which already accounts for 3% of output from a standing start. Favourable trade deals with the Americas and the Far East could be of huge benefit to Brompton, as indeed, to other British manufacturers. A new generation of Government ministers and opposition spokesmen are already following the well-trodden path to deliver soundbites from the Greenford factory floor, and who can blame them?

For all sorts of entirely practical reasons, Will Butler-Adams is adamant that Brompton will continue to build bikes in the UK:

"Ours is an intellectual property business. There are some 1,200 parts in a bike, and a lot are unique.

Describing our bike takes 30,000 to 40,000 drawings, but in describing the machines to make our bike there are maybe 300,000 - 400,000 drawings. So the cleverness is in the bike, yes, but there's far more cleverness in how to make the bike. As soon as you take that out to China, you teach people how to do it and they will leave, perhaps to work for Cannondale, who are out there already. So we haven't patented anything, but we keep our knowledge in-house in our staff. If you go out to China you make more money for a couple of years, then suddenly the copy from Dahon really is good because all your cleverness has gone into the Dahon. Suddenly you have to cut your margins, so you don't have enough money to do R & D, you don't have enough money to develop new ideas and it just stagnates and sits there. Game over."

Far from building bikes, Asia is increasingly being seen as a market. In Japan, where the Brompton costs ten times as much as some cheaper brands, consumers have demonstrated a willingness to pay a premium for a quality European product, and sales remain strong.

In March 2011, Japan became the test-bed for a new Brompton innovation when the 'Brompton Junction' retail concept was trialled in Kobe. This flagship store was an instant success, and stores followed in Hamburg, Amsterdam and, signalling the company's Far-Eastern aspirations, Shanghai. By 2016, these pathfinder stores had been joined by London (naturally), Milan, Beijing, Chengdu, Munich, Tokyo, Barcelona and Suzhou. The branded stores present the bike in a uniform and carefully manicured form, with expert staff willing and able to demonstrate the numerous options. Even if they weren't profitable in themselves (and they are), the Brompton Junction outlets are marketing gold - a priceless shop-window.

The opening of the Shanghai Brompton Junction store in July 2016 reinforced Brompton's commitment to becoming a global player.

As with the Docks, the risk is usually shared with local partners. Most Junction shops are based on existing bike shops that had found the majority of their sales were of Bromptons and Brompton spares. There are exceptions though, notably in China, where independent bicycle dealers simply didn't exist. The Chinese outlets had to be set up and paid for from scratch, a somewhat riskier business, and one shop has subsequently closed.

The Chinese market is different in almost every respect from the others. Folding bike commuting is unknown there, and as in much of Asia, the bike is seen as an expensive European toy ("Not just a premium product", says Will Butler-Adam, "It's a super-premium product!").

But China is a breathtakingly vast market and its giant cities are beset by pollution issues. The Brompton needs to become mainstream in China, and no doubt it will.

In China, as elsewhere, Butler-Adams believes that the continuing concern over global warming may see cars eliminated from some cities, with transport funding shifting to improved cycle infrastructure. Brompton starts with a unique product and expertise in dealing with transport planners and public transport providers, expertise that could be exported anywhere in the world.

What of the competition? "Forget the small-fry like Dahon. The real competition is going to come from the likes of Giant and Trek. They don't have serious folding bikes now, but they haven't really been trying. They're not stupid."

Throughout most of this story, Brompton has been one of a handful of small British cycle manufacturers, fighting for the market scraps left behind by three or four really big companies, such as Raleigh and Dawes. Today, only Brompton and Pashley manufacture bikes here in any number. Of the two, Pashley held top spot until it lost the Post Office bicycle contract. Since then, Brompton has found itself at the top of the tree - an almost unimaginable scenario, even ten years ago.

Earlier editions of this book ended with the bike's designer still very much involved, but sadly, on 3rd March 2016, Andrew Ritchie resigned as a director, citing differences with the Brompton management team. The company kept this resignation quiet, and it was not until September that the story broke in the conventional media and as a series of outlandish conspiracy theories on social media. In fact, Ritchie remained the biggest shareholder, with an 18% stake, although now a very long way from controlling the company.

Why did he feel the need to go? He had been frustrated by the occasional engineering own goals, but by 2016 the engineering expertise was reawakening. The truth seems to be nothing more than a difference in management style. Andrew had always controlled and overseen every single aspect of his small, then medium-sized company, from floor cleaning products through the purchase of nuts and bolts, to the design of jigs and work-stations.

Will Butler-Adams' style is about enabling the much bigger workforce to do their creative best. Perhaps the engineering hiccups had been exacerbated by Andrew's continuing presence. With such a strong and multi-talented character looking over their shoulders, the new team had never really felt willing to take responsibility, always expecting Andrew to fine-tune projects and sign them off. They really were on their own now.

Besides the bike itself, Andrew Ritchie designs are everywhere in the new factory. One of the last projects to carry the hallmarks of the Ritchie genius was the wonderfully Emett-esque 'rumbling machine'.

Grit blasting brazed components had always been a messy, dangerous and polluting process, with stray grit causing all sorts of issues at the painting stage. The rumblers are built around a ring of squash balls that expand to grasp the inside of frame tubes, allowing them to be lowered into a frothing, boiling mass of ceramic beads floating in lime juice. As the beads circulate, they cause the ring of components to float slowly round without outside assistance. The machines are supremely elegant, practical, and world-class in their effectiveness. Also hypnotically watchable.

Feeling the need to strengthen the boardroom with Andrew's departure. Butler-Adams brought in several new faces, including Dan Cobley former MD of Google UK, but the one that caused a minor media storm was 'serial entrepreneur' Luke Johnson. As Johnson is known in part as a successful venture capitalist, there was a great deal of suspicion at first about his intentions. Was he there to asset strip the company and flog the intellectual property to the Far East?

The reality is that Johnson's venture capital firm was not involved, and - apparently a bit of a Brompton nut - he had bought a small 3% personal shareholding to bring his considerable expertise to the board.

Johnson is a long way from the typical venture capitalist, and indeed, something of a philanthropist - chairman of the Institute of Cancer Research and a former Chairman of Action on Addiction. He has also involved himself with the arts, as chairman of Channel 4 from 2004 to 2010, and chairman of the Royal Society of Arts from 2009 to 2012.

He's a very big financial beast, and an extremely tough and able businessman. "Luke has made board meetings rather less comfortable… he holds us to account," says Will Butler-Adams. Crucially, his appointment has also met with the quiet approval of Andrew Ritchie.

And so, as the Brompton enters its third decade of production, the company looks secure, both financially and intellectually. But what of Andrew Ritchie, the brilliant engineer who started it all? In 2016, free at last, Andrew decided to start all over again, leasing a small workshop hidden away in a garden off the Goldhawk Road. It's The Arches all over again, but with a few quid in his pocket, Andrew has been able to buy slightly newer machinery.

What was he going to design? He wouldn't say, but then perhaps he didn't know. There's a whole world of industrial adventure out there waiting to be discovered. At some point - perhaps mulling over a pint in a favourite Chiswick watering hole - Andrew will hear a chance remark or spot the blindingly obvious thing that no-one else has spotted, and the spark of an idea will take root. We wait with trepidation.

2016 saw Andrew Ritchie return to his own workshop where he has a blank slate to turn his attention to any new engineering conundrums he might choose…

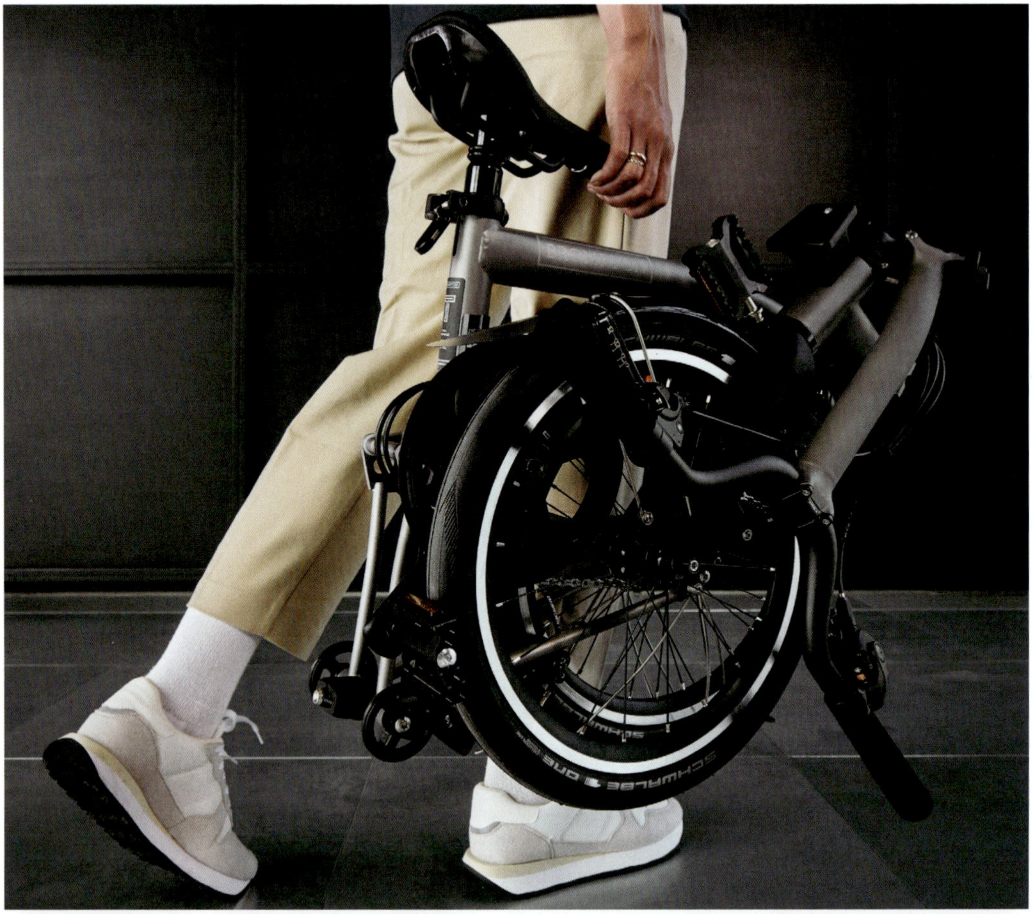

Brompton Bicycle

The All Titanium Bike & New Horizons Brompton's all titanium models were class-leadingly light

The All Titanium Bike and New Horizons
2021 - 2024

Russian Invasion, Inflation Worries

The pandemic could have been a nightmare for Brompton, but people had cash in their pockets, time on their hands, and in the new Covid/post Covid world, they were wary of their fellow citizens. People liked the idea of buying a mail-order bike in a box and finding their own way round the city. By the end of 2020 Brompton was booming and in the 2021-22 financial year, turnover rocketed, from £76 million in 20-21 to £107 million. Good going, but turning over a wad of cash doesn't show the whole picture. Profit fell from £9.6 to £7.3 million in the same period, slashing the bottom line from a healthy 12.7% to 6.8%. Even those 'celeb' endorsed special editions and superficial bag and colour options couldn't hold the line under these conditions. Staffing costs were up, and the company was having to increase stock levels as a hedge against turbulence in the supply chain. It was impressive stuff nonetheless - output increasing from 70,000 to 93,000 bikes in a year that saw many industrial groups throw in the towel altogether.

Interestingly, the Covid pandemic had accelerated Brompton's gradual annexation of bike distribution, from straight manufacturing to distributing and even retailing. In the 1990s, the company was desperate to bring retailers onboard. It was now dictating terms, and the terms were that it would continue to encourage direct sales to the public where this made financial and common sense. The old chestnut about shop technicians assembling the bike and fitting it to the customer just didn't make sense with this sort of machine. The customer could order online, open the box, unfold and start commuting. There was still plenty of business for dealers if they wanted it, but in the wired online age, Brompton no longer saw a need to divide and sub-divide the profit on each and every sale.

European business had fallen back post-Brexit, but the home market remained strong, and the second-largest market was now China (in 2023 it took the lead). This was a very different China to the repeat offender that had exported cheap copies to the West a decade before. Covid paranoia was fuelling a boom in the USA too, with sales increasing by 76% between 2019 and 2021.

It wasn't all plain sailing, and Brompton was working hard to control prices in turbulent times. In 2018, the basic M3L retailed for £1,000, and the price was held at this psychological barrier for 2019, increasing by only £45 in 2020, a fall in real terms of about 0.5% after inflation.

And then..... In February 2022, just as the Covid vaccines were being distributed, and the fearsome infection was abating, the world found itself facing a new and potentially even deadlier threat.

One consolation for many during the restrictions of the Covid pandemic was the freedom offered by bikes - leading to a sales boom for Brompton.

President Putin of Russia had been a figure of fun in the west for years. In deepest Siberia, a rather serious looking Putin was carefully stage-managing testosterone-heavy stunts aimed deep into the psyche of the Russian people: opening big projects from the cab of a monster truck, riding wild stallions, even (allegedly) wrestling bears. Some of it was generated in the West to poke gentle fun at the man and the state, but the Russian people really wanted to believe, and many of them loved every machismo-laden minute. The democracies had once made fun of the preposterously serious Herr Hitler, with his silly moustache and goose-stepping Sturmtruppen, but nations preparing for deadly serious global conflict may often look deceptively preposterous.

Putin had annexed Crimea in a bloodless coup back in 2014, and the west had largely shrugged, tut-tutted and moved on. Superficially still a democratic leader, but actually blossoming very effectively as a dictator, the Russian leader had made no secret of his territorial ambitions to annexe all Ukraine. There was even a hint of justification to his claim, because although Ukraine can follow its history back at least as far as Russia, some parts of modern Ukraine are an artificial construct. But modern history is littered with regimes that are given an inch and end up taking it all.

In February 2022, Putin launched a full-scale invasion, with the avowed intention of wiping Ukraine, a sovereign nation, from the map. Raw material prices were already high after Covid, but with the advent of a European war and loss of Russian oil and gas, inflation took off, passing 2.5% in 2020-21, then 9% in 2021-22, and just a shade lower in 2022-23. Brompton prices followed much the same pattern.

The T-Line Titanium Emerges

Did any of this really matter to a bicycle manufacturer far away in London? In a strange way it did, because a radical new bicycle was waiting in the wings that relied on a wonder material of which Russia was already a major supplier to Brompton.

From its inception, the Brompton had been built from steel. The metallurgy of the tubing was nothing special – something that Andrew Ritchie was happy to make clear, to the chagrin of his marketing department. Like most folding bikes, the Brompton relied for strength and rigidity on a single substantial main frame tube, rather than a triangulated structure of slim tubes like a conventional bicycle. Relatively simple to build, and easy to fold, but without a structure of interlinked tubes, it needed a lot of bulk in that tube to stay sufficiently rigid.

Various outsiders had tried building Bromptons from other materials, principally aluminium, carbon fibre and titanium, but few were practical, and the ones that were – such as Len Rubin's titanium creations – were prohibitively expensive. Aluminium lacked the necessary strength and toughness, so aluminium bikes were usually built using even thicker tubing and could come out as heavy as steel, with a lethargic 'dead' feel. Carbon fibre was good, but failure at stress-points could be catastrophic (almost explosive), and engineering the joints and hinges raises innumerable issues.

The only potentially viable material was titanium. It's expensive and difficult to refine, work and weld, but the superlatives go on forever. Titanium has the greatest strength/weight ratio of any common metal, it's effectively corrosion-proof, so it doesn't need painting (saving a few more grams), and unlike aluminium, it has a degree of 'liveliness'. All tributes that sound ideal for a bicycle frame. True, it's rarified and expensive, and thus more widely used in the supersonic aircraft field. But in the early 2020s, the basic material price was a reasonable $5/kg. Vastly more expensive than steel, but this doesn't matter too much in a little bicycle frame – the real costs are in the manufacturing. It was this material that Putin's invasion appeared to put at risk.

Brompton had developed a special expertise with handling the metal, since developing and equipping the titanium factory in Sheffield from 2013. The factory only made frame components (principally the hinged rear triangle), but beyond cost there were no particular engineering issues preventing manufacture of a full-titanium bike. Except one.

You could just swap out steel for titanium and keep the geometry of the frame the same, but this would fail to play to the strengths of the material. To get the best out of such an exotically different frame, it made sense to redesign the bike almost from scratch. And a thin-walled tubing of a larger diameter seemed to strike the best balance between weight, strength, price and 'feel'. So the saddle stem and mainframe tube were increased in size, the mainframe going from around 45mm (including paint) to 51mm, which meant that almost everything else had to change. Titanium behaves differently during and after welding, so the joints had to be different, the hinges and pins behaved differently, cutting threads into titanium was different – everything had to be changed.

Titanium wasn't used everywhere. The art with this sort of redesign is to specify the best material for each job. So forks were in carbon fibre, now an everyday material in this sort of application, and the seat pillar was manufactured from a carbon fibre core sheathed with chrome-plated steel to protect the plastic frame bush. The handlebars and wheel rims are aluminium, just as they have been for years... these are applications that suit aluminium very well. Brompton took the opportunity to eliminate some long-standing niggles at the same time: perhaps the most infamous being the frame and stem clamps which worked well enough if you had the time to position them carefully, but could be fiddly on a dark night in the pouring rain. The old clamp could be unwound until it fell off, but the new design only allowed the winder to go far enough for a recessed portion of the clamp to disengage, but not so far that the clamp spun round. This prevented loss of the clamp assembly through unwinding it at night and losing it down the drain, theft, or vibrating loose and falling off during a long-haul flight – all more common issues than you might think. Another very common issue was 'plastic fatigue' in the ball and clip that secured the folded bar-stem to the frame. The plastic ball was replaced with a notched stainless steel rod, held in the folded position by a pair of spring-loaded ball-bearings that dropped into the notches in the folded position. It was better, but not, as it turned out, infallible.

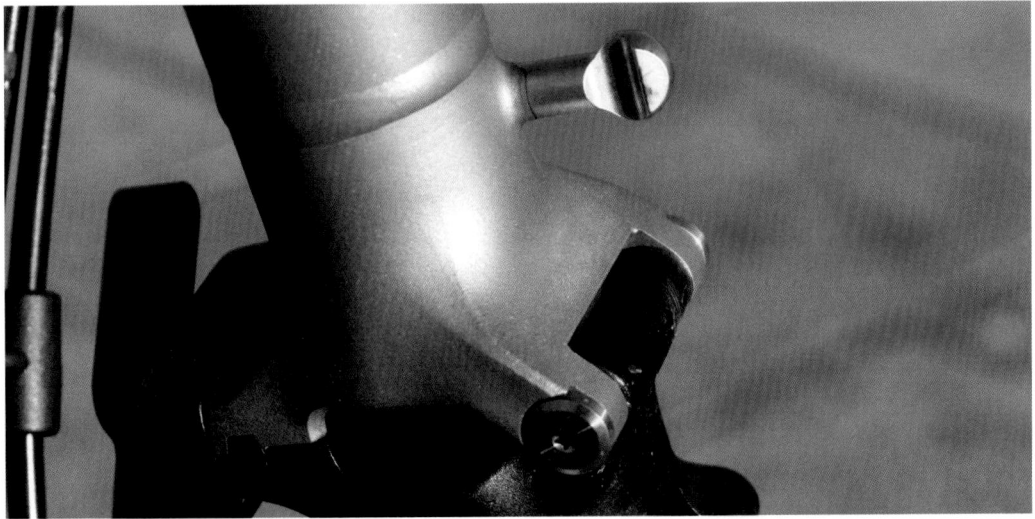

The T-Line saw a new one piece, more resilient all metal handlebar catch along with new frame and stem clamps

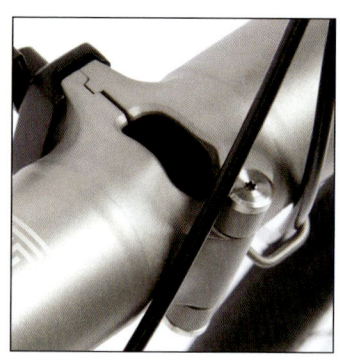

The new T-Lines of 2022 onwards were practically new from the ground up, with user-friendly frame clamps (right) just one new feature. The bike itself (below) used slightly larger frame tubing to take advantage of titanium's magical strength to weight ratio.

The new T-Lines also saw the introduction of Brompton's own design of 4-speed derailleur (left) and, in an effort to trim off every gram of weight possible, the replacement of the classic folding pedal with a removable one that magnetically retained itself in the fork crown.

New Model Names

This new super-lightweight bike was called the T-line, released as the final part of a major revamp of models and names that began in 2021. The basic model was now the A-line, available only from Halfords without mudguards, front carrier block or folding pedal for a reasonable £950. It was also the last resting place of the 3-speed AW (later the BSR or Brompton Standard Ratio) hub, fitted to most Bromptons for 42 years. The 3-speed option had vanished from the mainstream bikes, which were now available only in Urban derailleur 2- and 4-speed bikes or Explore 6-speeds in derailleur/BWR wide-ratio hub form. The Explore range later expanded to include a 12-speed option (again, using the BWR 3-speed hub). These gearing options were divided into C-line and P-Line ranges (the latter being the old XL lightweight bikes).

The 4-speed option was a major change that helped to explain why the 3-speed hub had been banished to the sidelines; Brompton had developed a compact and technologically innovative derailleur mechanism, introduced towards the end of 2021 on the P- and T-line bikes, and the C- and P-line electrics.

Opinion was mixed. The gear shift was light and quick, and the ratios were close, but the gear range was unusually limited – actually slightly less than the Sturmey-Archer AW 3-speed it replaced. Andrew Ritchie had always refused to fit a derailleur to the Brompton, despite the weight advantage, because the lack of space limited the gear range and folding bikes with derailleurs had a tendency to drop the chain during the fold, an issue that had publicly plagued Riese & Muller's Birdy. The Brompton derailleur wasn't too troublesome in this respect, but worries about the gear range inevitably remained.

With Andrew out of the picture, the way was clear to make the derailleur a standard fitting on the titanium T-Line, introduced from late 2021 at a breathtaking £3,750 in single-speed form, or £3,950 with the 4-speed derailleur. The exercise was all about weight, of course, and the new bikes broke all sorts of boundaries. The four-speed weighed exactly 8kg, and the basic single-speed 7.5kg, putting it in a very exclusive club of sub-8kg bicycles.

T-line output from the Sheffield factory had ramped up quite slowly, and was still a trickle in February 2022 when Putin struck Ukraine. In some ways, the world order would have found the shock easier to absorb if his blitzkrieg had succeeded as planned, but the Ukrainians fought fiercely and bravely, driving the invasion force back from the capital and much of the north. The conflict settled into trench warfare and a long game.

The new T-Lines meant the skills of Sheffield's titanium welders assumed even greater importance

Ukraine and Russia were both major exporters of titanium ore, together accounting for about a quarter of global trade in the early 2000s. Ukrainian production was hit hard by the war, and Russian exports were subject to Western sanctions. Titanium prices had risen three-fold by May 2022, threatening the whole titanium project, but the mining and refining of the metal is well spread around the globe, and other countries were quick to increase production. The peak price proved very short-lived and fell rapidly, but it was a warning that nothing could be taken for granted any more. Even steel and aluminium were in short supply for a while.

And with more than a third of the Brompton's parts and accessories coming from Taiwan (including the hub gearbox used on all the multigear models), there had already been a stark reminder in 2020-21 that political instability could occur almost anywhere, when China launched one of its periodic episodes of sabre rattling, threatening to take the islands back by force. Regular cycles of anti-independent Taiwan rhetoric and military manoeuvrers continued in the following years.

Consumer Reaction and 3x4=12

The T-line was the lightest folding bike Brompton had ever produced and – barring a few oddball machines – it was one of the lightest folding bikes to emerge anywhere, ever. Industry criticism again centred largely around the narrow gear range of the four-speed derailleur. The machine came with the long-established 50-tooth chainring, driving 11, 13, 15 and 18-tooth sprockets, giving gears of 45, 54, 62 and 74 inches and a modest 164-inch range. A larger 56-tooth chainring was available as an option for those in search of greater speed at the expense of hill-climbing, and amateur fiddlers soon found that a 20-tooth could be squeezed on to the derailleur in place of the 18- to give a lower first gear, and marginally widen the range, but it wasn't enough for some and sales were certainly lost. Generally though, consumer reaction was highly favourable, and for those who could afford the technology the prize was an impressively light machine.

With the new P- and T-line bikes much admired, the Brompton electric was having a less satisfactory time. It was selling well, and much improved after a rather disastrous start, but the technology was hardly state-of the-art. The motor was heavy and noisy by modern standards, and the sensitive multi-way connector under the battery was still causing issues, particularly on rough surfaces, which could result in momentary loss of connection. This was cured, or alleviated, with a more secure latch in 2022, but bugs in the software and motor continued to crop up, and there was another (rather unlucky) recall later in the year caused by insufficient mudguard clearance on electric models, which had resulted in a few locked front wheels caused by trapped debris. The number of voluntary or compulsory recalls had not been great, but with three in 2021-22 alone, they clearly weren't going away. It was not an ideal situation.

Gear options have been an issue since the Brompton was conceived. The bike started life with the venerable Sturmey-Archer AW 3-speed hub, a mechanism that has changed little since the early years of the 20th century. It was cheap, reasonably efficient and reliable, but heavy (in folder terms) and lacking gear range. The Sturmey 5-speed solved the range issue to some degree, but at the expense of almost everything else. When Sturmey was bankrupted, Brompton had to make do with a 3-speed SRAM and later, the clever, but complex, 3x2-speed using the SRAM (later the bespoke BWR wide ratio hub from Sturmey-Archer), in combination with Brompton's own 2-speed derailleur. The combination was heavy, but it worked well if you understood it. The 2-speed derailleur was light, easy to use and efficient. The wide-ratio Sturmey was heavier, but equally user-friendly, but putting the two together produced a bike with two shifters using two different systems. A lot of people simply didn't know how to use it.

The new four-speed derailleur was a skilfully executed bit of design, but trapped with a limited range and low ratios. The obvious answer was to combine the 4-speed derailleur with the BWR 3-speed

hub, to create a 12-speed, released by Brompton in late January 2024.
With both derailleur and hub systems onboard, this was the heaviest official option yet devised, adding around 800 grams to the 4-speed P-line and T-line, according to Brompton. But unlike most multi-gear derailleur bikes using a rear gear cluster and two or three front chainrings, there is very little gear overlap between the three ranges, so the system provides ten genuinely different gears, and a huge range, from the lowest to the highest gear ratios Brompton has ever provided.

All the parts are standard Brompton issue: 50-tooth chainring, BWR hub and 11, 13, 15 and 18-tooth derailleur, but put together they give an overall range of 408%, from 29" to 118".

Yes, of course the system could be lighter. Perhaps the company will succeed in skimming off the odd gram here and there, but apart from weight, this does seem a sensible solution, and it's hard to imagine any customer wanting more. The middle range alone is adequate for most day-to-day eventualities, with the lower range available for hill-climbing and high for spinning out on descents and taking advantage of tail-winds, all the more so on the electric P-line option, which tends to run out of gears at speed. According to Brompton's senior product manager Rafa Nascimento, some 70% of electric bike purchasers were asking for higher gearing.

Initially introduced on the P-line, electric C-line and titanium T-line, the 12-speed came at a premium of about £200 over the standard 4-speed, giving a base price on the P-Line Explore of £2,470. The 12-speed electric C-Line cost £3,150 (£170 more than the 4-speed), a relatively modest increase, although whether electric bike owners could ever really need a 408% range is debatable.

The premium on the T-line was a little more, lifting the price from £4,520 in 4-speed form to £4,745 as a 12-speed. This bike sounded quite a contradiction in some ways, as you were paying a very large sum of money to purchase an exquisitely light bicycle, then putting 800 grams back on for the extra gears. But for those who could afford it, here was a 12-speed Brompton with a substantial gear range, weighing just 8.8kg. Top of the range indeed.

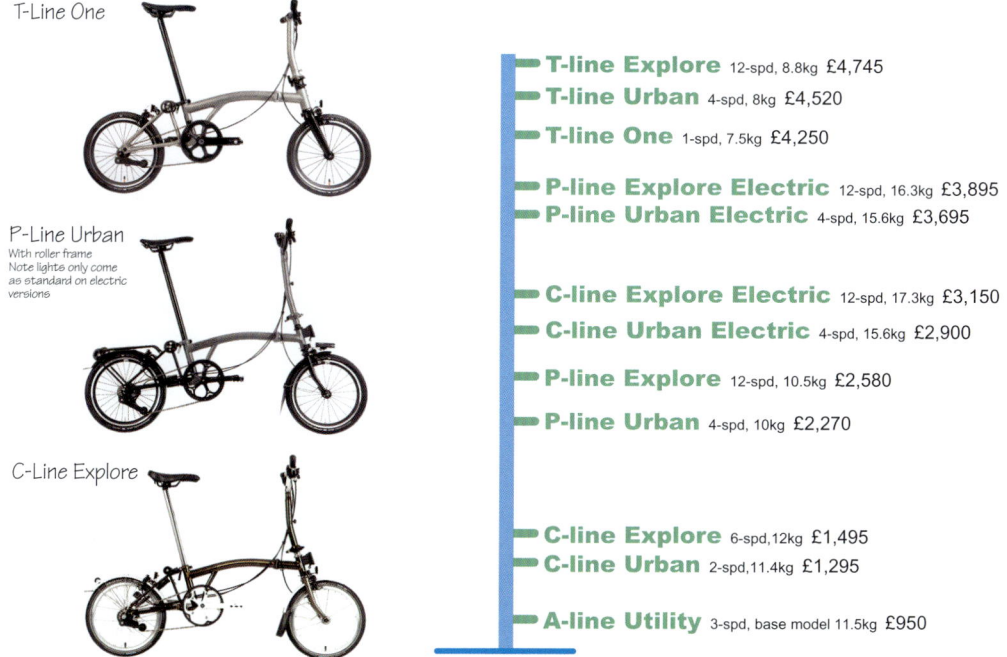

T-Line One

P-Line Urban
With roller frame
Note lights only come as standard on electric versions

C-Line Explore

T-line Explore 12-spd, 8.8kg £4,745
T-line Urban 4-spd, 8kg £4,520
T-line One 1-spd, 7.5kg £4,250

P-line Explore Electric 12-spd, 16.3kg £3,895
P-line Urban Electric 4-spd, 15.6kg £3,695

C-line Explore Electric 12-spd, 17.3kg £3,150
C-line Urban Electric 4-spd, 15.6kg £2,900

P-line Explore 12-spd, 10.5kg £2,580
P-line Urban 4-spd, 10kg £2,270

C-line Explore 6-spd, 12kg £1,495
C-line Urban 2-spd, 11.4kg £1,295

A-line Utility 3-spd, base model 11.5kg £950

Rider reports were good, barring the usual confusion over the different characteristics of the derailleur gear set on the left handlebar and the hub system on the right. Brompton has tried to get round this by suggesting riders treat the hub gears as 'overall terrain modes' for different circumstances, and reserving the left shifter for fine-tuning pedal cadence.

There are several downsides to this steady drift towards derailleur gears, including the virtual demise of the AW 3-speed hub. Lowly and forgotten perhaps, but offering much the same range as the 4-speed derailleur with greater reliability. Hopefully the solitary 3-speed model will continue ploughing its way through city filth and country mud for decades more, sustained by just a few drops of oil once in a while. Gear systems on small-wheeled bikes are particularly vulnerable to dirt and damage and Brompton's derailleur is already proving susceptible.

The Future

Where is Brompton heading in 2024, and what technology are we likely to see on new bikes in the future? After a tumultuous decade, it would be foolhardy to predict anything. Brexit, Coronavirus, global conflict and the accelerating climate crisis have changed the industrial picture out of all recognition. These events have demonstrated the folly of just-in-time delivery, particularly by sea over longer distances.

New cleaner engines, hybrid-power, partial wind-power and crew-less ships will become the norm, but freight charges will never fall back to the low levels we've come to expect. Brompton is already sourcing parts closer to home, from British or conveniently situated European countries, and this process looks bound to continue.

In 2022, Brompton comprehensively dealt with its long-standing retreat from design and manufacturing by developing and launching the T-line, a bike that reset the folding bike development clock to Year Zero – it really was as important in its way as the original Brompton. The 3x4 gear system is less innovative, and definitely not the final solution, but it gives the range consumers have been asking for. The world is still waiting for a wide-range automatic, lightweight, cheap and efficient gear system. Sadly, it looks as though we will have to keep waiting.

Whilst the recent launch of the 12-speed gearing system has given the Brompton true climbing ability it still really calls out for a built-from-scratch lightweight, wide-range and easy to operate system

Titanium is the future. The darker forces in world politics hold big reserves, but the ore is widely spread, and Britain has some refining capacity of its own and good friends overseas with huge ore reserves.

As a frame material it makes a lot of sense: it resists corrosion, it's immensely tough and it weighs half as much as steel. So how will Brompton use this wonder-material? The T-line shows what can be done, and it's hard to see how the bike's headline weight of 7.5kg could be reduced to any degree, but 7kg is probably doable with some very careful fine-tuning of the components. What we *will* see is titanium spreading down the line to the more basic models. The P-type has already adopted the T-line rear frame and other parts are bound to follow. Titanium fabrication is absolutely ideal for robot welding. With no human intervention, the operations could all be carried out in a sealed booth, eliminating oxygen, finger prints and other accidental contamination. The price could fall very sharply. At the bottom end, sales are much more price-sensitive, but as each T-line design element becomes cost-effective, the metal will spread to other models. In the new age of recycling, upcycling and sustainable design, a more or less indestructible, but easily recycled, material is bound to play a greater role. Where the steel Brompton was good for a lifetime (assuming early replacement of the rear frame, rims, seat pillar and other large components), we might expect to pass future machines down to our children and grandchildren.

There are a host of other technologies worth experimenting with, if only to rule them firmly out. The 1/2-inch pitch steel bicycle chain has been around for well over a century, and it works superlatively well, but it's resource-heavy, over-specified for the task, physically heavy and subject to rapid wear in poor weather conditions. Smaller pitch chains down to 6mm pitch and 7.4mm width (even smaller in the growing field of robotics) are now commonplace. A shorter pitch means smaller chainrings and sprockets, saving even more weight and potentially making the bike more compact. Carefully specified for the job, these micro-components can cut the weight of the transmission system in half. Perhaps more importantly, a narrower, shorter pitch chain would make a 5- or even 6-speed derailleur possible, giving a wider gear range, higher gears and reducing weight.

Retired UK engineer Derek Cranage (pages 162-163) managed to reduce the weight of his steel-framed Brompton to 7.3kg with the help of carbon forks, lightweight saddle and even a rebuilt chain tensioner featuring lightweight sprockets! Clearly weight reduction is a path Brompton should continue following to keep ahead of the pack. The T-Line has largely solved the issue if you can afford titanium but weight loss is important on lower-priced bikes too.

A quick and easy win would be a simple, cable-free two-speed automatic. Automatic two-speed hubs have been around for years, and in 2019 Sturmey-Archer developed a variant aimed specifically at the Brompton, although the company didn't choose to proceed with the project. Hubs are heavier than derailleurs, but a back-pedal brake version (not easy on the Brompton) would be left with only one short cable to the front brake, bringing the gross bicycle weight quite close to the existing 2-speed derailleur. The benefits would include simplicity of operation, a weather/wear proof rear brake and an end to rear rim replacement, all factors of importance to regular city commuters.

Chains will always need lubrication, but toothed polymer belts are oil-free, offering a clean(er!) drive, a big bonus on a folding bike. They have tended to be heavy and energy-sapping in the past, but again, the strength, weight and efficiency of micro-pitch belts has improved, and it's one of those areas where components can be carefully honed to minimise weight for the transmitted power.

This Sturmey Archer Duomatic hub geared converion from Kinetics of Glasgow has only one cable to the front brake and this is cleverly hidden in the handlebar stem post. Pedal backwards a small amount to change gear and a larger amount to brake. Brompton could no doubt develop their own cableless variant in future. Note the back pedal brake requires a special chain tensioner to cope with the forces.

Tyres are another area where weight can be saved and ride and handling improved. Back in 1999, Andrew Ritchie designed the Brompton tyre on the carcass of the lightweight Primo, giving a step-change in performance while reducing weight and rolling resistance, but Brompton is now reliant on outside suppliers.

An in-house design made sense in 1999, because 16-inch tyres varied from poor to downright dangerous, but a quarter of a century on, the breed has improved, and going back into the tyre business probably isn't worthwhile. Brompton is now big enough and powerful enough to order a custom spec, as none of the commercially available tyres are ideal. Schwalbe's Marathon and Marathon Plus might be described as 'puncture resistant', but they weigh a massive 400-500 grams apiece and they don't roll too well. Of the lighter tyres, Schwalbe's One and Kojak are both sub-200 grams, but on the frail side and over-priced. The Continental Contact Urban is probably the best all-rounder, and it's now starting to appear on Brompton models. Other options will arrive as technology advances.

There is massive public demand for a puncture-proof 'solid' tyre, particularly for a 16-inch wheeled bike like the Brompton, but perfecting the technology seems as far away as ever. If Brompton isn't keen on committing the manpower and resources at Greenford, how about a tie-in with a university-led team? Solid tyres have always been heavy, and hard work to pedal, but the best available today are broadly comparable with a typical pneumatic tyre, although they can wear quickly and unevenly. With access to state-of-the-art materials expertise, and the purchasing muscle that comes with an annual output of 90,000 machines, Brompton could realistically specify and market its own solid tyre if the technology was there.

Brakes are a fascinating field for development. On most modern bikes, cable or hydraulic disc brakes are now the norm, and they have revolutionised bicycle braking. Discs would make special sense on the Brompton because brake block and rim wear are such big issues. Disc

One hundred per cent puncture proof solid tyre technology has been developing in recent years and there are after market versions available for the Brompton. The examples above are from Tannus.

brakes are now much cheaper, but they're still relatively heavy and big clumsy things. This is simply because no-one thought to develop a disc for small wheels. The brake force exerted at the road/tyre interface is proportional to the size of the disc with respect to the size of the wheel, so where a 160mm disc might be essential with a 26-inch wheel, a 16-inch wheel would only require a 100mm disc, a size already in production for high performance electric scooters. Flexible hydraulic piping can be lighter than steel cable and better suited to the constant bending and flexing required on a folding bike. Not a cheap development exercise, but worthwhile in the long run.

The factory has been planning to introduce a single gear shifter on the 6-speed for years, but there are huge technical difficulties in sending precise movement commands to twin cables. The arrival of the more complex 12-speed adds extra layers of difficulty together with increased consumer demand. This issue really needs to be solved, and it's another field where hydraulic or electric activation might make sense and potentially be very reliable in the long-term, and lighter too. But it's hard to imagine that anything so sophisticated could pass the 'Brompton' test. This little bike has succeeded in part because the surplus fat has long been hewn from the design. All mobility machines – from pushchairs to jet aircraft – tend to become flabby and over-complex in middle age, as new ideas are bolted on. For a bike that has to be lifted and carried, middle-age spread would be the kiss of death.

Hub gears are old technology and they're heavy, but the ability to multiply gearing up beyond the chainring/sprocket ratio is a real asset on a small-wheeled bike. Derailleurs can't do this, and they're much more vulnerable to wear and damage when working close to the road surface. Brompton could replace the hub/derailleur 6-speed by looking again at the simpler, easier 5-speed Sturmey-Archer hub, and that might make sense now that the flagship 12-speed is available to customers looking for maximum range. For users, the primary advantage is a single shifter.

Another slightly off the wall solution to the gear issues would be to help Sturmey-Archer develop a narrower, lighter 3- or 5-speed hub - not as difficult as it sounds, because some models from the 1950s were lighter than today's hubs. As with so much else in the utility bicycle field, effort hasn't gone into lightweight technology, because weight isn't usually an issue. If hub gears were being fitted to racing bikes, they would have halved in weight years ago.

The electric Brompton is an interesting issue. After seven rather tumultuous years, the product is looking quite elderly, but still lacking the reliability people expect. The time may have come to start work on a completely revised Mark 2 electric variant. Everything needs to be lighter, more efficient and more resilient, right the way through the electric system. Broadly-speaking, a front motor is probably still the way to go, but the controls need to be within reach, and the power-assisted bike needs to share normal Brompton luggage. The complex multiway wiring connector on the front block will never be entirely satisfactory in all weathers, or dealing with dusty environments and rough road surfaces. Technology has moved on since the Brompton Electric was designed, and it might now be feasible to mount a solid-state battery (they can be any shape) in the triangle under the mainframe, so the bike wouldn't need a connector. With a smaller, lighter motor, such a bike would be easier to carry, with a simpler one piece wiring loom and compatible with normal Brompton luggage.

Brompton's original e-bike technology has been overtaken by third party kits, with the T-Line specific version of the Cytronex kit being state of the art at the time of writing (more detail on page 170).

Side Tracked?

After a decade side-tracked by marketing and gimmicks, Brompton seems to be returning to its innovative engineering roots which has to be welcome news. Perhaps less welcome is the project to move the entire factory out to Ashford in Kent, an expensive task that might be construed as a vanity project. The intention is to build an advanced new factory by 2027, and close the existing Greenford site by 2030.

The talk is all about setting a course away from car culture, but moving 90 miles from suburban London to deepest car-centric Kent rules out regular commuting from the Brentford/Greenford area where Brompton staff – some third generation – have always been drawn. By train or car, the journey takes at least two hours, and although Ashford International station has high-speed rail services from central London, it has no international services in 2024, and there are none planned.

A Holloways Studios concept sketch of the planned new factory in Ashford, Kent.

The only logistical advantage is proximity to the British motorway network for freight deliveries by lorry, but it's 90 miles further from the titanium factory in Sheffield on one of Europe's most congested and unpredictable motorways. In principle, deliveries by road from Europe would be easier via the Channel Tunnel but that makes a mockery of the green credentials of the Ashford move. There will be no car park, but most visitors and workers will inevitably arrive by car. A key design element is two miles of cycle path from the railway station, but this whole scheme does seem to do more to highlight the weaknesses of the public transport/folding bike lifestyle than herald a new age of green mobility.

Brompton may argue that the intended move gives them room to up production for the rapidly growing US and Chinese markets and escape the high rental costs associated with manufacturing in London. By 2022, some six years after moving to their current Greenford base, rent had increased from £11 per square foot to £30 per square foot. Butler-Adams told the Financial Times in 2022 that "Anything that is a potential distribution hub (in London) is going to get more and more expensive," adding "We will need to grow and we need more space." He doesn't mention that his company has already established a satellite factory in South Yorkshire, where industrial land and housing are relatively cheap, and transport links fast improving.

The Ashford scheme may prove at best a distraction, and at worst a route to financial collapse. It does at least keep Brompton in the media spotlight, albeit at quite a high financial cost, even if nothing ultimately gets built, but media and social media are fickle bed-fellows. Is Brompton burdening itself with a massive self-imposed financial folly at a time when the future is so bright, and the product so very very good?

The World of Brompton Specials This Juliane Neuß designed 'Brecki' recumbent is a superb example of the way the Brompton has inspired other cycle designers and engineers to come up with their own take on the machine.

The World of Brompton Specials

Steve Parry and the SP Specials

Inevitably, the neat fold and quality ride of the Brompton has attracted inventors of various kinds over the years. Perhaps the most prolific Brompton 'adaptor' was West Country gas fitter Steve Parry, who has produced a number of sporty SP derivatives over a couple of decades, generally with the blessing of the factory in the Andrew Ritchie era.

Parry had emigrated to Australia but returned to the UK in 1997 and began experimenting with the Moulton, Birdy and Brompton. He soon found that there was particular interest in customized versions of the Brompton and by 1998 the bike had become the core of the SP product range. The SP bikes built up quite a following amongst enthusiasts. Like the Brompton itself, machines were specified on an individual basis for customers. The more radical being completely reworked, with different seat pillars, handlebar stems, and even frame tubes, but customers could also buy a basic Brompton upgraded with a selection of 'go-faster' accessories. The first SP bikes were fitted with the 7-speed Shimano Nexus hub, but later machines used derailleur gears, offering a wider range and closer ratios than Brompton's own hubs. These conversions took on a special significance in 2001, when the supply of 5-speed Sturmey-Archer geared hubs dried up, and the factory output was limited to 3-speeds. Derailleurs can cause chain alignment problems when folding, so like the Birdy, the SP bikes needed to be folded with a little more care, but they certainly filled a gap in the market between the standard machines and the much more expensive Birdy and Bike Friday.

Other derivatives included a superb single-speed, a 6-speed (3-speed hub with dual-chainring), a Shimano Nexus 8-speed, and eventually the Rohloff 14-speed, which proved to be the most popular variant, with more than 50 sold by 2009.

Steve Parry's superb single speed.

The front of the SP trike is built from two mainframe tubes and two rearward-facing Brompton forks, but as trikes go, Steve Parry's Brompton tricycle is relatively compact when folded. Only one has been made to date.

Early SP bikes were often fitted with V-brakes, but when the Brompton brakes improved, these became largely redundant. Parry also fitted disc brakes to a few Brompton SPs.

Perhaps the most intriguing SP was the hingeless Brompton, which kept the standard rear triangle hinge, allowing the rear wheel to fold under the bike, but featured a long, custom-made frame tube of aluminium, with detachable handlebars. The basic fold was only in one plane, resulting in a long, tall, and very thin package, but the bicycle also came apart Bike Friday-style, and could be carried in a hard case.

Once Steve Parry's fertile imagination had settled on the Brompton, there was no stopping him, and the SP family were soon joined by a tricycle and a tandem. The extraordinary SP Trike was made for a friend with balance problems in 2004. The spidery machine was effectively a normal Brompton aft of the steering tube, where the conventional frame tube met two other mainframe tubes mounted at right angles, each carrying a front wheel at its outer end. Folding amounted to tucking the rear wheel under, dropping the seat pillar, and folding down the handlebars. This produced an unwieldy package measuring 92cm wide and 92cm long, but by trike standards it was pretty compact, and small enough to be manoeuvred through a wide door, or fit into an estate car.

The tandem was, in some ways, the most conventional SP design, being a standard Brompton and a half, with some additional cross-bracing to strengthen the, by now, very long mainframe. Folding wasn't quite to Brompton standards, because although the machine retained a rear hinge, this no longer served any purpose, but it wasn't bad. The rear wheel folded under, the stoker handlebar stem folded down to the left, and the captain's frame tube and handlebar stem folded to the right. Quite a large package, but like the trike, very small by the standards of its contemporaries, and surprisingly rigid and pleasant to ride. The prototype was equipped with a Rohloff hub (the extra width making no difference in this case), front hub dynamo and V-brakes.

The first SP trailer bike, produced as far back as 2001, was a superb machine - basically a standard Brompton with a double-length frame tube, terminating in a universal joint, cleverly produced from a Brompton head-set and rear frame bearings. The trailer bike clamped around the seat pillar using the front part of a frame tube and seat pillar clamp. This worked very well, and could even carry a small adult over moderate distances (one took part in the London-Brighton ride in 2007) but the cost of manufacture was prohibitive and it was destined to be a critical success, but a commercial failure. The SP child seat filled a major gap in the market, left when the Spanish distributor temporarily stopped producing the IT Chair (see following chapter).

The SP business relied on a steady stream of wealthy cycle enthusiasts, and was badly affected when Brompton began to produce up-market derivatives in-house in 2005, when the sportier part-titanium bikes were introduced. Business was further hit with the credit crunch of 2008 and arrival of the Brompton Wide Ratio hub, which made it possible to buy a wider gear range 'off the shelf'. Steve Parry produced a few more machines with exotic gear conversions, such as the 14-speed Rohloff and 9-speed SRAM, but the core business had gone and in the summer of 2009 he ceased trading. Others have followed where Steve led, (though undoubtedly lacking his true flair for innovation), with Kinetics of Glasgow currently still finding there is a market for such Brompton modifications as disc brakes, hub gears and, of late, larger wheeled versions with wider tyres (see pages 176-179).

Steve Parry demonstrates his folding tandem at the 2008 Brompton World Championships. Although the rear frame clamp is visible, it is only for show, as the frame tube aft of the front hinge and associated braces are brazed into one rigid unit. When folded, the rear wheel folds under, and the front wheel folds round, with a rigid frame in between! Total length is a little longer than two folded Bromptons. It's still more or less unique in tandem terms.

The SP Rohloff special with disc brakes.

Juliane Neuß

Juliane Neuß is one of a handful of female cycle engineers who have had a disproportionately large effect on the trade. Juliane, now based in Clausthal-Zellerfield in Germany's Harz mountains, was a recumbent enthusiast, who discovered the Brompton in 1993. As so often the case, her Brompton recumbent was born of necessity: local trains in Germany provide space for bicycles, but fast, long distance services usually do not. Unable to take her recumbent to a rally in Hamburg in May 1996, Juliane travelled with her Brompton. During the journey she began to ponder whether the Brompton itself could be turned into a recumbent, and later in the day, she pushed the saddle right down, thrust her feet forward to engage imaginary pedals, and coasted off. It worked!

Four weeks after this first trial, the prototype 'Brecki' recumbent was born. The Brecki was a clever adaptation utilizing a toothed rubber drive belt from a replacement chainring on the normal bottom bracket to a boom ahead of the front wheel. The saddle was replaced with a recumbent seat sat on top of the main frame tube, with the handlebars staying pretty much as Brompton intended. Luggage was either a backpack hanging from the back of the seat, or small panniers on the rear rack. The beauty of the conversion was that it came as a bolt-on kit, so the bike could be reconfigured in an hour or two, and indeed, the kit could be sold and transferred to another Brompton.

The Brecki worked quite well, and what's more, it folded into a package little bigger than a standard Brompton (L75cm x H67cm x W34cm), which in recumbent terms was (and still is) nothing short of miraculous.

As Andrew Ritchie had found, producing the prototype was the easy bit. After the first trials in June 1996, and an enthusiastic reception from recumbent enthusiasts, Juliane spent more than a year searching for a manufacturer, before deciding to go it alone. After a draftsman friend had risked his job producing CNC-compatible drawings at work early one morning, Juliane and her boyfriend, Ingo Kollibay, were able to start home manufacture, and the first production machine was tested in August 1998.

By 2004, nearly 90 had been produced, but Juliane lost a lot of money making the kits, and seems to have been relieved when Brompton altered the frame making the kit impossible to fit, thus bringing manufacture to an end!

Like Steve Parry, Juliane Neuß has adapted as the market for Bromptons and Brompton accessories has changed. Since 2004, her main business has been fitting the 8-speed Shimano Nexus hub to give a wider gear range (albeit on a wider bike!). But although the Brecki is long gone, she continues to receive regular enquiries, and doesn't rule out relaunching an improved kit: "During all those years, several people tried to make a folding recumbent, but none folded as small as the Brecki!" In 2017, she became Brompton's mechanic-in-chief in Germany, training other bicycle mechanics.

Juliane Neuß email: info@junik-hpv.de   tel: +49 (0)5323 - 96 32 486
junik-hpv.de

The World of Brompton Specials

Juliane Neuß's Brompton recumbent, the Brecki, was a great feat of engineering, folding to little larger than a standard Brompton package. As Juliane demonstrates with the prototype below, it rode pretty well too. When Brompton introduced the long wheelbase frame in 2004 the kit could no longer be fitted and production ceased.

Weight Watchers

Weight is a far more serious problem with folding bikes than conventional machines, and numerous engineers, both amateur and professional, have turned their attention to the Brompton. Bromptons today weigh between 11.5kg (the A-Line) and 7.45kg (T-Line Urban) single speed, with 8kg-10kg the range of the 4-speed lightweight T-Line and P-Line variants. In the early days, it was possible to trim weight from the bike fairly easily, but as the factory sourced lighter components, this became increasingly difficult and Brompton's 2022 introduction of the T-Line has meant lightweight conversions are now more likely to be older, heavier bikes, modified with the use of 3rd-party aftermarket options. With some effort and expense, a 1990s-vintage Mark 2 L3 could be lightened from 12kg to about 10.4kg, but going beyond this was expensive. With a fair amount of pricey technology, it was possible to produce a fully-equipped bike (ie, with mudguards, a front carrier block and at least two gears) weighing about 9.2kg. To go further required a titanium mainframe, and the expert in this field is Len Rubin...

Len describes himself as "a proponent of car-free and 'car-light' human-powered & multi-modal transit, and a lifelong folding bike fanatic" and has been riding and tinkering with folding bicycles for the better part of half a century. Rubin has had a long involvement with the bike trade, having owned several bike shops over the decades, as well as being a Technical Editor of Sutherland's handbook for Bicycle Mechanics, though, in his own words, he has "no formal training or natural aptitude for engineering or construction". This hasn't stopped Len from devoting much of his spare time to developing a better folding bike. Like Steve Parry, he quickly became captivated by the Brompton, but he caught the bug much earlier, writing to Andrew Ritchie in 1986, before the bike was even in mainstream production.

The first Rubin 'SuperBrompton', produced in 1996, was more an exercise in improving the brakes and gears of the bike than removing weight. But gradually the machines became more sophisticated, utilizing the latest and lightest V-brakes, derailleur gears, wheel rims and tyres, plus a treasure-trove of custom-made goodies such as double-butted spokes, lightweight hubs, and a unique adjustable stem, together with a number of other custom-made parts.

The original 27-speed SuperBrompton weighed 9.7kg, and went on to be shown all over the world. Priced from around US$6,000, Rubin sold about twenty in the next few years, before moving on to other projects. In 2001, he married and moved to Portland, Oregon to "take a break - from the Bay Area car-centric culture, and raise a family in a more bicycle-centric city". But as so many people close to the Brompton story have found, the possibilities kept nagging him and in 2002 he unveiled a full titanium prototype, then in 2007 a full titanium version at the Rohloff booth at the Interbike show which - at 9.2kg - was believed to be the lightest Rohloff-equipped bicycle in the world. The entire frame of the SuperBrompton was made from beautifully-crafted titanium, broadly similar in appearance to the factory-made steel frame, but with thin-walled oversize tubes.

Rubin then returned to his much lighter derailleur-based transmission, using a 27-speed drivetrain for which he claimed a weight of around 7.3kg, making it almost certainly the lightest multi-speed folding bike ever made, bearing the moniker Ultimate Folding Bike. Rubin also built a single speed version that weighed just 7kg. Only on the west coast of America would a designer have the sheer nerve to call a machine the UFB, or 'Ultimate Folding Bike', but Rubin was probably right.

Rubin says that customers shelled out many thousands of dollars for UFB conversions that ranged from $7,000 to nearly $15,000 — a stratospheric price for a folding bike in those days — even on the US West Coast, storied land of celebrities and billionaires.

You might expect the introduction of Brompton's T-Line to finally bring UFB production to an

The World of Brompton Specials

Len Rubin and an enthusiastic customer with two early 'SuperBromptons' (above) and his latest ultralightweight 'UFB' or Ultimate Folding Bike (below).

end, but Rubin saw an opportunity to leverage the availability of a lightweight production titanium mainframe in the form of upgrade kits that could be conveniently shipped to a customer anywhere in the world, and installed by any good Brompton-competent mechanic without requiring the customer to physically visit his shop.

Recent emphasis is on a UFB Adventurer kit which holds out the possibility of a lightweight, all-titanium wide-tyred version. This so-called ATB variant is based on an 18" tyre for ETRTO 355 rims, for which there are lightweight folding fat tires available, but Len says the existing high-perfomance ultralight 'asphalt-optimized' upgrades based on the lighter narrow rims (ETRTO 349) will also now be available in a DIY kit form. For more information on off-road conversions see pgs 176-179.

Len Rubin e-mail: len@ufbco.com   tel & text: +1 (0)503-702-2708   www.ufbco.com

In 2024 Len Rubin produced this T-Line conversion using his UFB Adventurer kit.

We should also mention retired British engineer Derek Cranage, who built a 7.3kg Brompton relatively easily (admittedly a mudguard-less single-speed), and went on to slice the weight down to 5.9kg, but this did require some serious engineering, including a carbon fibre rear frame. Note though, that the standard steel mainframe was used, albeit with some judicious lightening proving there's no inherent need for a titanium frame if weight is carefully hewn away elsewhere.

In late 2018, Derek went on to produce arguably the lightest electric folding bike in the world by adding a carefully sourced motor and battery combo to the bike, producing a machine weighing 9.8kg with a reasonable 72Wh battery. If that doesn't sound very exciting, it was almost a kilogram lighter than Brompton's lightest unassisted Superlight bike of the time. It was also nearly 2kg less than the Cytronex-adapted T-Line, although that's a somewhat more practical electric machine with four gears and a 33-mile range. Derek doesn't produce anything commercially, but most of the parts are easily available online, though again, the T-Line factory version has made the majority of such weight saving projects unnecessary.

The World of Brompton Specials

Left and middle is UK pensioner Derek Cranage's first attempt at a lightweight Brompton, weighing 7.3kg. Whilst it used a standard Brompton steel mainframe much of the rest of the bike was made up of special non-standard Brompton parts. More details of the project can be found in A to B magazine, issue 119, February 2018.

Derek Cranage's remarkably light homemade electric Brompton weighing only 9.8kg came next (bottom).

Power Assistance

Although considered a purist, Andrew Ritchie made it clear in his original patent that the Brompton might at some stage be fitted 'with an electrical or internal combustion engine', although his personal view was that the technology was some way off. How right he was! It was to be another 15 years before electrically-assisted bicycles became commonplace, and practical folding versions have taken much longer to arrive. The problem is weight, the old enemy of the folding bike. It's difficult enough to make a pedal-powered bike that can be carried with ease, but bringing batteries and motors into the equation takes another whole layer of cutting edge technology.

Several appalling power-assisted Chinese folders were produced in the first years of the new millennium, none being light enough, or compact enough to be regarded as practical machines. The breakthrough came in 2000 with the SRAM Sparc, a 5-speed hub incorporating an electric motor, which was adopted by Dahon and fitted to the 20-inch Roo in 2002. This Roo EL variant was powered by a tiny battery on the rear rack, feeding power to the motorized rear hub.

This original Sparc system had limited range, and offered weak assistance, but it was redesigned in 2005, making the EL quite an effective machine. At 18kg, the bike was a touch heavy to lift, and the cost of the Sparc system had pushed the UK price up to £1,200, which in 2005 was pretty expensive. Despite a reasonable power-assisted range of about 20 miles, it failed to sell well, although it had demonstrated what could be achieved. The Roo EL remained in limited production until 2009, by which time it cost £1,400 and was selling in very small numbers.

After this promising start, Dahon's electric adventure seems to have involved a succession of duds, at least in terms of sales. The Boost utilised a relatively advanced Sunstar crank-drive motor in 2010, but it weighed 19.6kg, cost £2,000, and inevitably sold in very small numbers, if at all.

In 2013, the company teamed up with Currie Technologies to produce the single-speed IZIP E3 Compact, a conventional machine with a front hub motor and rear rack-mounted battery. The following year, the company experimented with the BionX EPS system, producing the 17kg Formula S18, which was certainly listed for a while in the USA at around $3,000. For certain other markets, Dahon introduced the Ikon, a rather cruder design, similar to the IZIP, with a TranzX front hub motor and rear rack battery. At 21kg, this was not a very practical machine. 2021 saw the announcement of the more promising Unio E9 whicAerAas 16.1 kg, but this rapidly faded from view, to be replaced by the 20"-wheeled Unio E20 that claimed a similar weight but kept the small, neat-looking mid-drive and the seatpost-enclosed battery of the E9. The E20 was still on sale in 2024 with substantial discounts on the £2271 RRP available, substantially undercutting Brompton's cheapest e-folder at the time, the £3695 4-speed P-Line. But compared to the Brompton, the E20 fold was bulky at 69cm×38cm×75cm.

Other early 21st century attempts at popularising a folding electric bike included the Japanese produced Panasonic Will and the largely British Airnimal Joey Move. The former was a well-designed high quality folding pedelec (an unusual beast indeed) but suffered from being underpowered compared to full size pedelecs with a rather small battery.

The Joey used the Canadian BionX EPS system, which boasted regenerative braking and a sophisticated computer console allowing the rider to adjust the power and regeneration (electric braking via the motor) settings. This was undoubtedly a nice ride, but the 24" Airnimal folder was never intended to have a quick, compact fold like the Brompton and you had to carry the front wheel separately. Like the Panasonic Will, it weighed around 17kg, which was fairly light, but still something of a problem for many potential users. You could remove the hefty 4.5kg battery from the Airnimal's frame, but you were still faced with the challenge of carrying three separate components - bike, front wheel and battery. Despite this relatively cumbersome folding performance, Airnimal's offering seems to have found a niche and sold fitfully for a few years before being quietly withdrawn.

Cautiously eyeing these rather disappointing developments, Brompton (perhaps wisely) did nothing officially for a while, but in June 2007 an independent conversion was introduced by electronics engineer Tony Castles. The Nano-Brompton made use of the Tongxin, the lightest, most effective motor technology then available. This little motor went in the front wheel, and the battery in a normal front pannier bag. The brilliant lateral thinking was the self-cleaning electrical contacts on the tapered front carrier block linking the two key components. With the battery in the bag, the only extra weight to carry on the bike was the motor and control electronics - around 3kg. A typical Nano-Brompton might weigh 14.4kg, but using an S2L-X as a donor bike could reduce that to less than 13kg. The battery and pannier might add 2-4kg to that, but the bag could be carried in the other hand. It was still a relatively heavy package, but much more practical than anything that had come before.

With low motor gearing (it was designed to run at 15mph in a bigger 26-inch wheel), the Nano-Brompton wasn't very fast, with a top assisted speed of only 12mph, but it was an impressive hill-climber, and it could go great distances, with a range of up to 50 miles. Unfortunately, Tony Castles' small company was not prepared for the deluge of orders it received throughout 2007

The Nano hub motor generates great torque and so is good for heavy loads. But have plenty of towing experience before you take on a dinghy!

and 2008, and problems with motor supply and battery reliability soon brought the project to a premature close. But the Nano had demonstrated the viability of an electric folding bike, and that there was plenty of demand for the right machine.

In 2008 Tongxin introduced a narrower, lighter motor (the original 100mm Nano motor needed custom forks to fit the Brompton) and updated kits to suit the Brompton (and other bikes) were introduced by the Electric Wheel Company. Sadly the reliability issues with motors and batteries soon resurfaced, and by 2010 production of the kits had been brought to a standstill by outstanding warranty claims, principally over batteries. In February 2012, Tony Castles helped relaunch the machine as Nano 2.0, with numerous improvements, and the Nano Electric Bike company has sold conversions ever since. An increasingly popular option is a smaller Bosch 144Wh power-tool battery. This cuts range to 8-16 miles, but weighs only a kilogram, reducing the weight of the front pannier to around 2.5kg. A key advantage is that the Bosch battery is small enough to circumvent the ban on carrying lithium-ion batteries by air, and is accepted by most airlines as hold or carry-on luggage.

For a while the Nano had no real competition, but its success didn't go unnoticed, and the Electric Transport Shop chain launched the Brompton Sparticle, with a similar front motor layout, but a rather clumsy saddle stem battery pack. The battery was later moved to the front pannier, but the system still lacks the finesse and light weight of the Nano. It can, however, be purchased in (technically illegal) over-powered form.

Frustrated with Brompton's inability to supply an electric option, NYCeWheels of New York introduced a power-assist kit broadly similar to the Sparticle, but with a quieter (but weaker and heavier) direct drive motor. The battery went in the front pannier, but like the Sparticle, this design lacked automatic contacts on the pannier block, so the battery had to be clumsily disconnected before taking the pannier off the bike. NYCeWheels got round the airline regulations with a twin 72Wh battery option, the two smaller batteries going in the pannier rear pockets. December 2019 saw the closure of the New York store and the effective demise of the kit.

Back in the UK, Cambridge-based ARCC Innovations introduced a neat looking front hub motor in 2015, initially only for demountable Moultons and the non-folding Cinelli. By 2016 they had extended their offering to Bromptons but retro-fit kit prices starting at £1799 in 2020 mean the conversion costs

Tony Castles engineered the Tongxin hub motor Nano kit for the Brompton. Features included a protected cable run inside the front wheel catch and a luggage mounting block adapted to act as a battery connector. Unfortunately the kit was a victim of its own success and the project was overwhelmed by demand.

The World of Brompton Specials

At a cursory glance it isn't at all obvious the Nano-Brompton is electrically-assisted. The battery powering the front hub motor is hidden in the front pannier whilst the controller is fixed to the handlebars.

alone come to significantly more than many brand new Brompton models, making it one of the priciest retrofit kits available. The ARCC system borrowed heavily from the Nano design, utilising Bosch power tool batteries with the option of carrying the battery in the front bag which features an electrical connection.

Canada-based GRIN Technologies has pioneered some quite sophisticated retrofit e-bike technology over recent decades. They offer a direct drive front hub using an unusually thin Crystalyte front motor. These are well-considered kits, that can be configured to include a crank-based torque-sensor and a large display screen, but they add a lot of complication to the Brompton and add complications to folding. Please bear in mind that they are illegal in most countries in terms of power (500 watts) and speed (around 25mph). The company is constantly working on new options, and its latest developments are always worth checking out.

One particularly light power-assist kit for the Brompton utilises some clever design elements. Velological of Germany makes a neat and extremely efficient rim-driven bottle dynamo recognised as one of the best lighting options around if you can afford it. In 2015, the company developed the technology to provide rather than generate power, with the Velospeeder. This utilises two tiny motors sprung inwards against the rims of the front or rear wheel (rather than the tyre, like many friction drives), which can be fitted to a wide range of bicycles. Junik-HPV, run by Brompton specialist Juliane Neuß has produced a mounting kit to fit the Velospeeder motors onto an adapted Brompton rear rack. The entire kit weighs 1.7kg but the original Velospeeder was always going to be limted to fairweather cycling (due to potential traction slippage in the wet) and over only moderate hills given the tiny size of the motors. A design overhaul in 2018 sought to address these problems, though in-depth reviews to assess the effectiveness of the redesign are very thin on the ground.

Germany's Velospeeder friction drive

The Pendix - also from Germany - is extremely well made and simple in conception but really just too heavy for the Brompton

One of the most cleanly integrated retrofit kits is from German firm Pendix, albeit at the opposite end of the weight spectrum to the Velospeeder. The Pendix system cleverly fits a gearless motor onto the non-chain side of the bottom bracket. In practice the Pendix proved to be pretty heavy, not very efficient and to have an idiosyncratic torque sensing system, so - despite it's smooth minimalist look - its appeal was always going to be limited.

Other lightweight Brompton conversion systems were launched after Brompton's own electric bike rolled out in 2018. First came Swytch, majoring on the relative ease with which the customer can fit it themselves and featuring three main elements. Early examples came with a small, handlebar-mounted battery and controller, which proved under-powered, unstable

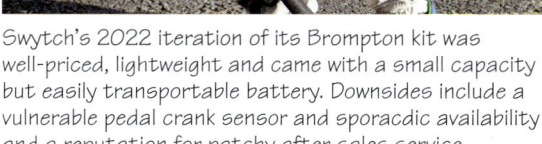

Swytch's 2022 iteration of its Brompton kit was well-priced, lightweight and came with a small capacity but easily transportable battery. Downsides include a vulnerable pedal crank sensor and sporacdic availability and a reputation for patchy after sales service.

and inconvenient, and were moved to the front luggage block mounting in mid-2020. The battery bag connects to a small front geared hub motor, and a motion-sensing ring which fits at the base of the non-drive side crank. The eye-catching £500 price for the smaller battery option was due in part to Far Eastern manufacture and also, presumably, the fact that the lead time of several months allowed for bulk buying and surface delivery, hence the low price.

2022 saw Swytch downsize the battery option and move it back to the handlebars with the choice of 'Air' and 'Max' options at 98Wh and 180Wh respectively. Whilst the handlebars aren't ideal places to mount a battery, due to extra weight potentially affecting handling, the relatively insubstantial 700g and 1070g of these particular ones didn't really pose too many problems whilst riding. The neat alloy handlebar-clamped battery mount is a good quality piece of engineering but may foul getting larger items of luggage on and off the mounting block - it's likely only smaller ones will easily fit. It also means using a longer than standard handlebar catch to accommodate the battery mount and results in a slightly wider folded package. One option to allow a larger front bag would be to fit the battery on the 'inside' of the the handlebars, facing the rider and using a standard length handlebar catch if you can live with the fact the mount is now protruding from the outside of the folded package.

More potentially troublesome is the fact the pedal crank motion sensor is rather easily knocked and a little fiddly to fit in place - certainly downsides where the magnetic sensor ring rotates a few millimetres from a sensor that itself relies on adhesive to stay in situ on the frame!

Still, adding only around 2.6kg for the 98Wh option, the Swytch remains one of the lightest and lowest-priced options out there for those looking to electrify an existing Brompton. The only caveat is that the pricing and availability can be opaque and at the time of writing it wasn't even possible to join the Swytch website.

At a cursory glance the Cyrtronex system, launched in 2020 after a long and meticulous development, was similar to the Swytch, using a similarly discreet geared front hub motor and added a total of just over 3kg to the Brompton. On closer inspection though, it couldn't have been a more different beast, incorporating a plethora of original design features, from the marine-grade stainless steel mounting mechanism for the aluminium battery bottle to the tiny sprocket movement sensor, responsible for delivering power.

Whilst Swytch and Cytronex both took the same lightweight approach, giving perky performance and a lighter, easier bike to carry, the high quality of the Cytronex and impressively smooth power delivery are much more in keeping with Brompton's engineering heritage, and like the Brompton it is designed and manufactured in the UK. One can't help wondering of this might not have been a better approach for Brompton's own engineers to have followed... In 2024 Cytronex prices started at £1145 for those self-fitting (the kits can also be fitted by Cytronex at its Winchester workshop).

In January 2023, A to B magazine tested a Cytronex kit adapted to suit the 4-speed T-line Brompton.

The 2023 world class, 11.7kg T-line specific version took e-bike portability to unprecedented levels.

This machine has to rank amongst the best folding electric bikes ever, weighing just 11.7kg including battery, with a range of just over 30 miles. On the downside, the recipient bike currently costs £4,520 and the power-kit starts at £1,270 (all at 2024 prices). It clearly isn't the cheapest option.

2022 saw the emergence of the very simple looking Boost retrofit system consisting of only two main components; a geared rear hub motor with a magnetic motion sensor integrated into the axle and freehub and a separately mounted 126Wh battery and controller unit sitting neatly inside the rear triangle, with a cable connecting the two that carries both power and sensor information. There is also a wireless handlebar control and an app which has similar functions with regards to altering power settings and data feedback. Claimed additional weight was 2.5kg. At the time of writing the kit was in 'pre-order' phase at a discounted price of £799.

Launched in spring 2020, the Cytronex retrofit kit looked like yet another hub and battery system but on closer inspection featured a raft of UK designed and manufactured original technology, including alloy casing for the battery bottle unit, marine grade stainless steel for the bottle mounting levers and a sprocket movement sensor by the gear indicator chain.

Whilst this looks a very neat, simple and well-balanced solution, the obvious flaw is that hub geared recipient bikes will not be suitable. Indeed at the time of writing the Boost's Brompton kit was only offered ready laced into a two-speed derailleur wheel. More of a problem for most people is the limited range, claimed (probably accurately) to be in the region of 30km, or 19 miles. It sounds a lot, but electric bikes tend to make longer trips, and with this design you can't carry a spare battery.

This prototype of the rear hub motored Boost kit used a very small battery permanently fixed to the front of the rear triangle with the option of a wireless handlebar control. It looks nicely minimalist but was only advertised as a two speed model during its 2024 launch phase.

A final mention should go to Ebike Solutions of Germany. Despite being a conventional retrofit kit along the lines of the Grin kit from Canada, it looks thoughtfully conceived, as you might expect from a German-based company with long experience in the e-bike world (they have been producing the Bromptonaut kit since 2018). Ebike Solutions use a small, light AKM front hub motor and a choice of modular 98Wh Grin Li-Go batteries or their own design of 500Wh battery - either way they are placed in the front luggage bag and disconnect to stay in the bag once the bike is folded. A separate but very discreet control unit is attached to the bike frame and there is a choice of two displays, one even featuring a walk assist function.

The Bromptonaut kit has a bag enclosed battery, frame-mounted controller and neat handlebar unit. There's a choice of clip-on and bottom bracket integrated pedal sensors (the latter requires professional installation.)

To see how the Brompton Electric (not a retrofitable system unfortunately) measures up against the existing retrofit kits see the table overleaf. For thoughts on what an electric Brompton of the future might look like see page 150.

Meanwhile, the race is on amongst other manufacturers to introduce a practical, and reasonably priced off-the-peg folding electric bike to compete with both Brompton's own offering and the burgeoning number of Brompton-specific kits.

Despite the emergence of smaller, lighter hub motors, the mainstream competition is still mainly composed of larger heavier fold-in-half machines. In 2017 the Tern Vektron electric folder, powered by a Bosch crank drive went on sale, going on to become one of the market leaders. But weighing in excess of 22kg, and costing £3,000 plus, the Vektron hardly fulfilled the brief of mass-market portable assistance on which a true folding electric bike should be judged.

A number of smaller electric folder brands each with their own take on how to lose weight are emerging, but no single product appears pre-eminent. Some of the more promising are Hummingbird and Carbo. The former uses an 'all-in-one' gearless rear hub. It is a wonderfully simple carbon fibre machine and weighs a headline-grabbing 10.9kg, but the single gear, small 155Wh battery and similarly gearless motor mean range and hill-climbing are limited. This tends to throw the retail price of £4495 into stark relief!

Brompton's own e-bike, launched in 2017 - and just as important its subsequent refinement - have undoubtedly made life tougher for the competition, but with the lightest model costing £3695 and weighing 15.6kg, there's plenty of room for lighter or cheaper electric folders to

The UK's Hummingbird Electric currently sets the standard for lightweight folding electric bikes at 10.9kg. It is the brainchild of UK-based Romanian Petre Cranium.

make their mark. In 2024, the Hummingbird is still the lightest, but the Cytronex-T-line Brompton runs it a close second and is an altogether more practical machine. These machines *should* be good because they both cost many thousands of pounds. Cheaper off-the-peg models are starting to emerge, like the weld-free FLIT M2 from Cambridge, which is claimed to weigh 14kg. It has a frame-concealed but removable 230Wh battery and a folded size of 80 x 60 x 30 cm, the only real potential shortcoming being the single gear. It was reduced from £2,499 to £1,999 on a 'pre-order' basis at the time of writing in early 2024.

In short there is still everything to play for in the quest to produce the world's best electric folder. Perhaps Brompton will produce a lighter and more efficient 'Gen2' electric model that will help establish its preeminence in the world of e-folders in the same way it has conquered the non-electric folding world.

Without being worldbeating, the FLIT M2 hits a practical sweetspot between weight, price and functionality

Brompton E-bike Kits Compared to the Brompton Electric

	Motor Type	Technical Notes	Additonal electric weight / weight of typical size battery	Prices excl delivery	Contact
Brompton Electric	Geared front hub	Torque sensor. No titanium options. LED lighting powered by main battery as standard. 300Wh battery	Total weight 5.7kg including 3kg 300Wh battery and LED lights	From £2900 for an Electric C Line Urban 4 speed	brompton.com
ARCC	Geared front hub	Torque sensor and wireless Bluetooth handlebar power level control. System features launch control feature for quick acceleration from a standing start. Must be fitted at ARCC, Cambridge. 144/216/324 Wh Bosch powertool battery options Bag conversion kit optional extra. USB C charging output ports UK spec only. T-Line compatible.	Total weight 3.9kg including 1.3kg 216Wh battery	From £1899 kit price including fitting (note app control only available for Apple iPhones)	arccbikes.com
Boost	Geared rear hub.	Motion sensor integrated within the hub motor.	Total weight from 2.5kg say Boost, including battery - capacity unknown.	From £995 kit price self-fitting. Note pre-order only at time of writing	boostbike.uk
Bromptonaut	Lightweight geared front hub. The heavier, gearless SAW20 motor is also available (as used by Grin below)	Pedal motion sensor - plastic magent disc and a pedal sensor set. The latter is a more robust solution but needs professional installation as it needs removal of the bottom bracket to fit the sensor parts.	Circa 4.5kg including 500Wh battery (smaller battery optios may be available). Also Grin Li-Go batteries will be avaialble (at the time	From €1289 kit self-fitting (ordered direct from Germany). International shipping free on orders over €1000 (though there may be customs duties)	ebike-solutions.com
Cytronex	Geared front hub	Cytronex patented sprocket movement sensor and patented frame mounted combined battery & control unit.	Total weight 3.2kg including 1.5kg 198Wh battery. Hardwired LED lighting system adds 170g.	From £1330 fitted	cytronex.com
Grin	Gearless (Crystalyte)	Choice of throttle, crank motion sensor or torque sensor (US spec 20mph).	Total weight circa 5.5kg (depending on options chosen) for SAW20 gearless motor option with 360Wh battery	From circa US$1017 kit inc 360Wh bottle battery. Shipping / tax ex-USA not inc.	ebikes.ca

The World of Brompton Specials

	Motor Type	Technical Notes	Additonal electric weight / weight of typical size battery	Prices: Kit only / fitting / price including M2L June 2020 prices Postage exc	Contact
Nano	Geared front hub	Choice of throttle (must be pedaling to activate) or motion sensor pedelec LED lighting option Battery choice: 144Wh / 216Wh powertool or 481Wh Chinese Hailong. Not titanium compatible as fork spreading required.	Total weight circa 3.3kg including 1.3kg 144Wh battery.	From £820 Fitting £100-£170	nanoelectricbikes.co.uk **Note: All details subject to change due to business restructuring in 2024**
Pendix	Gearless crank drive	Fitting only by approved dealer. Torque sensor. Battery choice: various options from 140Wh to 1000Wh dual battery Titanium compatible.	6.5 kg inc 2.3 kg, 330Wh battery	£1649 Pendix insist on approved dealer fitting and prices vary	pendix.com
Sparticle V9 S886	Geared front hub	Throttle only and crank sensor options 390, 555, 960Wh batteries Higher 'peak power' rated motor options available Self-fitting or shop fitted	8.2kg inc 555Wh battery weighing 5.6kg	From £750 Fitting £100 Self-fitting available	electricbikesales.co.uk
Swytch	Geared front hub	Crank motion sensor (small Brompton specific option available). 180Wh / 252Wh batteries.	Circa 3.4kg including 1.78kg 180Wh battery	Price not available at time of writing	swytchbike.com
Velospeeder	Friction drive	Dual motor system acting on opposite sides of the rear wheel rim.	Circa 1.64kg including 0.89kg for a 188Wh battery.	From €1255 for the kit only	velogical-engineering.com

Note: Prices quoted in this table are for kit only. Non-electric Brompton price range at time of table compilation in May 2024 was £950 for the A-Line to £4745 for the 12-speed T-Line. For indicative second hand prices see pages 182-185.

Bigger Wheels and Off-road Capability

Despite Brompton's advances over the years in widening the gear range and improving brakes and tyres, there still appears to be a demand for after market conversions. With the introduction of the full titanium T-Line in 2022 there seems to be little incentive for far eastern manufacturers to continue copying the Brompton design using this super light and super strong metal. Focus looks like it may be shifting to bigger-wheeled conversions, achieved by swapping out the factory-fitted front forks and rear triangle for bigger versions. These will accommodate larger wheels and wider tyres, plus a wide range of mass-produced bike parts such as Gates carbon belt drive, hydraulic disc brakes and wide-range hub gears with a single control lever (unlike the twin shifters used on the Brompton 6 and 12 speeds).

Why is there a demand? Most Brompton riders adjust to its smaller-wheeled handling, but some clearly yearn for larger wheels and the more stable handling they afford. However, judging from the bigger-wheeled conversions currently on offer, the accent is on wider (often knobbly) tyres giving greater off-road capability, or at least more comfort over bumpier surfaces. A Brompton can do a surprisingly good job off-road, but it's never going to outpace an MTB with larger wheels and full-suspension. Nevertheless, these upgrades have a strong appeal and if things like hydraulic disc brakes and more intuitive-to-operate wide ratio gearing (with electronic shifting if desired) help persuade potential customers this really is the Brompton they need, so be it.

Other reasons for bigger-wheeled conversions include customisation for much larger riders. Brompton's telescopic seatpost option allows for a maximum height of 6'8" with an inside leg measurement of up to 39", but people are getting steadily taller and heavier. Perhaps – a potentially overlooked area – the bike will become popular for fast touring, or even long distance racing. A like-for-like 20" tyre will have significantly less rolling resistance than a 16" Brompton-sized version, as rolling resistance is inversely proportional to tyre radius, and there is a much bigger range available at 20". On the downside, most big-wheeled conversions – especially those with fat tyres or multi-speed hub gears - are likely to add several kg to a standard build Brompton and inevitably result in a bigger folded package .

Two specialist outlets, working independently and in different countries, both self-taught yet highly skilled - pioneered this market. Vincent van Eerd's Eerder Metaal is based in Amersfoort, central Netherlands and the former Brompton dealer has a background in mechanical engineering and worked for one of the country's biggest bike manufacturers, Sparta (designing and prototyping a 24" folding bike for the Accell bicycle group which sadly never came to market in it's original pure form, just a 'look a bit alike' made by Dahon).

After starting his Brompton modification experiments in 2003 and going on to make telescopic stems for taller riders and repair bridges for rear frames, from 2018 he began modifying Brompton's own rear frames and forks to accept disc brakes and derailleur gears using his self-acquired brazing and welding skills (his father's profession of goldsmith was helpful in passing on brazing tips).

Vincent says 'I have been a believer in bigger wheels than 16"….. Rear derailleurs don't hit the ground and break on 20" wheels and a bumpy road is evened out by bigger wheels. My first Brompton conversion of 2005 with derailleur gears still featured the original 16" wheels size. Being almost a full time stabilizer builder (bespoke ones for bigger kids bikes and full size bikes), it took some 14 years for a serious follow up with disc brakes and a little more tyre clearance for 40mm wide, 16" (349mm) tyres. Vincent experimented with the 18" (355mm) wheel size but ultimately settled on a completely redesigned fork and rear frame accommodating 2.25" x 20" tyres plus mudguards – the 20" version became the Xplorer and Vincent has produced a number of bespoke conversions of customers' Bromptons at this size. The Xplorer conversion is not a straightforward job, however, as it involves shortening the headtube of a post 2004 Brompton mainframe (2004 saw the Brompton wheelbase lengthened) in order to keep the bike acceptably low once 2.6" wide tyres are fitted. This involves reaming and facing the headtube. Due to the long lead time in making the Xplorer conversions and the fact there is a clear demand for an off-road capable Brompton, Vincent is concentrating on fulfilling current orders. He now passes all new off-road Brompton enquiries to another expert brazer, based in Scotland, who is able to produce the widened forks necessary at a steadier pace.

Eeder Metaal eerdermetaal.nl

The distinctive raw brazing of Eerder Metaal's Xplorer custom front and rear frames allow for tyres up to 2.25" wide. Typical stats are a fold of 75 cm (L) x 66 cm (H) x 35 cm (W) and a 14.5kg weight - though of course everything depends on the bespoke spec.

In 1998 Glasgow's Ben Cooper graduated from a university course and moved on to own a bike shop, Kinetics. Over the years his business grew and changed to the point where retail sales no longer predominated and small scale parts manufacture – in particular Brompton large wheel conversions – made up a significant chunk of his business, although still a speck on the current level of Brompton's factory output. In Ben's case he simply responded to light-hearted comments about putting fat tyres on a Brompton by making such a modification out of curiosity to see how it would ride. Kinetic's current Brompton-compatible 304 marine-grade stainless steel rear triangles were designed for their Rohloff Brompton kits, but are suitable for fitting most standard 135mm-wide rear hubs to a Brompton. The design has been refined over 10 years of making hundreds of Rohloff Bromptons. Their rear frames also have IS disc brake mounts and enough space for a 160mm rotor. They work with normal Brompton frame rollers and Eazy wheels, brakes, and the standard elastomer. Standard Brompton mudguards and rear rack will also fit, and if you fit a 14-speed Rohloff hub it can also use the standard Brompton single-speed tensioner (Ben makes bespoke tensioners for belt drive conversions). The Kinetics MTBrompton is one of the simplest ways of getting a larger-wheeled, wider-tyred Brompton, with kits to retrofit available, as well as a full fitting service for both used and new Bromptons. The MTBrompton is, as the name suggests, intended to be a mountain bike version of the Brompton – with space for 20" tyres up to 2.4" wide.

Kinetics' MT Brompton is available as a conversion kit (RRP £1445 in 2024) or a bespoke offering. Using an unaltered Brompton mainframe means a high bottom bracket, giving plenty of ground clearance!

As you would expect, the folded package is a fair bit bigger than a standard 16"-wheeled Brompton fold and it adds a fair bit of weight too. Kinetics' website gives respective figures of 74cm (L) x 65.5cm (H) x 38cm (W) with convereted bikes usually starting at around 14kg.

Given the clear demand for bigger wheeled (or at the very least wider-tyred) Bromptons, it's certainly conceivable the company itself could produce such a machine. It would need to convince itself there really was enough demand to set up what would be in effect a whole new production line for a new model (if they opted for an 18" or 20" wheeled version), with many of the parts likely to be different to the original 16"-wheeled machine.

As bigger wheeled machines would inevitably move the Brompton away from its original strengths - a superbly compact and potentially very lightweight folding bike - it looks to be much more of a debateable prospect. The resulting bike would be heavier and produce a larger fold, albeit, as Eerder Metaal and Kinetics have demonstrated, retaining the magic of the Brompton 'tri-fold'.

The new heavier and larger folding machines would also suddenly find themselves up against a select band of competitors who have already gone down this route and honed designs accordingly. Probably the most notable of these are the Birdy GT10 and the Bike Friday All-Packa.

We've already looked at the genesis of the Birdy (see pages 68-70) and despite its early travails, writing in 2024 it appears to be prospering in Asia where Birdys are manufactured under license by Pacific Cycles. The latter produce an off-road variant, the GT, with Schwalbe Black Jack 18"×1.9" knobbly tyres and a claimed weight of 11.4 kg and a folded size of 60cm x 39cm x 72cm. That weight significantly undercuts most if not all Eerder/Brompton conversions and produces a package of similar folded volume. The US$2,800 price tag also undercuts the bespoke conversions, as you would expect from a mass-manufactured machine.

Birdy's GT10 would give stiff competition to any production off-road capable Brompton offering - on paper at least - a relatively lightweight, compact and well-priced package. At the time of writing if appeared to be available in Asia only.

Whilst it lacks the full suspension of the Birdy GT, Bike Friday's All-Packa boasts frame clearance for enormous 20 x 2.8" wide off-road tyres and offers several derailleur gear options alongside a 14-speed Rohloff hub option. Whilst no weight is given, the 81cm x 61cm x 30cm folded package size is competitive for this kind of machine in terms of volume, even if the folded package looks somewhat ungainly. A price of $2,595 is pretty reasonable against similar machines too. Note there are no attachment points for mudguards though there is a factory-fitted electric assist option.

Using and Maintaining a Brompton The Brompton can be serviced in a small space and with a surprisingly basic list of tools. The exact make-up of the Brompton toolbox will vary according to the age of the bike, with a general move from spanners and screwdrivers to Allen keys, but this is a typical list (from left to right): pliers, crank extractor tool, 8mm and 10mm combination spanners, 13 x 15mm open-ended spanner (older front axle and saddle securing nuts may be different), 6mm x 100mm slotted screwdriver, Phillips #2 x 100mm screwdriver, chainlink extractor, 110mm Mole wrench (optional), 6mm, 5mm, 4mm, 3mm and 2.5mm Allen keys. Other items that might get infrequent use are a 10mm Allen key or 24mm AF socket to release the left-hand folding pedal, Sturmey-Archer cone spanner for hub adjustment, and a thin 32mm or 34mm open-ended spanner for adjusting the headset.

Using and Maintaining a Brompton

Note: The following maintenance and usage tips are not intended to be comprehensive.

Versatility and Handling

Over the years, the Brompton has found all sorts of roles way beyond the original brief of a car boot or rail commuter machine. Not only is the bike used to get to work, but increasingly it has *become* the office for many people. The Brompton quickly found a niche amongst surveyors, map-makers and other transport professionals who need to get around a small area quickly, with the convenience of being able to pack the bike away into a car, bus or train. A Brompton has even found its way to the Australian observatory at the South Pole. Other Bromptons are used for serious touring, the machine being quite capable of 60 to 70 miles in a day, and much more if set up carefully.

The bike is easy to ride, but for those who have never tried small wheels, the almost total lack of gyroscopic action from the front wheel can be unnerving at first. Some people never really acclimatize to this twitchy steering behaviour but most soon adapt, after which the cumbersome response of a big-wheeled bike will seem strange! A little more care is needed on pot-holes and rough surfaces, but in general, a Brompton can go anywhere and do anything a big-wheeled bike can do, even in surprisingly rough (but not muddy) off-road conditions. In city traffic, the short length of the machine, hub gears, and quick steering give a real advantage in traffic.

The bikes are easy and cheap to maintain and the factory's ability to provide spares for older models means a healthy resale value. However, there are a few points to watch, especially on older machines.

A modern lightweight Brompton like the T-Line (left), used in conjunction with public transport, is probably the fastest and easiest way of getting about most modern cities.
Perhaps more surprisingly they have also proved extremely strong and reliable world tourers, as used by the globetrotting Heinz Stücke who has covered hundreds of thousands of miles by bike.

Buying Secondhand

With the exception of certain rarified Bike Friday and Birdy variants, folding bikes don't tend to keep their value, but the Brompton is an exception. All Bromptons, from the very earliest prototypes to the titanium T-line, and the ordinary everyday L3 (later the M3L, and now the C-line), can be expected to sell for at least the original price, losing only inflation. Brompton mileage varies far more than most bikes – or cars, come to that – because they were used by everyone from long-distance tourists to commuters and Sunday park wobblers. Interestingly, prices don't vary much, so the 'best buy' will be something like 'his and hers' red L3s, possibly without a luggage block and/or folding pedal. This more or less guarantees low mileage. Pricewise, the most impressive are the 1981 pre-production bikes, produced in very small numbers, mostly as a reward for those who helped to fund the project in the early days. These come up only rarely, and will set you back between £10,000 and £20,000, but they're heavy and relatively wobbly. One for serious collectors only.

The oldest of the viable riding machines are the Mark 1s, produced in 1981. Recognisable by their distinctive main-frame kink, these really can be used on a daily basis, but the hand-made parts mean they're difficult to maintain, and you could be paying £2,500-£3,500 for something that originally cost about £200.

A Mark 1 in unusually good condition, shown off in Brompton's Long Acre shop in 2023

Even in poor condition like this one with a missing chain, Mark 2s can certainly be worth repairing and even upgrading with modern parts

The oldest really practical bikes are the Mark 2s, produced from 1988 to 1999. These are effectively the same as today's line-up, give or take improved brakes, tyres, handlebars and other components, so they can be upgraded very easily. The only real issue is that the bottom bracket bearings were changed from ISO to the near identical JIS standard in 2013, and the older type is no longer made. New bearings will fit your old frame, but you will need a new chainring, spider and right-hand pedal arm to match. In all probability you will also need a new chain, tensioner and rear sprocket too. A complete transmission is expensive, but console yourself with the thought that if the bottom bracket was beyond use, everything else will have been pretty worn, and you will have effectively future-proofed your bike.

A small number of main-frames have failed just forward of the frame hinge over the years. Brompton has always been willing to replace this short section of frame, but as the bikes are now 30 years old, the company offers a 10% reduction off a new C-line instead. Reasonable enough, but should we be scrapping serviceable bikes which were previously considered repairable? Well used Mark 2s can also suffer from corrosion in the rear triangle tubes, caused by winter salt spray, but that part of the frame can be replaced, as can almost everything else, usually for something lighter and more effective. The Mark 2 bikes originally cost £200-£300, but the average cost in 2024 is £570. Most of the frame numbers can be found in Appendix IV if you want to check provenance.

This early Brompton marketing shot (probably for Mark 2 bikes) interestingly features the idea of towing with a Brompton - something that hasn't really been promoted in marketing literature since.

The Mark 3, made from 2000-2004 was upgraded in numerous ways, but just as sales were taking off, Sturmey-Archer was put out of business, throwing Brompton's expansion plans into doubt. In the event, Brompton managed to liberate a van-load of three speeds, but far fewer 5s, so these (more fragile) hubs were soon getting rare. A particularly unfortunate affair, because the 5-speed hub had just been improved. Luckily, SRAM stepped in, enabling 3-speed production to continue without a pause and Ritchie had soon engineered a clever 2-speed derailleur to turn the 3-speed into a 6-speed. Later on, Sturmey manufacture restarted in Taiwan and Brompton jumped ship (it was a better hub), and later helped to engineer the BWR wide-ratio variant.

Today, all of the 2-, 3-, 5- and 6-speed Mark 3s can all be kept on the road one way or another, but mud sticks, and the Mark 3 bikes (originally £450-£550) sell today for about £450. Avoid SRAM because in 2017, the company announced it would end production of its internal gear hubs due to declining sales. However, older 3- and 5- speed Sturmeys are fine (see Upgrades below).

The Mark 4, produced from 2005-2017, is arguably the best value Brompton variant, with many new and improved parts, especially on earlier bikes. These are lovely machines, and effectively very similar to a modern Brompton. Best of all are the early LX lightweights, with many titanium components, but if you're looking for one, take a magnet. Later bikes had steel seat pillars and steel folding pedal nuts. You really want these in titanium and of course the front forks and rear frame should be checked too. If you are very lucky you may find an early one with all the right bits, and if you pay less than £1,300 for it you have one of the best Brompton variants at a fair price. The ordinary steel Mark 4s cost £500-£600 at the time, and fetch about £670 today. Worth every penny, unless the bike has had a very hard life.

Later bikes made between 2018 and 2022 (let's call them Mark 4a for argument's sake) are a hard bunch to judge, because apart from the introduction of the electric variant, the changes were mainly cosmetic, such as bag options, frame colour schemes and celebrity-endorsed special editions. There were a few withdrawals too, such as Brompton's own-brand tyre in favour of a near-exclusive deal with Schwalbe, and other small changes, some of which left the bike slightly heavier and more expensive.

It's a bit early to judge what effect this will have on the second-hand value of these bikes. Presumably celebrity-endorsement is only valuable while the celebrity is still in the news, so prices might even go negative in the longer-term. Colour schemes are likewise linked to public whims. Pink could be 'in' one year and fall off a cliff the next.

The effect of the major engineering-led revamp of 2022-23 is much more interesting. These machines deserve to carry the Mark 5 epithet, because they are significantly different. The P-line is a worthy successor to the old lightweight, even though the new 4-speed is probably a little heavier than its (albeit two-speed) 2005-2010 forebears. So a tad heavier perhaps, but it seems unlikely this bike will lose much value. And what of the T-line? All the gear variants – single-speed, 4-speed and 12-speed are special in different ways, and they all have the cache of being expensively crafted from a near-precious metal. A titanium bike, like a diamond, is forever. Robotic welding, or some astonishing new 3D printing technique might yet make ready-formed frames as cheap as steel, but the bikes will always keep their value.

Whilst the current titanium-framed T-Line bikes seem a very good bet in keeping their value, the humble 3-speed A-Line also appears a sound choice if you want a bike that at least holds its value.

An interesting case is the humble A-line. It costs just under £1,000 in 2024, and as Brompton points out, it's shorn of all non-essential parts, even coloured paint. On the other hand, it's a genuine 2024 Brompton, with a seven-year frame warranty, and it comes with the standard-ratio BSR three-speed Sturmey-Archer hub and optional 44-tooth chain ring, a combination ideally suited to hillier places. Not everyone wants a folding pedal or even a front carrier block, although opinions might differ about mudguards! This plain little bike is unlikely to go up in value, and if it does go down, it won't fall far.

Upgrades

Almost any post-1988 bike can be upgraded to modern spec with a few provisos, and spares are widely available, sometimes for garage clearance prices, so it's well worth keeping an eye on online auction and sales sites such as eBay. There are a few issues to bear in mind. The failure of Sturmey-Archer caused some complications for a while, and there has been continued fallout in terms of spares. Mark 2 and early Mark 3 rear frames will only accept 3- or 5-speed Sturmey hubs, while later Mark 3 frames will only officially accept the SRAM 3-speed hub (or 6-speed variant). Luckily they can be adapted to accept Sturmey hubs too, because SRAM has now ceased hub production and parts are getting rare. More recent bikes (post January 2005) have a universal rear frame. If an old bike needs a new frame, you should be able to fit this part to any older Brompton, whatever the age or gear system. There were certainly problems for the years that the Sturmey hubs were not available, especially for owners of Mark 2 5-speeds for whom hub failure (not unknown) could mean replacing the entire rear frame. With the 5-speed hub back in production this is no longer the case, but Brompton's unique short axle variant is no longer made. Fortunately, the longer axle fits perfectly well, leaving a slight protrusion from the folded package. This can be cut off without causing harm to the hub (the axle is very hard, so use an angle-grinder with diamond-impregnated disc or similar). Any rear frame fitted with the derailleur changer braze-on can be upgraded to 6-speed spec, but later Mark 3 frames will require a little modification to accept the more desirable BWR wide-ratio hub, which gives evenly-spaced gears. Older frames without the braze-on will need to be replaced if you want six gears. This is unlikely to be worthwhile unless the bike has sentimental value, because these older 3- or 5-speed machines are quite valuable secondhand. If you really want a 6-speed, it makes more sense to sell the bike and buy a newer 6-speed. Or just upgrade to a new 5-speed hub.

The derailleur changer braze-on (needed to convert 3-speeds into 6-speeds) is arrowed here. It was introduced as standard in spring 2001. Without it the rear frame will have to be replaced for one with the braze-on.

What are the best modern upgrades? This is bound to be a rather subjective list, because everyone has different aims and priorities. The Continental Contact Urban tyre ticks most boxes and by shopping around, you can find them for less than £20 each. They weigh about 320g each and do most things pretty well. Too new to judge accurately is the Aceoffix Flyer, a slick folding tyre rather like the old Primo. They are 32 x 349mm, are rated at 100psi and weigh an excellent 210 grams apiece. Like the Continental, you should be able to find them for £20 each. There are now quite a range of inner-tubes, but again – in terms of ticking boxes for most people - the Schwalbe AV4 (SV4 for a Presta rim) seems to come out top: tough enough for daily use, weighing only 85g and less than £10 apiece.

Brompton's folding pedal is the best in the world, and they were originally an accessory, so older bikes do not always have them. It's a very worthwhile upgrade, but they're not cheap, even secondhand. If you really can't afford it, the economical answer is to buy a cheap-and-cheerful 'brand-less' folding pedal. The same goes for the conventional non-folding side. An authentic Brompton pedal looks nice and folds well, but it won't work any better. A well-used older bike will probably need a new saddle stem frame bush. They are easy to buy from Brompton or a dealer, and fitting it is a fairly straightforward engineering task. See 'Common Problems' overleaf. A nice set of mudguards will cheer up an older bike very nicely for about £30 a pair from Brompton, but do make sure to look after the stays (they can be straightened in a vice!) and grease all the little nuts, bolts and washers when reassembling, because the stay/fastening kits are expensive. Always inspect the handlebars on a Mark 2 bike, and with a bit less rigour on a Mark 3 or 4, looking for indications that a hairline crack might be starting, or there's a deep scratch that might promote one, particularly where the bar enters the stem. If at all in doubt, replace the handlebars. There were failures in the early days (thankfully very few) and all subsequent bars, including modern replacements are fine. Replacing the bars might cost £40, but you have hopefully eliminated this very small, but rather dangerous weakness. Rear frames can fail through corrosion, but they tend to sag slowly out of shape, and a worn rim should likewise give fair warning with a rhythmic click or knock that varies with wheel speed. You may also feel a slight bump through the brake lever, especially after pumping up the tyres (caused by the weakest section of rim distorting). Don't ignore these tell-tale signs! Stop riding until it's sorted, but it's admissible to get home with reduced tyre pressure. In both cases, you will need the Brompton parts. Rims are relatively cheap, but rear frames are not. There are variations with the frames, and older rear frames haven't been produced for a while, although adaptation should be fairly straightforward. A bigger worry (literally) is the mainframe. These look as though they'll last forever, and they might, but a minority of older frames with forged hinge assemblies have failed through stress and corrosion just forward of the forging. These strange failures have always been rare, but they might increase as elderly frames enter their fifth decade. Brompton can supply a new 'long wheelbase' mainframe onto which it's feasible to bolt all the old parts if you want a challenge, or leave it to your friendly local bike shop, but neither option will be cheap. It probably makes more sense to dismantle the bike for spares (keep everything - some parts are getting rare), and buy another Brompton of similar vintage. Generally speaking, newer bikes are more rigid, freer running, lighter and roomier, so although an early Mark 1 will match your Carnaby Street flares and in theory do everything a modern bike can do for less than half the price, it will never be quite as good. The same is true to a lesser degree with newer machines. There are exceptions, with the right bike and the right components, but do choose carefully when buying secondhand. Bromptons are upgradable, but there comes a point where it would have been cheaper and easier to buy a new or newer bike.

This 1997 5-speed Mark 2 model was selling with only gear two working and a loose front hinge pin. As long as the hinge pin wear is not excessive, what might seem at a casual glance to be irreparable faults might in fact be a good opportunity for a repairing and upgrading project - if the price is right!

Brompton Bicycle

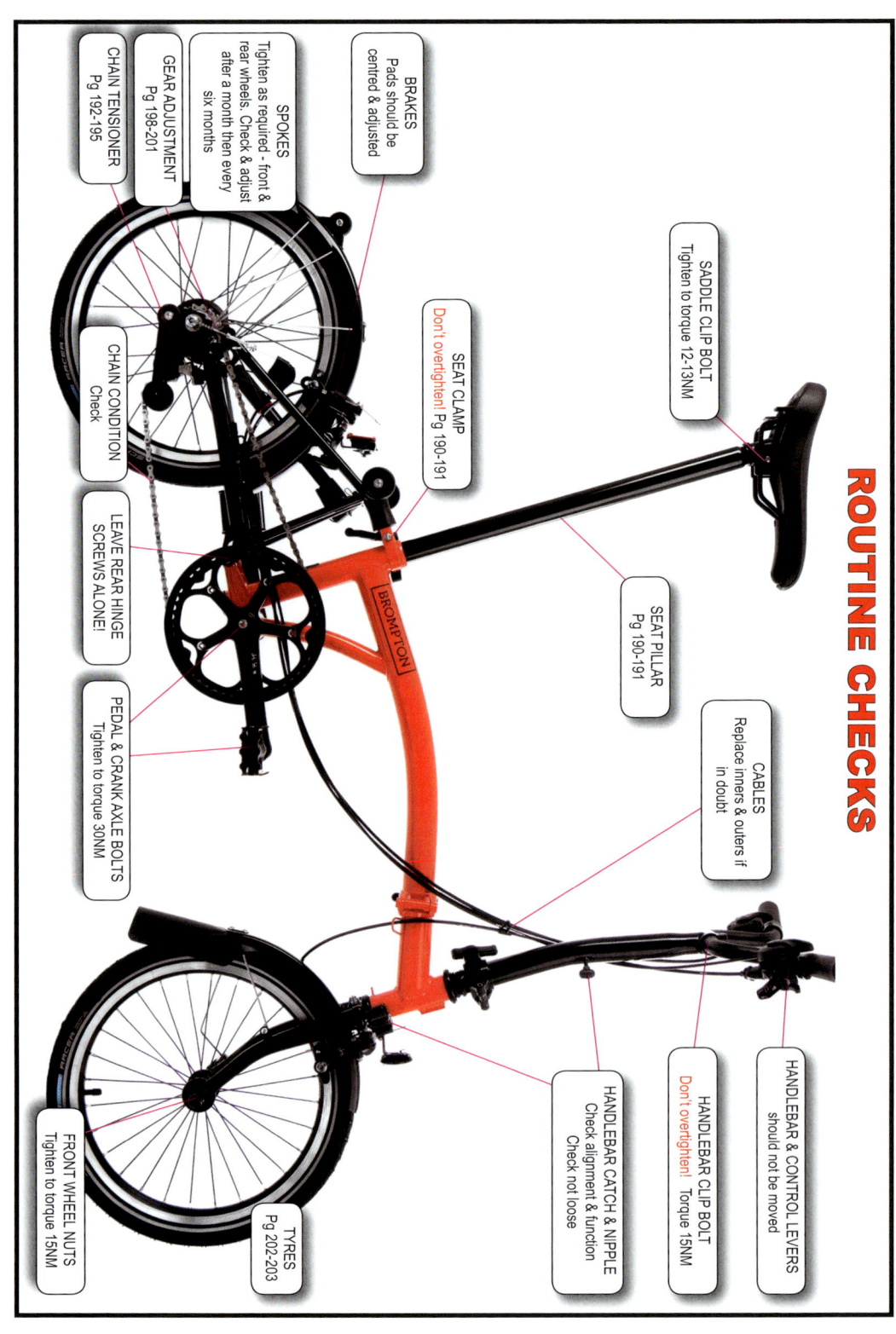

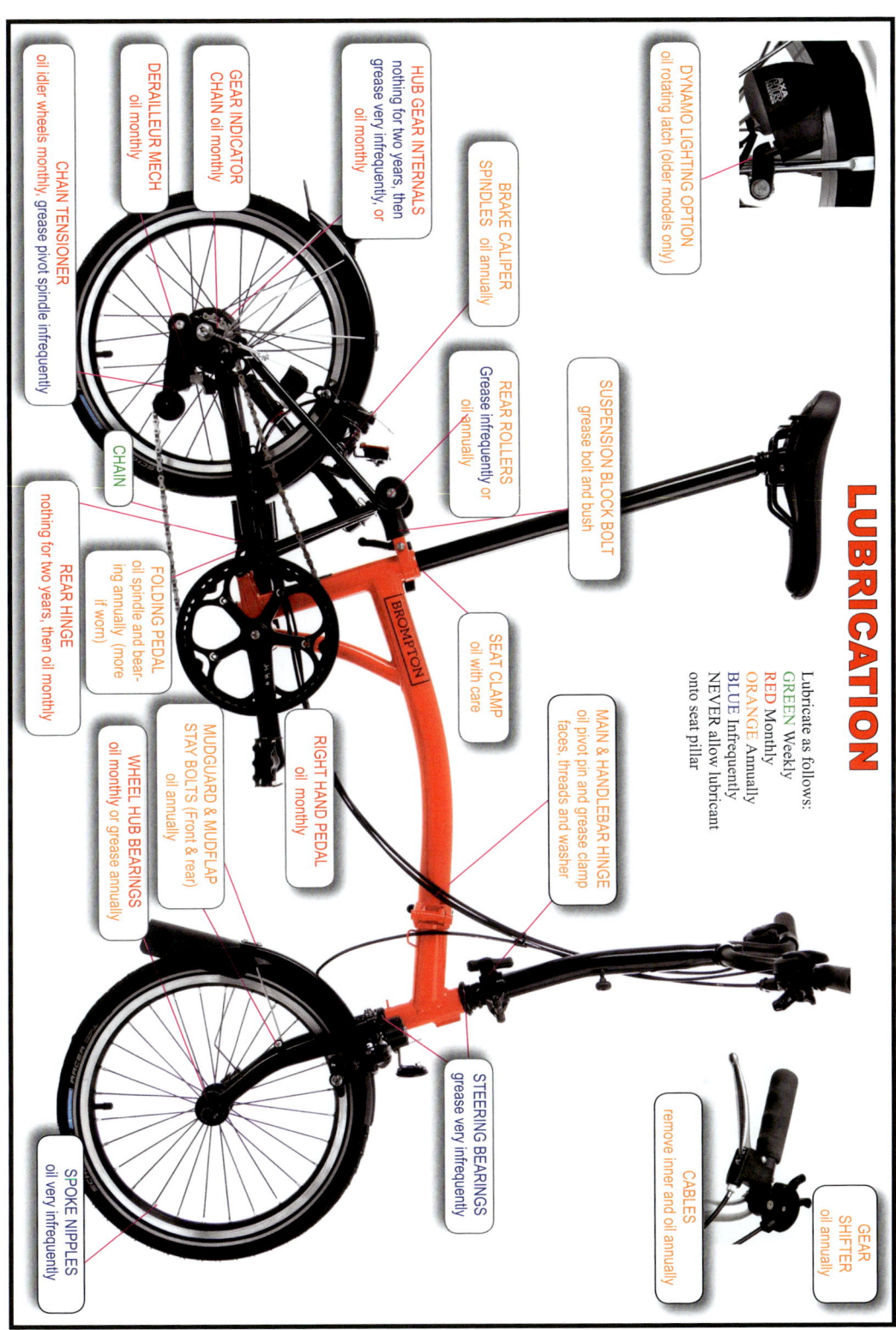

Common Problems

There are a number of ailments common to all Bromptons, many of which can be cured with a drop of oil or a minor adjustment. Starting with the most frequent issues:

Suspension Block Bolt
After a certain mileage, the bolt in the centre of the suspension block will begin to squeak rhythmically as the rider pedals, a sound that can be extremely hard to trace. This is caused by the factory-applied grease being washed out, so it will occur relatively rapidly on a commuter machine used daily in wet conditions, and may never occur on a leisure bike ridden only on sunny days.

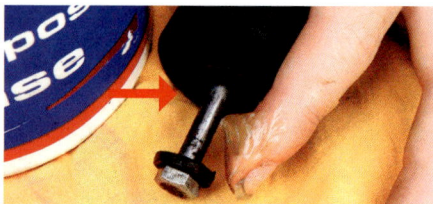

With the rear suspension assembly removed from the bike, the bolt shaft and bush (arrowed) can be greased. If the bush or bolt shaft are badly worn, they will need to be replaced. These examples are marginal!

An immediate cure is to simply grab the suspension block and turn it around, presenting a new face to the bearing, which should instantly stop the noise. As soon as possible, the assembly should be stripped down and the bolt thoroughly greased before reassembly. In bad cases, the bolt and/or plastic bush may be badly worn and need renewing.

Lighter riders may prefer a softer suspension block. Standard blocks post-2008 are supposed to be softer than the older block. If this still feels hard, suitable polymer or rubber blocks, steel springs (available in a variety of strengths), and even drilled cork (very light, but frail) may suit you better. A bit of experimentation should yield something that works well for you. Since 2009, Brompton has produced an optional harder block, ideal for heavier riders or anyone riding hard who doesn't want to waste energy bouncing the suspension.

Seat Pillar
The seat pillar and bush can be affected by two contrasting conditions: slippage when fully tightened, and seizure when loose. If you're really unlucky, your bike may suffer from both conditions at the same time!

If the seat pillar slips, or the clamp is stiff to operate, a few drops of oil in the clamp eccentric will help it to move freely and increase clamping pressure. But oil MUST NOT be allowed to get near the seat pillar! The bush is inside the top of the frame, and on an elderly bike like this, may well need replacing.

Slippage
This is usually caused by oil or grease contamination of the pillar and bush - even a tiny drop of hand cream or sun tan lotion is enough to make the pillar slip, but problems are much less common on bikes built after July 2007, which are fitted with a new clamp design. Before dismantling anything, check the condition of the clamp assembly. If the action is stiff, or the parts look dry or rusty, apply a drop or two of oil very sparingly to the eccentric, making sure oil is kept well away from the seat pillar. With the action working smoothly, check the tightness of the adjusting nut in the clamp. On older pre-2007 bikes this is a big self-locking nut, leading heavy-handed owners to overtighten it, which can distort or damage the frame. Adjustment may be required after the first few months of service, but extremely rarely thereafter. Movement of the nut must be made in very small increments, no more than one face (1/6 turn) at a time before rechecking the tightness of the clamp, and the sliding action of the pillar both clamped and unclamped. As a very rough guide, the early clamp - once properly lubricated - should close with the pressure of two fingers, and the later one - which clamps more efficiently - should close with one finger.

If the pillar continues to slip after lubrication and adjustment of the clamp, remove the saddle, slide the pillar out from under the bike, and degrease both the pillar and the bush inside the frame with an old toothbrush and dilute detergent or an industrial solvent such as ketone (also useful for binding pillars - see following section). If this fails to work, it may be worth trying a different pillar, as the metallurgy can vary, or even fitting a new frame bush, but cleaning and adjustment should work in 90% of cases.

Binding
A binding seat pillar can be caused by a number of factors. The most common is a worn or partially collapsed frame bush, or a bush distorted by underlying rust inside the frame, but other less common causes include a bent or badly scored seat pillar, or a distorted frame, usually caused by overzealous tightening of the clamp, as above. If a new bush is required, it will have to be 'superglued' into place, after all traces of old glue and rust have been removed. When the bushes are factory fitted, they are reamed to precisely the correct size, but this can also be done by hand. Insert the pillar as far as possible, tighten the clamp a couple of times, turning the pillar if you can, remove the pillar, and using a torch, look for shiny high spots. When these have been filed down, repeat the operation until the pillar runs freely when unclamped and locks firmly when clamped.

Frame and Stem Hinges
The alloy hinge clamp plates have tapered faces, so they tend to bend outwards as they are tightened, this regular flexing giving the plates a finite life. Look closely for signs of cracking on the corners, and replace the plates immediately if even a tiny crack appears, or if the plates are sufficiently worn to 'bottom out' when fully tightened. When reassembling, put a smear of grease on both faces of the washer, on the screw threads and the mating faces of the plate.

Over time, the hinge pin will wear, particularly if the grease has been washed out after extended use in wet conditions. As with all moving parts, a regular drop of oil will greatly extend the pin life. Some wear is not a serious issue, but the increased flexing in use will tend to wear out the hinge clamp plates at a faster rate. Brompton can supply oversize pins, eliminating the wear (up to a point), but the frame needs to be reamed to suit, making this a job for a specialist engineer.

Rear Hinge
The hinge linking the main frame to the rear frame will gradually wear over time, at a rate of around 1mm (measured at the extreme rear of the bike) every 2,000 miles. The bearings are grease packed from new, but once they have become a little worn, the remaining grease will soon be washed out, and regular lubrication with a few drops of heavy oil or spray grease is the only way to extend the life of the bearings. Modest play in the bearing has little effect on handling, so replacement can wait until sideways movement at the rear of the bike exceeds 6mm. But do check carefully if you find a sudden increase in movement. The shaft inside the hinge is secured by two countersunk screws thread-locked into place at the factory. If one or both of these screws come loose, movement in the bearing will rapidly increase and the screw head may begin to stand visibly proud of the frame. Under these circumstances, the screw must be removed, and the screw and shaft thoroughly degreased before the screw is locked back in place with a drop of thread-locking fluid, provided it is not badly worn. Failure to thread-lock the bolt back into place can result in the suspension collapsing.

Chain Tensioner
Like the more complex derailleur, the tensioner has a hard life on the Brompton, particularly in wet and muddy conditions, but it can continue to work for a considerable mileage, with very limited maintenance. All the same, an hour or two every six months dismantling and cleaning the tensioner will extend its life and improve its action. If the chain falls off when folding and/or unfolding the bike, suspect tensioner problems - the Brompton chain should never fall off. The tensioner pivot may be partially seized, or the tensioner arm bent.
With the bike part-folded and standing on its rear rollers, remove the chain from the long tensioner arm and check the action of the tensioner. It should have a strong spring action and flick back instantly when released. If the spring is weak, or the action sluggish, the tensioner will have to be stripped and checked.
A common error is to loosen the centre screw of the tensioner while removing the rear wheel. This bolt supports the tensioner bearing, which is clamped between two washers. If the bolt is taken out too far, one of these washers may slip out, causing the tensioner to seize when the bolt is retightened. An inexperienced mechanic will then leave the bolt loose, which can result in the tensioner flying apart or breaking after a few weeks. On older tensioners, the threads were cut into the plastic, resulting in stripped threads if overtightened - another cause of the assembly falling apart. This older design can be replaced with the newer type which has a steel captive nut and other improvements. If there is wear in several parts this might be the best course of action.
A common but easily cured problem with older bikes is seizure or partial seizure of the pivot bush. Carefully strip the assembly down, taking note of the order and condition of the parts. The bush is in the centre of the long arm, and should be easy to push out by hand. If seized, knock the bush out, clean it and - provided it is in reasonable condition - regrease and reassemble. Reassembly looks extremely difficult, but it's easy once you know the procedure. Assemble the spring (taking care that the spring ends have located in their respective housings), the two washers and the bush, then partly tighten the centre bolt. With the assembly part tightened, the long arm can be turned against the spring, past the raised centre boss on the short arm, after which the screw can be fully tightened. The tensioner should now have a strong spring action and instant response when released.
Tensioner idler wheels on early Mark 2 bikes are fitted with 6mm centre bolts. There are no

Using and Maintaining a Brompton

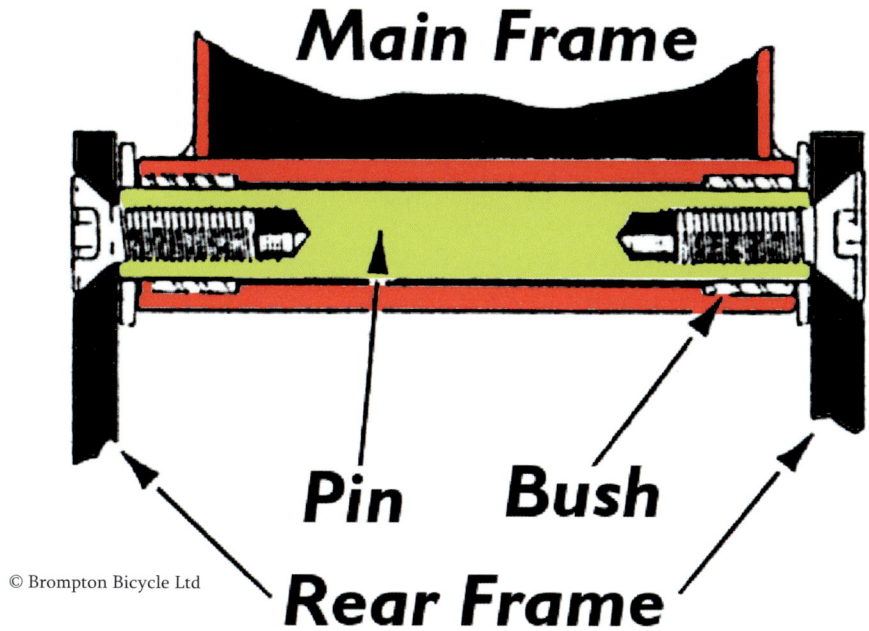

© Brompton Bicycle Ltd

Once play becomes apparent in the rear pivot, the bushes can be sparingly oiled as below. The Allen head screw in the foreground must not be touched, and should be flush with the paintwork as here. Note the low frame number of 7110, traceable to 1992 (see appendix IV).

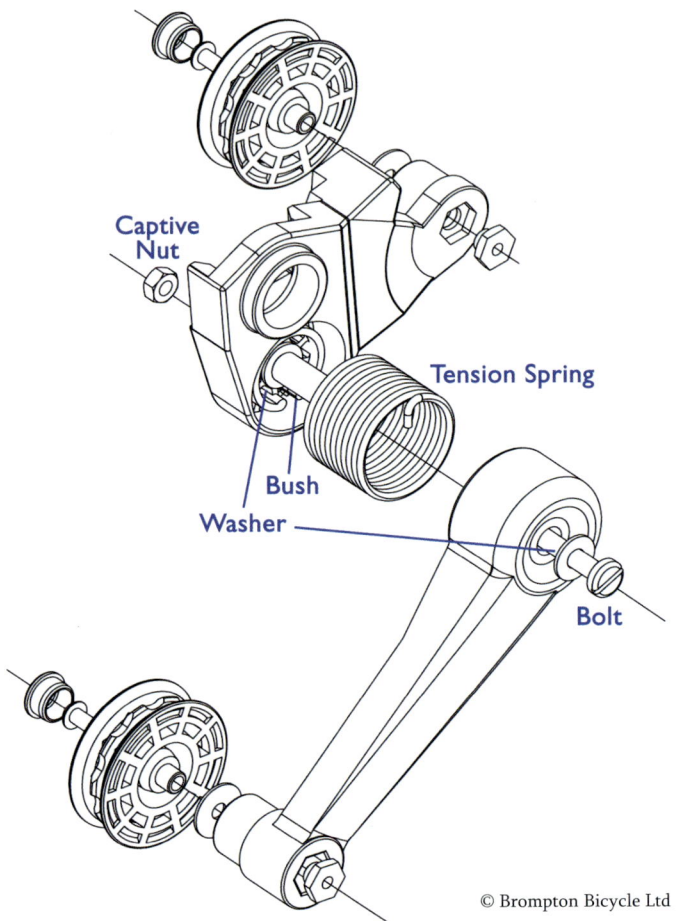

This exploded view is of the latest 6-speed chain tensioner. Earlier tensioners do not have the floating idler pulleys, and very early examples have threads cut into the plastic, rather than replaceable captive nuts, but the basic design is the same. The spring must be assembled with the ends engaged in the slots, and the bolt partly tightened. The arm can then be flipped over the raised boss, and the bolt fully tightened. The jockey pulleys can also be dismantled for cleaning and lubrication.

spares available for these, so the whole tensioner assembly will have to be replaced if problems occur. The same is true for slightly more recent tensioners with 5mm bolts, which can suffer from stripped threads, and again the only practical answer is to replace the assembly. Tensioner idler wheels can become partially clogged with road dirt and muck, although this doesn't usually cause problems, other than rough running. Dismantle each wheel, checking the position of all washers, and check the steel bearing bushes. If these are badly worn or corroded, the idler wheel will need to be replaced. If satisfactory (some play is fine) thoroughly remove all traces of road dirt and grit - a small saw blade will help remove trapped debris in bad cases. Oil the bearings, reassemble the idler wheels, and with the tensioner back on the bike (but the chain off) check that the wheels, rear sprocket and chainring line up with each other with the tensioner in the folded and unfolded position. Small alignment problems can be dealt with by fitting or removing washers, but in a bad case the tensioner arm may be bent, and possibly cracked, and will have to be replaced. All the above also applies to the 'floating' idler wheels fitted to the 2,4,6 and 12-speed, but in this case the wheels also need to float freely along their shaft as well as revolving smoothly.

Worn chains, chainrings and sprockets can also cause problems. The Brompton chainring will last for years, but chains and smaller 12- or 13-tooth sprockets need regular replacement, and must be replaced together. In an emergency a worn sprocket can usually be turned around and put on backwards. A build up of dirt, grass or mud around the sprocket can cause the chain to jump mysteriously and intermittently, but this is easily solved by careful cleaning. Again, the smaller sprockets are particularly vulnerable to this.

Lighting

The Brompton has always suffered from lighting problems. Wiring looms have a tough life as the bike folds and unfolds, rear filament lamp bulbs failed if the rear frame was folded under carelessly, and dynamos suffered from vibration and water ingress. From 2010, Brompton eradicated the bottle dynamos and troublesome old-fashioned bulbs, offering instead a special narrow version of Shimano's hub dynamo, allied to a halogen front lamp and LED rear standlight, or for those with £338.50 to spare, a SON hub dynamo, light-sensing Busch & Muller front LED lamp and rear standlight. The latest option is a Shutter Precision SV-8 hub dynamo, Busch & Muller front light and cheaper (but perfectly adequate) Spaninga rear stand light. This set will weigh more than an old bottle dynamo, but otherwise ticks all the boxes: powerful, reliable, efficient and reasonably light. Electric variants are self-powered by the traction battery... an excellent solution.

New SP dynamo hubs (above) are very reliable and light compared to many other hub dynamos. However they involve extra wiring and mounting fittings (above left) so battery powered lights like the Cateye Volt 400 are a lighter solution.

For leisure or infrequent users, for whom lifting the bike in and out of a car-boot is more important than daily all-weather commuting, a hub dynamo set is heavy and expensive, so battery-powered LED lights probably make more sense. Brompton introduced a battery lighting set with the Mark 4, but the two versions of the Spaninga LED rear light and diminutive S-sun LED front light were never more than adequately powerful, and reliability left much to be desired. The front light was later replaced by a much better Cateye Volt 300, which fitted in place of the reflector above the mudguard… a better position on a bike that needs to fold regularly and rapidly.
The latest Cateye 500LM is compact and powerful, and the internal lithium-ion 18650 battery can be recharged via a USB port. These batteries may only survive for a year or two of hard use, but the battery cartridge is replaceable, and you can buy spares, and keep one in the pannier for emergencies or longer journeys. The 500LM costs £55, but don't be tempted to save a few pounds by buying it elsewhere, as the Brompton version comes with a model-specific bracket.
Brompton's optional Spaninga LED rear light is excellent: it fits in place of the rear reflector, costs £25 and is bright and reliable, although charging three AAA batteries can be fiddly.

Brake Problems
The brakes on the Brompton have gradually improved over the years, although by modern commuter bike standards, Mark 1 and 2 brakes are positively dangerous. If you can afford it, upgrade to the latest caliper and brake blocks, which will have a near miraculous effect. A cheaper option is to fit the latest cartridge-type brake blocks (currently the Brompton-specific Fibrax ASH410-BR), which will give much better braking.

The early design of side-pull brake (above left) was inefficient when compared to the modern dual-pivot brake (above right).

In 2013 more compact and powerful brake levers were introduced replacing older style levers which were of an alloy and plastic construction and a bit flexible. Post 2013 levers are a worthwhile upgrade but you will need to change inner cables as well.
Older cables are heavy and extremely inefficient, unless well lubricated. Even on newer bikes, water ingress can be a problem, and if the cable isn't well oiled, it will quickly corrode. The only answer is to remove and clean the inner cable and feed it back with lashings of oil. If in doubt, replace the inner - again with plenty of oil. It isn't expensive, so replace it before it fails, because failure can be serious… There isn't usually any need to replace the outer cable unless

Changing from pre-2013 brake levers (above) to post-2013 levers (right) will result in more powerful braking. Post 2016 levers also feature threaded attachment points for gear changers.

it's clearly damaged, but modern cables, such as the Alligator I-Link weigh only half as much as traditional types and are more efficient too. They're not expensive (especially if bought direct from China) and worth every penny. Precise cable routing is essential and must exactly follow the original. The new cable must also be exactly the right length - watch out, newer long-wheelbase bikes have a different cable. But in most cases removing, oiling and refitting the inner will cure any problems.

Alloy wheel rims have been fitted to Bromptons from early Mark 2 days. These offer much improved wet weather braking over steel, but have a tendency to wear. The alloy rims on the Brompton and other small-wheeled bikes are particularly vulnerable, due to their reduced surface area, and on a well-used commuter bike they may need replacing every couple of years. Cleaning (pick out any grit or metal particles) and/or replacing brake blocks regularly will help reduce rim wear, but in the end, it's just something users have to put up with.

Keep an eye on rim wear and as with brake cables, aim to replace the rims long before they fail. On pre-Mark 4 bikes, judging the degree of wear is a matter of experience. Any obvious wear lip either side of the rubbing surfaces, early signs of rim distortion, or a rhythmic knock under braking, particularly after inflating the tyres, can mean imminent rim failure. This is a job for a dealer, unless you are experienced at wheel building. On later bikes, a telltale indicator groove is machined into the rim, the idea being that the rim should be replaced when the groove is no longer visible, but this is not a 100% accurate system, so regular inspection is still important. Overheating of rims can be a potential problem after severe and prolonged braking. Most commuters will be doing well to get their rims lukewarm, but ride down a twisty mountain pass on 16-inch wheels with alloy rims and after descending several thousand feet, tyre failure becomes a real possibility through the build-up of heat from the brakes. Quite simply, there's less rim to absorb the heat, so it can build up to dangerous levels more quickly than it would on a big-wheeled bike. The answer is to take it easy, or adopt one of the alternatives...

Failure of alloy rims is probably the Brompton's primary weakness today, and there are two permanent solutions for bikes that get very hard use. In dry conditions, steel rims offer a complete cure, but be prepared for braking efficiency to plummet in the wet. Modern high-efficiency brake blocks will improve matters, but little research has been done into this. A small disk brake is the best option - Kinetics in Glasgow produces several kits (you need replacement forks), both cable and hydraulic, but expect to pay nearly as much as for the bike!

Gears

Hub gears are more reliable and much less susceptible to dirt and damp than derailleurs, and as long as the sprocket is replaced at the same time as the chain, the hub itself should last for a considerable mileage - in the tens or even hundreds of thousands of miles. Sturmey-Archer hubs made before July 1987 were fitted with an oiling point, so Mark 1 Bromptons and very early Mark 2s can be topped up as required. More recent hubs are pre-greased at the factory, the manufacturers claiming that routine lubrication is not required between major services, when the hub should be stripped and reassembled with fresh grease. True enough, a hub that has seen gentle leisure use will last for years or even decades without fresh lubricant, but hard-ridden commuter bikes need better lubrication than old grease can provide.

The most important element of servicing is to replace the grease once it has gone hard or been washed out. Quite when this might be is a matter for judgement. A very noisy hub can mean a lack of grease, but partially seized pawls and ratchets can also go ominously quiet, suggesting hardened grease. If a well-used hub develops a problem, such as a sticky unreliable change or a missing gear, lack of lubrication may well be the cause, so don't replace the hub without investigating. In any event, oiling will do no harm, but once you start, you have to continue. Neither Sturmey nor SRAM hub gears are sealed, so with oil lubrication they effectively operate on the 'total loss' principle, as car engines and gearboxes once did. As there is no oiling point, the bicycle must be laid on its side, the indicator chain removed, and a few drops of light oil run into the hole. It makes sense to do this whenever the wheel is off for other purposes, such as mending a puncture. Don't overdo it, because the oil that runs out of the hub will be as black as ink, but make sure to oil the hub at least every six months, and immediately after riding through heavy rain or floods.

With the bike lying on its side and the indicator unscrewed and removed, oil can be dripped into the hole. This is an early 3-speed, but the technique is much the same for newer bikes. A few drops will last quite a while in dry weather.

Adjustment is not too precise an art with any of the 3-speed hubs. As a general rule, if the cable is just tight in first gear, and just slack in third gear, it's right. The 5-speed Sturmey hubs are much more critical and need to be carefully adjusted using a coloured band on the indicator chain, which should be flush with, or up to 1.5mm proud of the axle in second gear. The indicator chain should be just slack in gear five.

Another common problem with the 5-speed is failure to align the guide roller with the cable pulley assembly after replacing the rear wheel. Poor alignment or lubrication will result in an inconsistent change, and possible damage to the hub.

Above: Gear triggers, from left to right, 'Classic' Sturmey-Archer 3-speed (up to April 2001), Sturmey-Archer 5-speed (1994-early 2001), SRAM 3-speed (April 2001- January 2005), Brompton 3-speed (from January 2005), Brompton 2-speed (from April 2002).

The Brompton has used three gear shifters over the years. From the very start of production until April 2001, all 3-speed Sturmey bikes were fitted with Sturmey-Archer's wonderful 'Classic' 3-speed trigger. Developed in the late 1930s, the Classic is arguably the most successful gear trigger ever devised, and still in production, after more than 70 years. In the 1930s, most gear shifters relied on friction to select and hold gears, but the Classic was 'indexed', so that the shifter moved to each gear precisely and stayed there. If properly adjusted and treated to a drop of oil every few months, these triggers rarely go wrong, and if they do, replacements and basic spares are cheap and easy to find almost anywhere in the world. Early 5-speeds were fitted with a pair of 3-speed triggers, which was a less than ideal solution - difficult to understand, and difficult to adjust for the less mechanically minded, but at least the triggers were reliable.

From June 1994, the single-cable 5-speed was introduced, and Brompton had to choose between a twistgrip or the 'Nimbus' thumb shifter. To ease the cable run, and keep weight to a minimum, the company opted for the Nimbus, but it was a rather crude thing, the gears being locked in position largely by friction rather than positive stops. With age, the action of these triggers can become quite sloppy, but more friction can be applied by removing the large red centre cap, and tightening the crosshead screw beneath. If the controller still won't hold onto first or second gear reliably, it's best replaced, as inaccurate gear selection can damage the hub.

With the demise of the 5-speed in early 2001, it was back to the archetypal 3-speed trigger until April 2001, after which all bikes were fitted with the SRAM 3-speed hub and 'Torpedo' shifter. This was broadly similar to the Sturmey-Archer trigger, but less precise, and certainly less robust.

From April 2002, the '2x3' 6-speed model was introduced, the 2-speed derailleur element being controlled by a new shifter designed by Brompton. This has been generally quite successful but it's made largely of plastic and open to the elements at the top, so it needs a drop of light oil every few months, or whenever the action becomes heavy.

There is a widespread assumption that plastic components do not need lubrication - they do! The only difference to metals is that some plastics are damaged by mineral oils, so it's generally safer to use something plant-based such as olive oil. Oil sparingly, but the oil will be washed out quickly, so make sure to repeat in poor weather.

From January 2005, Brompton introduced the 'universal' rear frame, suitable for either SRAM or Sturmey hubs, and matched it with a new universal 'Y' shifter, compatible with either hub. This met with a less enthusiastic response than the 2-speed shifter, mainly because it replaced the supremely ergonomic and effective Sturmey Classic shifter, which was bound to be a hard act to follow. As with the 2-speed, a drop of oil will keep the mechanism running smoothly but note that Brompton says lubrication is not recommended, and may cause the shifter to jump past gear 2 when changing up.

From 2016 the separate 2x3 gear changers were redesigned and integrated with the brake levers. They were masterpieces of CAD design, but made almost entirely from plastic and prone to sticking. If light oiling fails to cure 3-speed problems, it's quite acceptable to fit something else. Sturmey-Archer produces several 3-speed triggers, of which the Classic is still probably the best.

Integrated 2x3 dual shifters are - for some - complicated to use but are also prone to sticking.

Happily, the 4-speed shifter fitted to some P- and T-line bikes seems to work much better. This may encourage Brompton to return to the concept of a single integrated gear-shifter operating both the hub and derailleur on 6- and 12-speed bikes. A real technical challenge.

Like most derailleurs, the new 4 speed derailleur P and T Line models have their own built in set of adjustment controls needed to keep them working smoothly. The derailleur itself features upper and lower limiter screws to make sure the chain does not come off at either end of the sprocket and there is a barrel adjuster attached to the 4-speed shifter that will help you tighten or loosen the inner cable tension to make sure your gear shifts are smooth.

Brompton's derailleur system, launched in 2021, has both limiter screw adjusters (the small silver screws at the top of the derailleur body, far left) and an inline cable length adjuster (left) allowing you to easily dial in smoother shifting.

Dismantling hubs is best avoided. Even the humble 3-speed hub is a complex piece of precision machinery, and stripping and reassembly is only practical for those with some engineering knowledge. The 5-speed is even more delicate, and servicing really is a matter for an engineer familiar with hub gears, an endangered species these days. If you really do want to have a go at repairing the hub, Sturmey-Archer keep .pdf files covering maintenance of all new and recent hub gears

Below: Brompton has used both SRAM (left) and Sturmey-Archer (right) 3-speed hubs but bikes from January 2005 have universal rear frames that will accept either make.

Fortunately, internal hub failures are rare, and apart from lubrication and cable adjustment, the only regular servicing necessary is adjustment of the hub bearings, which can be done by a home mechanic with care. A very small amount of 'play' or looseness at the rim is normal, but adjustment will be necessary when this play becomes excessive.

Ideally, the hub should be mounted in a vice, but adjustment can also be made on the bicycle. In both the 3- and 5-speed, the right-hand bearing (the one under the sprocket) should be left alone, and adjustment carried out on the other side. If making the adjustment on the bike, loosen the left-hand axle nut sufficiently for the rear frame to spring away from the hub slightly - it may need to be gently knocked to accomplish this. With the hub secured on the right side - either in the Brompton frame or a vice - but the left side loose, the amount of play will probably have increased, but it will reduce as the wheel is refitted and/or the axle nuts are fully tightened, so it must be adjusted slightly loose at this stage.

To adjust the bearings, you will need a Sturmey-Archer cone spanner, or similar very thin 5/8"AF or 16mm metric spanner. Carefully loosen the outer locknut, and make the adjustment with the underlying bearing cone. This should be carefully tightened (preferably by hand) until resistance is felt, then backed off a little and the lock nut retightened. If correctly adjusted, the sprocket should spin easily, with noticeable side-to-side play, and the wheel should rotate freely, with a little play at the wheel rim. Finally, either refit the hub to the bike, or tighten the left-hand axle nut and recheck for freedom of rotation and play. The hub should be completely free running, and there should now be just discernible play at the rim. Final adjustment may take a few attempts. If in doubt, err towards loose bearings, as tight bearings will damage the hub. If you're not sure of your abilities make sure you use a bike shop with experience of working on hub gears.

Tyres

Tyres are a subject of endless debate, and have changed quite rapidly over the last decade or so. The first of the new breed of light and free-rolling 349mm tyres was the Primo, which arrived in 1996, and single-handedly changed the prospects for bikes with 16-inch wheels, which could now roll as well as a typical 26-inch bike. Brompton's own 'Yellow Flash' tyre followed, using much the same technology, but with a light sporty tread. There was also a 'Green Flash' option featuring a kevlar under layer to improve puncture resistance, although it was a little slower and less sprightly on the road. These tyres weighed about 240 grams each, a huge advance for the day.

In 2008/9 the small tyre market was thoroughly shaken up when Schwalbe discontinued the unsatisfactory Stelvio and announced that the existing Kojak range would be extended to include 349mm. During the same period, Brompton altered both its tyres after a few cornering scares. The newer tyres can be distinguished by the change from black to grey shoulders, made of a softer rubber to improve grip when cornering hard.

In 2010, Brompton discontinued the Yellow Flash, leaving the kevlar tyre as the definitive base-level option. Options included the heavier, but tough Schwalbe Marathon. For ultimate puncture resistance, albeit with a considerable weight and rolling penalty, the Schwalbe Marathon Plus provided an even tougher option.

In early 2018, Brompton rather controversially dropped its own tyre altogether, leaving it totally reliant on Schwalbe, which thenceforth supplied the existing Marathon Racer in a 35x349mm size as the standard Brompton tyre, with the Kojak as a sportier option (joined by the One in 2019), and Marathon Plus as a more puncture-proof variant. Continental spotted this rather unhealthy monopoly, and responded with the 35x349mm Urban in early 2020. This tyre has a remarkable 116psi rating (don't try it!), weighs a mid-range 267g, and has relatively thick rubber under the centre of the tyre, and nice flexible walls, attributes suggesting good puncture-proofing and a fast tyre. It's a good 'jack-of-all-trades' for someone who wants a fairly fast tyre with the security of a decent amount of tread (most of the racy tyres are slicks). As mentioned in the 'Upgrades' section above, the latest arrival is the 32 x 349mm Aceoffix Flyer, a 210 gram folding tyre, which seems to tick every box, but it will be a while before tyre life and safety have been verified. By all means try it.

Continental's Urban tyre (left) has grown in popularity since its 2020 introduction, largely down to its great jack-of-all-trades properties. It strikes a nice balance between weight, comfort, puncture protection and grippy tread. The Aceoffix Flyer tyre (right) looks to compete with the Urban and weighs around 57 grams less per tyre.

Rather a niche use for a Brompton, but if riding on muddy or snowy surfaces very regularly, you may want to consider Schwalbe's Winter tyre, introduced in 2014 as a rather narrow 30x349mm knobbly tyre with metal studs implanted in the surface. Schwalbe say it is suitable for on-road riding as well, if somewhat noisy. There are anecdotal reports of the studs dropping out after heavy use on tarmac and Schwalbe themselves note '...to ensure that spikes are permanently fixed, tyres should be run-in for about 40km on asphalt/tarmac, while avoiding any fast acceleration or heavy braking.'

Even should the studs all eventually drop out you are still left with a knobbly tyre for use on slippy mud, within the limits of what a small, narrow tyre can handle. Despite this - and the fact the tyres are really designed for compacted snow and glassy ice - they seem to have found a niche in the UK's temperate climate and are still for sale in 2024 but cost over £80 per pair. Note they are heavy (465g per tyre), slow on tarmac and you'll need to tape up your frame to prevent the studs scratching it when folded.

If you want an 'off-road lite' tyre you might consider Schwalbe's kevlar-beaded Almotion, introduced in 2023 as an after-market option. It has the impressive statistics of only 239g for a 35x349mm treaded tyre that has the same puncture rating as the Schwalbe Marathon. It actually appeared the previous year, available only on one of the 'special editions', the Brompton Barbour. Whilst it looks good on paper only time will tell if it stands up to heavy real-world Brompton-style use.

Schwalbe's Brompton-sized Winter tyre (left) is heavy and not ideal for use on tarmac but has found a niche as it is still for sale ten years after its introduction.

The later Almotion (far left) has a much less heavy duty off-road tread but is much lighter and freer-rolling. Introduced in 2023, the jury is still out on its longevity.

If you've bought a bike fitted with very early tyres like the Raleigh Record or cheap unbranded modern ones, do upgrade them as soon as possible. Primo and Brompton Yellow Flash are rare today, but they're good tyres that can be left on the bike. Kojak is slightly heavier, but more durable, and still reasonably fast. The Schwalbe One and the Continental are impressive tyres. The One seems to be the fastest option, but the Continental is cheaper and is more durable. At the other end of the scale, the Marathon is heavy and frumpy on the road, but should be relatively durable and puncture-proof, and the Marathon Plus is indestructible, but the downsides go on forever, so only for the puncture-paranoid!

Whatever tyre you use, tyre pressures are far more critical than they would be on a big-wheeled conventional bike, particularly with heavier, less free-running tyres.

As a guide, the rear tyres should be inflated to around 70psi, the actual pressure depending on your weight, and the road conditions. A harsh ride suggests overinflation, while a 'soggy' bouncy ride and increased pedal effort suggests under-inflation. The front tyre needs about 15psi less, but add a bit more if carrying a heavy pannier. Paradoxically, it's particularly important to keep the 'slower' puncture-protected tyres well-inflated, because they don't flex as well as the sportier ones and will be hard work.

A final word on tyres... don't assume that a narrow section tyre is going to be faster than a wider, sporty one! Some very wide tyres, like the 40mm Greenspeed Scorcher, work well on the Brompton and some narrow ones like the Schwalbe Stelvio do not.

Brompton Bicycle

Handlebars

Slight fore and aft adjustment of the handlebars is permissible, but this must be done very sparingly, and the cable runs and handlebar catch adjustment carefully checked with the bike folded. There is no vertical adjustment, but this is less important today, with three height options, from the flat straight Low 'S' bars, through the original Mid 'M' to the extra-tall High 'H'. The multi-position 'P' has been withdrawn, but you might find a set with a dealer if you want to try this odd, but comfortable option.

If buying an older bike second-hand, check carefully against the chart. Older bars - whether braced or not - should be replaced with the latest design, as aluminium handlebars have a finite fatigue life, and with a second-hand bike, you have no way to judge how the bike has been (mis)used. At the very least, examine the handlebars carefully – if there are any cuts, cracks or other damage, they must be replaced straight away. If upgrading to alternative bars, bear in mind that the inner and outer brake and gear cables will probably also have to be changed, as they are a different length. Older short wheelbase bikes have different rear cables too, and on bikes with Saccon brakes, the cables are different again. Cable length and routing must be exactly right, or there may be problems folding.

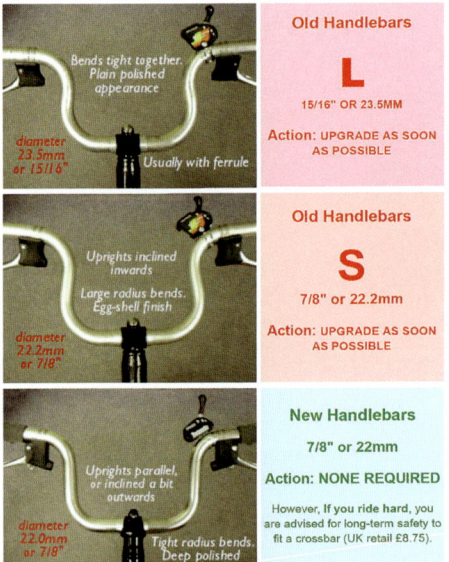

When handlebar failures became a problem in 2000, Brompton produced a chart to assist users and dealers identify whether they needed to be concerned. The 'L' bars are the early GB Cycles bars, few of which will remain in use today, the 'S' bars are the Neobike bars used from 1995-1999, and the modern Humpert bars are at the bottom. 'L' or 'S' bars are still eligible for the free crossbar upgrade, but after all this time, new bars would be strongly recommended anyway. The age of a bike can be confirmed by checking the date stamped on the Sturmey hub shell, and comparing the frame number with the dates listed in appendix V, but neither of these methods provide a guarantee. The latest bars are extremely strong, but you might be lucky to find a crossbar still for sale (part number QXBARS-D, £13.50 at 2020 prices) for those who ride hard and want extra security.

The crossbar (right) is being fitted between the two vertical parts of the handlebars, and will now be clamped in position. This 1998 bike has Neobike bars (and some telltale scoring on the surface) and should certainly be braced or replaced as soon as possible.

Folding Pedal

After a high mileage (or quite a low mileage if you ride hard), the bearing in the folding pedal will require replacement. Once play becomes evident, the life of the bearing can be extended by running a few drops of oil past the dust seal once in a while, with the bike lying on its side. Another option is spray grease inserted past the seal using a slim application tube. If you succeed, this sort of treatment can double the pedal life. Brompton used to recondition the pedals at a reasonable price, and it was possible to buy the bearing in its alloy block and do it yourself, but your only option today is a complete new pedal, currently £55. Removal requires a 24mm AF socket, and when replacing the pedal, make sure to fit the washer first.

If you find yourself getting through Brompton folding pedals, a cheaper folding, demountable or conventional pedal can be fitted instead, but at the expense of a wider folded package.

Front Mudguard Stay Hook

On older bikes these were made from a bent section of mudguard stay. These are easily bent out of shape, but just as easily straightened. A loose hook can cause the bike to fall apart when folded, and a tight one will fit too snugly around the chainstay, making the bike difficult to unfold. It's worth noting that two slightly different stays were produced for 3- and 5-speed, bikes, the 5-speed example being longer, to accommodate the wider 5-speed gear shifter mechanism. Since early 2000, a moulded nylon block has been fitted instead and these are retrofittable to all older bikes, except the 5-speed.

Handlebar Catch

This small catch performs a vital role, keeping the handlebars clamped against the folded package. For many years, the catches caused problems, giving insufficient clamping pressure after prolonged use. This can be permanently solved very easily by looping a small cable-tie through the holes and gently tightening it. Modern catches are more durable, but may still need a cable-tie if the bike is folded very frequently. The catch must enter the nipple completely square for best results. The nipple can be screwed in and out to allow for slight variations in package width caused by altered handlebar or brake lever position. Note too that the handlebar catch securing screw has a tendency to work loose, or even fall off. If it doesn't work, check that it's still there! T-line bikes use a completely different system that can be adjusted with a small allen key, but the clamping pressure is still barely adequate for the job and the new catches are just as unpredictable.

Lower Stop Disc

The other key adjustment with respect to folding is the lower stop disc that traps the lowered seat pillar, thus holding the folded bike together. Early eccentric discs have a tendency to work loose and must always be offset to the left, so that pressure from the seat pillar tightens the screw. Clearance between the pillar and stop when fully folded should be 3mm. If problems persist, a later-style concentric disc is a worthwhile upgrade. Clearance on these can be reduced to 1-2mm.

Rear Mudguard Stays

The rear mudguard stays on the 'L' type are very vulnerable to clumsy folding, and can become quite badly bent. In mild cases, the stays can simply be pushed towards the tyre, lifting the mudguard clear of the tread, but if the stays are seriously buckled, they will have to be removed, straightened in a vice and refitted. Note that the three stays are different lengths (shortest at the front) and must be refitted exactly as they came off the bike. If the stays are badly bent or corroded, treat yourself to a set of titanium stays, which will cost over £40, but they are less likely to bend and will never corrode.

Other Weak Spots
Brompton has been lucky, or perhaps it's down to Andrew Ritchie's dogged attention to detail, but major failures have been rare. Apart from the handlebar issue, breakages have been mercifully few. A handful of frames failed just forward of the hinge, a metallurgy issue that seems to have been resolved, and older rear frames may fail through invisible internal corrosion if used regularly on salted winter roads. A recent failure has been the short-lived nickel-plated alloy seatpost that replaced the titanium post in late 2010. Much cheaper than the titanium post, and only a few grams heavier, these proved to be vulnerable to pitting in use and were rapidly withdrawn. There are no safety issues, but a badly pitted seatpost will damage the frame bush and should be replaced. The only alternative is a steel pillar or an aftermarket titanium pillar from the Far East.

An odd occasional failure on early Superlight titanium forks is a split or bulge in the steerer-tube where it has been gripped by the 'quill' in the handlebar stem. The main symptom is an inability to tighten the stem properly, but none appear to have failed, Replacement with later, stronger forks should be easy, but the distorted parts may have locked together, making removal a real headache. If the tube is undamaged, it can be reinforced with an aftermarket steel sleeve, for peace of mind.

Other cycle parts, like cranks and chains, may break once a while, just as they do on conventional bicycles, but there are no specific problem areas. The unusually low bottom bracket bearing seems particularly vulnerable to mud and salt spray, but they're not expensive to replace.

Using the Brompton

Rail Commuting
This is the classic reason for owning a Brompton, and in most people's eyes, the raison d'être of the bike, although as we have seen, Andrew Ritchie also perceived the bike as a tool for motorists hemmed in by parking restrictions. Some motorists certainly do park on the edge of town and ride in by Brompton, but the big market turned out to be amongst rail commuters. When the Brompton was being developed, most trains had spacious luggage areas in at least one carriage. These areas had been designed to carry parcels, but were being used almost exclusively for bicycles by the early 1990s. However, on newer trains luggage space largely evaporated, and commuters began to look for practical alternatives.

Today, most trains have space for two or three non-folding bicycles, but there are complex peak hour restrictions, and at other times the number of bikes is usually strictly limited. There are no restrictions on the carriage of folding bikes, but for all sorts of practical reasons, if travelling at peak times, it makes sense to use the most compact design, and this is where the Brompton excels.

The front pannier system is essential for commuting, so there is very little point in purchasing a rack-equipped bike, because the rack serves little purpose. The classic mid-height bars are ideal for urban use, and there is little advantage in buying anything too fancy unless you are cycling some distance, or in a very hilly area, so a C-Line is ideal for rail commuting. If you can afford the extra £1,000 or so, a P-Line will be significantly lighter, and thus easier to carry. Some railway companies have placed peak hour restrictions on wheeling bikes within the station, so weight has become increasingly important. The Brompton offers a bonus over most other folding bikes in that it can be wheeled like a small suitcase, and this can be useful when crossing large railway or airport concourses.

A little known Brompton characteristic is that it can be used as a seat on a busy commuter train or platform, thus liberating a seat for someone else, much to the delight of the railway companies. The seat should be lowered right down, so that your weight passes to the floor via the seat pillar and not the rear rollers, which are easily broken. Lock the seat in this low position on a skew of about 45° and you should be able to sit on the mainframe. Folding bikes no longer need to be covered on trains in the UK, but it might make sense to use a cover on very busy services.

Donald Wilson, station master at Marylebone, gives the Brompton his seal of approval on Bike to Work Day during the late 1990s.

One of the Brompton's better known trademarks is the little trolley wheels - four on variants with a rear rack, and three on lightweight models, as here. The wheels are unsuitable for rough surfaces, but cope well with airport concourses and similar smooth surfaces. Brompton can supply larger 'Eazy Wheels' for bikes that are frequently used on rougher surfaces. Waiting for a train? Many owners aren't aware that the bike can be turned into a practical seat while waiting at a railway station, or even on the train itself. The saddle needs to be pushed right down, tilted towards the handlebars at about 45°, and locked with the pillar touching the ground (in contrast to pulling the bike along, when it should be raised a centimetre or so). The stem then carries most of the weight, and locks against the floor, preventing the bike from rolling away. Not enormously comfortable, but better than standing on a long train journey.

Buses and Aircraft
Bus and coach companies generally expect folding bikes to be covered, and as the door is usually beside the driver, cover the bike well in advance, and keep a low profile. Never use the word bicycle, and try to avoid conflict. Unlike a railway guard, a bus driver has complete autonomy when away from base, and can turn anyone away for any reason, so argument is futile. With these provisos, the Brompton can easily and conveniently be carried by bus, particularly the newer low-floor models.

Air transport causes many headaches. The Brompton used to be accepted as hold luggage in many places, but those carefree days are long-gone. It's certainly not impossible though, and should cost nothing, provided you travel with a lightweight machine and not much else. US manufacturer Bike Friday knows this market well, and that's why their bikes mostly dismantle and pack into a hard case, which will stand the rigours of automated and manual baggage handling.

Brompton finally gave in to consumer demand and announced its own 'Brompton Pod' hardcase in 2010, but like so many projects in the modern era, it didn't see the light of day as promised, although case manufacturer Polaris went it alone, launching the case as the EVA Brompton folding bike pod. The pod weighs less than 5kg, so complete with bike and a few clothes it should come in under the 23kg weight limit and typical 200+cm length+height+width restriction imposed by most airlines. Travelling by air is easier with a 'naked' bike, but damage is always a possibility. Putting the seat pillar right down will help, because this channels the weight of stacked luggage safely down the pillar. As Brompton discovered, weakened 'sacrificial' rear rollers can be helpful where the bike is likely to see rough handling. It can make sense to remove lights and reflectors too, as these are easily damaged. Beyond that, you are in the lap of the gods. Perhaps one in three air trips will see minor damage, but one in ten will result in serious problems, and very occasionally the frame will be distorted badly enough to make the bike unrideable. Rather unfairly, many airlines - principally the cheaper carriers - will impose an extra charge for a folding bike, even when it's within the size and weight limit of the free luggage allowance. Like many such rules, it's discriminatory, but there's nothing you can do. In some cases, if the check-in person is either sympathetic or stupid, it may help to describe the contents of the bag as 'sports goods'...

All airlines will expect the bike to be covered. The Brompton Pod will give the greatest protection, but it adds weight, and makes riding away from the airport almost impossible. A more practical alternative is the Brompton 'B' bag, a soft bag with 5mm of padding, but this will only really protect the machine against scratches. More recently Brompton introduced the more protective Transit Travel bag, made of heavy padded cordura with roller wheels - but at 3.6kg it's not something you'll want to be carrying around much when not in use. Some regular travellers argue that an ultra-thin membranous cover is the best option: cheap, light to transport and leaving the machine looking vulnerable, which might just prevent the baggage handlers from throwing it too hard. Most airlines will provide stickers to verify that the luggage is delicate, and there's not much else you can do but pray.

Electric bikes add an extra tier of complication. Local buses seem to have little experience with compact eBikes, but national operator National Express bans all eBikes. The railways have recently banned electric scooters, skateboards and other equipment, but in the UK at least, made it clear that eBikes are still welcome.

For air travellers, the bike (or power kit) must have passed a set of stringent tests known as UN38.3, but issues remain over the batteries. Packs of up to 100Wh (typically in lap-tops and other devices) are allowed with limited restrictions. Batteries of 100-160Wh are allowed with more rigorous restrictions, and larger batteries are not allowed at all. The Brompton battery is clearly outside the limit, and the company makes no smaller sizes, so the Brompton Electric would be more or less impossible to carry. The battery box of the Cytronex contains two 98Wh battery packs, which should be acceptable, because it's permissible to carry spares. Make sure to check before making a booking. The picture, both in terms of bikes and airlines, is pretty complex.

Riding

To anyone used to a conventional bike, small wheels might seem odd at first, but don't be misled - this isn't instability as such, but a reduced gyroscopic action from the smaller, lighter wheels. After getting acclimatized, most people learn to appreciate the faster steering and more rapid acceleration, but there's no escaping the fact that riding one-handed - as when indicating - requires more care. Extra vigilance is needed too, because smaller wheels are more likely to be affected by potholes and kerbs. On the other hand, the faster steering makes holes easier to avoid, and the smaller, lighter front wheel is more easily lifted up small kerbs. Riding a Brompton isn't more difficult, but you may find the techniques a little different.

Some cyclists criticize the Brompton for being hard work to ride, but this usually means they haven't actually ridden one, or have ridden it wrongly. Tyre pressures are of enormous importance, and as on page 203, it's worth making a few experiments to find the perfect pressures for your weight, tyres and regular commute. Never let the pressure drop too low. Saddle height is also very important, and arguably more important than it would be on a big-wheeled bike. The complication is that the saddle has to be brought up to the correct height every time it is unfolded, and finding that height can be difficult. There is quite a bit of adjustment available at the saddle end of the seat pillar, so with luck you can tweak the height by a centimetre or two until full extension of either the standard or extended pillar suits your build. This will make unfolding a quicker operation, and do your knees a real favour. Most people should be able to achieve this, if necessary by adding the Brompton saddle adapter pin (no longer made, but you might find one second-hand), which gives even greater adjustability. For shorter people, Brompton's 'Saddle Height Insert' only costs a few pounds and can solve the issue at a stroke, provided your height is within a certain range. It's a corrugated plastic tube that can be cut to the correct length, then located inside the frame, under the seat bush. A more drastic permanent alternative, is to cut off the base of the standard seat pillar, then form a new flare at the right height. You can make the pillar very short this way, but if you go too far, the bike will fail to lock together when folded. This is a job for a skilled engineer, and it makes the bike unrideable for taller people, but will bring the saddle up to the correct height every time.

It sounds obvious, but taller people using the telescopic seat pillar can put the main pillar at full extension, make the final adjustment using the telescopic section, then fold the bike using the main adjuster. This will leave a section sticking out from the folded bike, but the height will always be correct. In September 2011 Brompton announced the new High bar configuration for taller riders or those who want a more upright riding position. As well as taller handlebars, the stem was made a little longer. From 2017, the taller stem was altered again to move the hinge up by 30mm. This left the hinge protruding further from the folded package (but still lower than the saddle), while doubling the effect of a slightly taller stem, enabling universal handlebar to be fitted, hence the title M/H bar. Both options are claimed to lift the bars by 60mm and increase forward reach to the grips from the saddle increased by around 13mm. The post-2017 high model fits into all existing transportation bags and covers. The weight increase over an M-type is approximately 100g.

Riding style is important. Since 2008, Brompton has produced two different grades of rear suspension, with soft being the default on a new bike. Accepted wisdom is that the hard block suits hard riding, and the soft block suits gentler pottering, but this isn't necessarily the case. The hard block is only necessary with a rather aggressive riding style, which can otherwise make the rear of the bike bob wastefully up and down. With practice, smooth, steady pedal pressure works best, and doesn't need firm suspension.

Tyres we've mentioned already. The rolling resistance of the tyre can have a huge effect on the enjoyment of riding a small-wheeled bike, and if you don't enjoy it you will avoid using it, making the effort seem all the greater when you do, creating a negative spiral. Set a Brompton up correctly, and you can expect to ride at least 75% as far and as fast as you would with a good conventional bike.

Gearing has caused numerous queries and complaints in the past, but with the BWR wide-ratio hub now fitted to all six- and 12-speed variants these have been largely answered. The ordinary 3-speed hub is surprisingly effective for most purposes, and if you can live with a low top gear, the overall gearing can be reduced by fitting a larger rear sprocket, smaller chainring or both. The 6-speed now offers a sufficient range of gears for touring and commuting in hillier country, and again, the overall gearing can be reduced quite easily at the expense of a lower top gear. A

Using and Maintaining a Brompton

Above: The P6RX with touring pannier on the front and Rack Sack on the rear - ideal for extended touring, especially where you want to combine cycling and other forms of transport. The Rack Pack is specifically designed for the Brompton rear rack, with tall, stiffened sides. Sleeker options for lighter loads include the C-bag (above centre right) and the S-bag (above top right), the only bag that will fit the S-bars.

If you want even more capacity simple use of bungees will allow a surprisingly large amount to be carried on the rear rack if you can find your own suitably shaped bag (left). Even full camping gear can be accommodated though the example above looks a little 'tail heavy'.

Attaching various kinds of box is an extremely practical way for carrying everything from the small but valued to very sizeable loads indeed. The space over both front and rear wheels will carry loads of about equal size.

© Dave Holladay

Opposite above: Axelle Presse and Vincent Burgeon crossed Switzerland's Furka Pass with standard Brompton 6-speed gearing, the first time they had ridden such high mountains. It was 'very hard' according to Vincent.

simpler, lighter and cheaper solution is to fit a wide-ratio BWR in place of the AW hub. This has rather wide gaps between gears, but can give a very low first gear.

If none of these options is suitable, and you need to reduce gearing down to walking pace or even lower, a Mountain Drive internally-geared chainring will double the number of gears to six or twelve, and provide some extremely low ratios without compromising the high gears. But it's an expensive and heavy option. Hopefully, Brompton's new 12-speed will eliminate the need for such serious engineering. This utilises the existing 4-speed derailleur *and* 3-speed BWR hub.

Luggage & Touring
Brompton and a few aftermarket manufacturers produce a vast and ever growing range of panniers and bags for the front of the Brompton, and Steve Parry (see previous chapter) has made a few luggage block carriers designed to be fitted on the rear of the seat pillar to put another bag behind. An alternative is Brompton's own rear rack (now rather confusingly called the 'roller frame', which also facilitates the fitting of dynamo lights. The rack can either be fitted with twin miniature panniers or Brompton's own Rack Sack bag. With suitably shaped luggage and a few bungees it's possible to get a surprisingly large amount on top of the rack, the long length of the seatpost also providing some handy, extra support for big rear touring loads.

If you need even more space, for the likes of a fully loaded camping trip for example, one of the best trailer options is the Chubby (part of Dutch firm Radical Designs' Cyclone range of bike trailers). It has a plethora of user-friendly features, and its tough Cordura bag will accommodate a folded Brompton. What's more, with Brompton size wheels and a towbar quick-release (it fits in the trailer top pocket), the trailer makes a convenient carry-bag for the Brompton, with the addition of a shoulder strap. The bike remains very manoeuvrable with the trailer on, and the ball hitch system means one handed disconnection is possible and its Brompton-specific design means it doesn't stick out and add to the folded dimensions of the bike. The bag itself is removeable from the alloy frame for washing or should you want the option of using it as a flatbed too (you would need to add a load carrying platform of some kind to the bare aluminium frame). Aside of the extra rolling resistance of pulling two more tyres behind you, the only real downside is the cost of €600.

© Vincent Burgeon

The Chubby trailer from Radical Designs (above) is a pretty practical option for touring. It features a strong canvas bag that can also double as a carrying bag for the Brompton itself. Wheels and towbar can be accommodated in the top pocket so you are left with a piece of luggage that can be taken on other forms of transport.

The growth in long distance loaded touring has been one of the surprises of the Brompton story. From the pioneering rides of a few adventurous souls in the 1980s and '90s, the concept of touring on a folding bike with 16-inch wheels has become quite common today. The ability to combine cycling with other forms of transport - train, bus, taxi, ferry (even a foot ferry), hydrofoil and air - can greatly enhance the touring experience, and eliminate the uncertainty of booking cycle spaces ahead. It can also save a surprising amount of money, as folding bikes nearly always travel free.

The Folding Society has long excelled at demonstrating complex multimodal day trips and short tours, including some unusual transport, such as narrow gauge trains, electric trams, horse-drawn trams and a mountain railway, as well as the more obvious ferries and aircraft. The Brompton excels at this sort of thing, but a bike cover (not necessarily a bag) makes a lot of sense in places where big luggage might cause problems.

Touring Emergency Kit

In the early days, Brompton recommended touring with a pile of spares because so much on the Brompton was unusual or unique. If something went wrong, there were few dealers in the UK, let alone overseas, where some countries had to make do with a single outlet, and others had no Brompton dealer at all. Today, Brompton spares are available right around the world, and can be ordered from a number of internet mail-order specialists. Inevitably, of course, if you do have a problem it will be somewhere remote. Whether you're stuck in the Outer Hebrides or crossing Afghanistan, a few basic spares can save a great deal of legwork and delay. Top of the list must come tyres and inner tubes, both of which fail relatively frequently. You can get away with fitting a smaller tube, but the tyres must be accurately sized, and the Brompton's 349mm tyre is almost unknown in many countries. 16-inch tyres are not unusual, but there are different types, with a variety of 'bead seat' diameters and only the 349mm will fit the Brompton rims. Nominally 16-inch tyres can be anything from 305mm (very common), through 317mm, 335mm, 337mm (all quite rare) and 340mm (a French 400A) to 349mm, which is actually closer to 17-inch!

A spare tube folds up very small and weighs just over 100 grams. Whatever tyres you have fitted to the bike, consider carrying at least one Schwalbe Kojak or Continental Contact with foldable kevlar bead as a spare (Brompton part number: QTYRKOJAK). These weigh 175-215 grams, fold up quite small, and cost £30-40, but mail order experts like St John Street, Brilliant Bicycles and Condor may well charge less. You might never need it, but if you shred the sidewall on a Brompton tyre, a spare will provide excellent insurance. After tyres, spokes are probably the most common failure, and an hour spent oiling (a drop on the threads and a drop under each rivet head), then adjusting spokes *before you go* is a very worthwhile investment. And taking half a dozen spare spokes (and a tightening tool) should see your bike through the most gruelling tour. In theory there are several different lengths, but most failures occur in the rear wheel, and the 146mm rear spokes fitted to recent hub-geared bikes (QSPOK-146-SB-13G) will also fit most front wheels at a pinch. Superlight wheels, and the rear of all 1- or 2-speed bikes will need slightly longer spokes. Hub gear sprockets are a bit hard to find these days, but sprockets can be reversed in an emergency. Most Bromptons now use a 1/2"x3/16" chain,which is very common. The 4- and 12-speed derailleur use a slightly narrower 10-speed chain, but this is, again, pretty easy to find.

A smaller and lighter part that's very vulnerable is the Sturmey or SRAM hub gear indicator chain. If this breaks, or falls down a roadside drain during a puncture repair, you will be stuck in top gear, and hub gear parts are rare in most countries. There are five chains, so make sure to carry the right one. In an emergency, the actual chain links can be repaired with a bent nail or similar.

In terms of frequency, wheel rim failures probably come next, but if you depart with new or as-new rims, you should be able to travel many thousands of miles without a failure (serious accidents excepted of course). If a rim begins to fail, it usually bulges outwards long before catastrophic failure occurs. The bulge makes itself known as a rhythmic judder when the brakes are applied. If you're somewhere remote, and the failure has been caught at this early stage, it should be possible to carry on very cautiously with reduced tyre pressure, even for hundreds of miles. Another occasional failure point is the chain tensioner. This can get smashed in an accident, and bits sometimes drop off or seize up, especially in wet and/or freezing weather, so a complete spare tensioner (plus the vulnerable securing nut on the Sturmey-Archer 3-speed) will, once again, provide good insurance. The 2- and 6-speed derailleur tensioner is part number QCTADR, while all others are QCTA. Gear and brake cables are pretty standard, but it makes sense to carry at least one of each inner cable because they're light and take up little space. Front and rear mudflaps fail quite often, and the handlebar catch and bolt can drop off or break, but a failure won't leave you stranded. The same can't be said for the 'L' type rear mudguard, which might appear to be in good condition, but can shatter into pieces the first time you fold the bike clumsily. If undertaking a long tour, a spare mudguard (QMGBL-RL) might be worth considering.

Finally, prevention is always the best repair tip. Check the bike over carefully before undertaking a major expedition. We've already mentioned spokes as a priority, but if items like wheel rims, brake blocks or tyres look worn, replace them before you go! Once on the road, keep the tyres well inflated, and carry a small oil can and a tiny pot of grease. With well-inflated tyres, and occasional lubrication (frequent in wet weather) a Brompton can run for thousands of miles without a single reliability issue developing.

This example emergency repair kit (above) weighs about 1kg and comprises adjustable spanner, multitool, gear and brake cables, mini high pressure pump, spoke key, spokes and nipples, chain, hub gear indicator chain, inner tube and Schwalbe Kojak foldable tyre.

With the right kit a surprising range of repairs can be made roadside (right). © Andy & Sue Black

Flatbed trailers - above and below - are useful for unusually shaped and sized loads, whilst the rear rack can also be pressed into service as passenger space (left)!

Riding with Children
This is another growth area that Brompton simply hadn't expected, but child carriers are one of the most frequently requested accessories. Rear-mounted child seats will fit on the Brompton, just as they do on most other bikes, and being well clear of the rear wheel, they're also safer. The only point to watch is that the clamp will need to adapt to fit the Brompton's 32mm seat pillar.

By far the best solution for all children from babes-in-arms to small eight-year-olds is the ITChair, invented by Spanish Brompton distributor Bike Tech SL. It's a clever device that fits between the seat pillar and main frame tube, complete with saddle and folding foot rests (the latest aluminium version has fixed foot rests). Children absolutely love travelling this way, and once you've used it, you will be hooked too. The only minor downside is having to ride with your knees further apart than usual if carrying older children, but it's still a great way of - for example - getting from the station to a camping site. It is not a Brompton-approved accessory, but puts little additional strain on the bike, and provides a very safe space for a child. The Chair is not in regular production, and they are not always easy to find, new or second-hand. The only UK stockist is BikeFix of Emerald Street, London, and they should be able to help. Many users have fitted Brompton's handlebar strengthening crossbar (Brompton part number QXBARS-D) to give the child a safe handhold. These are now discontinued, but you might find one.

The Brompton itself can be adapted quite easily for older children. With shorter cranks, smaller pedals, lowered suspension (this puts the pedals closer to the ground) and straight 'S' type bars on a normal stem, the Brompton can be converted into an excellent folding child's bike, and all the elements are reversible as the child grows.

When the child grows too old to carry as a passenger a Brompton can be converted to produce a superb folding child's bike. The short handlebar stem shown on this early conversion can now be replaced with flat bars on a standard stem, but everything else is obligatory to produce a safe and reliable conversion.

If you really want a front-mounted seat, choose one that can clamp around the handlebar stem. In this design (left), the seat quick-releases, and the mounting block stays in place when the bike is folded. A front seat is sociable, but it's difficult to avoid bumps, and impossible to lift the wheel over small kerbs.

What not to do (below). This child seat has been fitted to the Brompton front carrier block. It looks convenient, but this is a dangerous place to carry a child, and the block (rated at 10kg) is really not strong enough to cope.

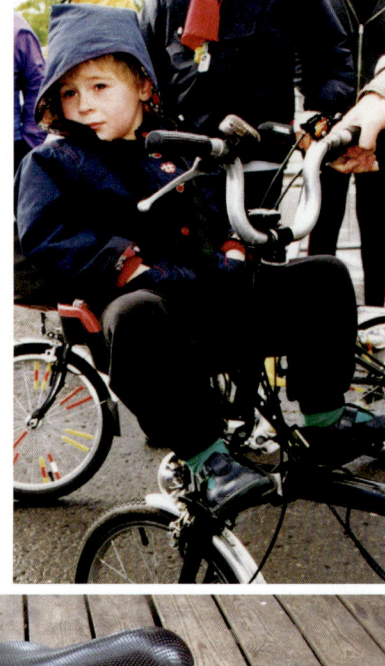

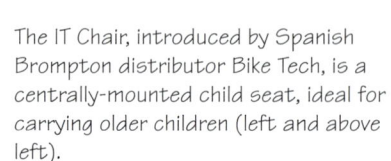

The IT Chair, introduced by Spanish Brompton distributor Bike Tech, is a centrally-mounted child seat, ideal for carrying older children (left and above left).

Using and Maintaining a Brompton

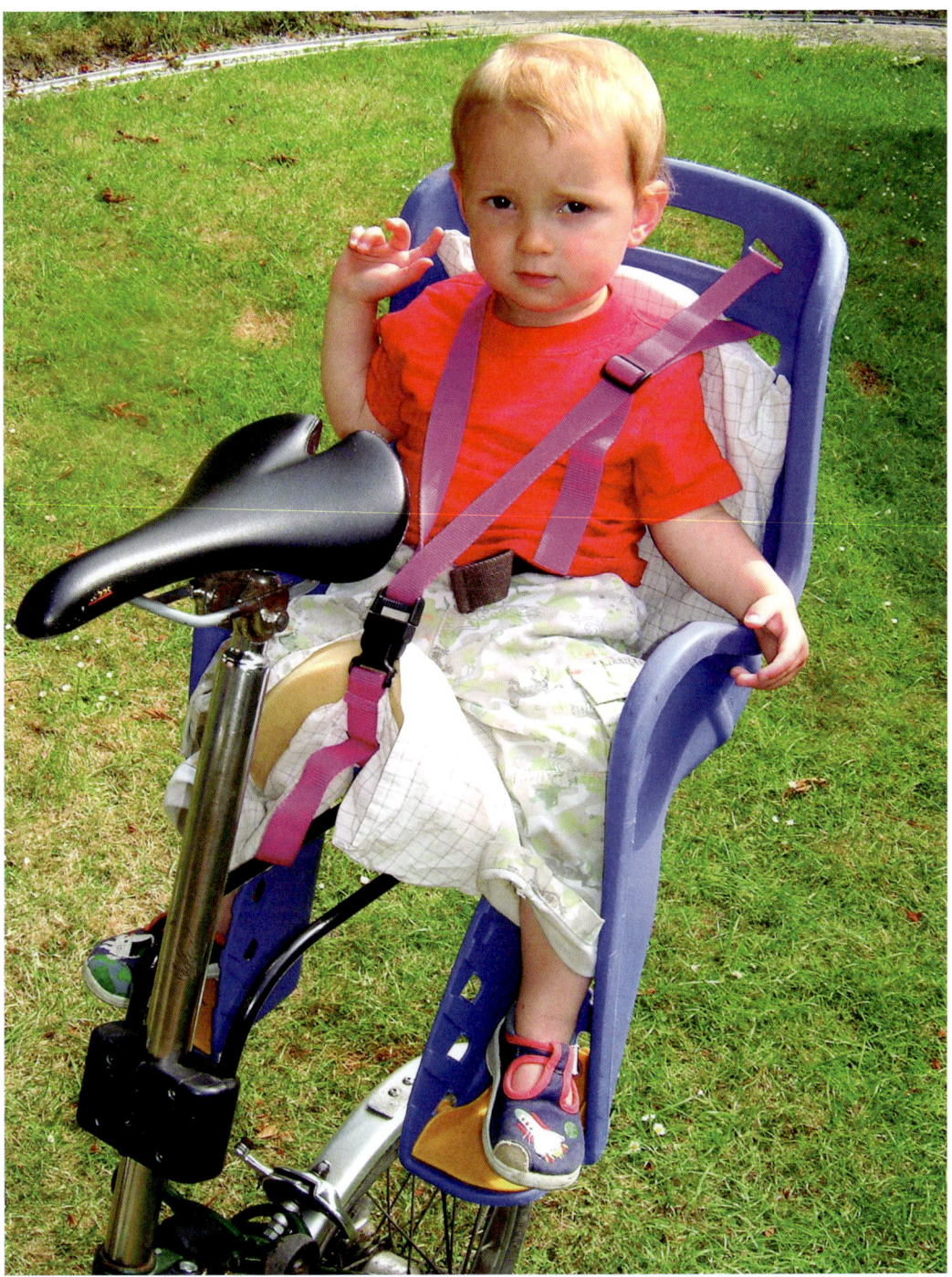

Rear-mounted child seat. The mounting block is now round the seat pillar, so it has to be slid to the top or removed when the bike is folded, but this is by far the best way to carry a child. The bike responds as normal, and the child sits in the empty space where a big rear wheel would normally be, so their hands and feet are well clear of danger. The clamp can be fitted lower to accommodate bigger children - up to four years old.

Brompton People & Places

The Early UK Brompton Scene

In the late 90s the Folding Society ran a series of three 'Folder Forum' shows - two at Weymouth, and the last at Ventnor on the Isle of Wight. The Folder Forums were open to all folding bikes, but had a strong Brompton influence, attracting an international crowd of enthusiasts.

(Left) Taking part in an agility test at Weymouth in 1996 is the late Channell Wasson, at that time the exclusive distributor for Brompton Bicycle in the United States.

Although billed as entertainment, the Folder Forum shows had a serious practical purpose, demonstrating that folding bikes (and perhaps the Brompton in particular) could change the way we travelled. In 1997, more than 100 cyclists departed from Weymouth by train for Wareham, where the party cycled to Norden to catch another train to Swanage on the Swanage Railway. Fitting that number of conventional bicycles on a normal service train would have been impossible, and the resulting television and magazine coverage put folding bikes firmly on the map.

The 1997 Folder Forum ride put folding bikes firmly on the map in the UK.

In 1997, with folding bikes still a relatively new and outlandish concept, the Natural Theatre Company's 'Cone Heads' were chosen to promote the second Weymouth show (below). The publicity stunts might have caught the attention of the media, but for the participants, the enduring image is of the visitors from outer space inspecting and photographing the Brompton (right).

The Folder (the Folding Society magazine) was relaunched as A to B in 1997, and is still regarded as the best source of information on folding bikes, including news and reviews of Bromptons.

A to B Magazine   email: atob@atob.org.uk   web: atob.org.uk   tel: 01305 259998

Making a Brompton

Making a Brompton consists of several stages:
* Organising the supply of components - for example wheels were still being handbuilt for the company in Wolverhampton in early 2017 (below left), but this has now been brought in-house.
* Frame brazing (below right) is a critical and highly skilled stage. In the time-honoured Brompton method steel frame tubes are secured in a jig and high temperature liquid copper alloy is run around the joints to 'glue' the tubes together. Unlike welding, the alloy in the brazing rods melts and flows at a lower temperature than the steel tubes, so the steel does not melt.
* After brazing, the finished frames and other parts are sent out to the factory's paint shop.

© Olivier Pascaud

* After the frames and other major assemblies have been powder-coated, everything arrives at the assembly stations where the bikes are built on rotatable bike stands. The photo on the left shows the old 'batch' method, where one builder built one bike at a time.

Left: Brompton has continued the tradition of training key personnel to build bikes, the assembly practice giving a priceless insight into the way the bicycle is built and why. Here, in summer 2009, the company's new US agent Ed Rae, takes his turn at one of the assembly stations. Avid Brompton watchers may have worked out that Ed is building one of the most expensive variants, an S6L-X.

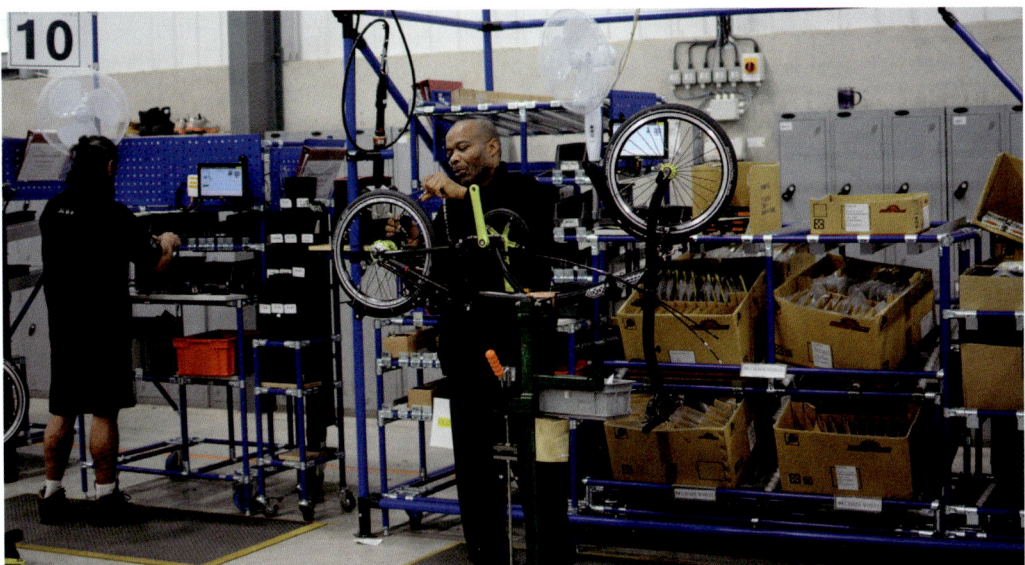

* Assembly lines at the Greenford factory have been designed from the ground up. Here 'production line' manufacture - ironically the process that revolutionised car manufacturing in the early 20th century and helped the car become an economic choice for the masses - sees one worker specialise in becoming as efficient as possible at one aspect on bike building. In contrast to car production lines however, the Brompton bike builders are free to move up and down the line to clear log-jams. This doesn't mean Brompton has gone entirely high-tech - there is still a place for the Victorian hand presses bought cheaply by Andrew Ritchie in the 1980s!

One of the new auto-brazing machines in action; cameras are used to detect the optimum temperature for the braze metal that flows into the joints, creating the strongest bond possible.

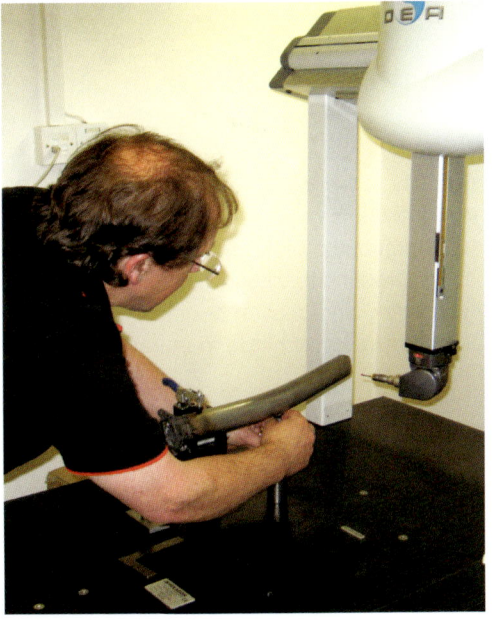

Computerised quality control; here a CMM (Co-ordinate Measuring Machine) checks the dimensions of a manufactured part against a computer image of the ideal dimensions. Previously the process involved clamping the piece in a jig and measuring by hand.

Appendix I - Chronology

1975 Andrew Ritchie first comes up with the folding bike idea.

1976 Brompton company formed, with friends as shareholders. **Prototypes P1 and P2 produced.** P1 has Bowden cables linking the folding sections, both have 18-inch wheels.

1977 Prototypes P3 and P4 produced, both with 16-inch wheels.

The P3 prototype from 1977

1978 Andrew decides to raise cash and produce the bike himself.

1979 Efforts to raise cash fail.

1981 First batch of 30 **pre-production bikes** pre-sold to shareholders to raise capital. Another 20 pre-production bikes were also sold.

1982 Mark 1 production begins in batches of 100.

1983 Cessation of hinge manufacture brings production of Mark 1 to an end after 450 have been made.

1984 Brompton approached by potential licensee which falls through. Attempts to raise capital fail.

1985 Julian Vereker joins Brompton.

1986 Finance package is pulled together, and tooling produced for production.

1987 In March the Mark 2 Brompton wins the Cyclex award. In November, **the first factory** is established in the Arches, Brentford.

1988 In March **the first Mark 2** bikes are sold. The bike is now in two forms: 'L', without a rear rack, and 'T', with a rack. Attempts are made to build a dealer network.

1991 Brompton takes over second arch, and **Nicola McGregor** arrives. Steel wheels replaced by polished aluminium. GB Cycles handlebars introduced.

1992 Chain tensioner assembly improved and in September handlebar stem diameter increased from 30mm to 35mm.

1993 In April the headset was increased in size from 1" to $1^{1/8}$". In December, Brompton moved to a **bigger factory in Chiswick Park**.

1994 From June, the 5-speed Brompton changed from the dual-cable Sturmey-Archer 5-Star hub to the new single-cable Sprinter. In October, the Sachs brakes were replaced with Saccon.

1995 Brompton wins the **Queen's Award for Export Achievement.** The forged bottom bracket assembly was replaced by a FAG cartridge, and the Soubitez dynamo replaced by a Union. Neobike handlebars introduced.

1996 Introduction of a basic 'C' type is investigated, but the idea is quietly shelved. Steel front hub replaced by KEYIN alloy hub. In August, the dynamo changes from Union to Jos, then in December, from Jos to Axa. In December, polished alloy rims replaced by anodised alloy.

1997 In June a new concave alloy hub replaces the KEYIN, and in November the mudguards were temporarily replaced with a round profile. Brompton wins **ADFC Bike of the Year Award** in Germany.

1998 In February, the anodised rims were replaced with milled-finish alloy. In October, Brompton moves to the **bigger Brentford factory**.

1999 Julian Vereker falls ill and withdraws from Brompton. Tim Guinness joins the board, then becomes Chairman. Stronger Humpert handlebars introduced in September.

2000 In March the **Mark 3** is introduced. New Brompton tyres, dual-pivot brakes, rear mudflap, battery light option, wider standard and optional colour range. Basic 'C' type finally introduced. Handlebar brace issued to owners of older bikes. In May, the 'ball-locking' version of the Sprinter hub is introduced. In June, the handlebar hinge was changed from a forging to a casting for auto-brazing. In September, **Sturmey-Archer ceases trading.** The 5-speed is withdrawn when stocks of hubs are exhausted.

2001 In April the 3-speed changes over to **SRAM hubs**.

Mark 3 Brompton

2002 In April the **Brompton 2 x 3-speed** is introduced. Will Butler-Adams arrives.

2003 New Axa dynamo in May, new handlebar catch in June, new lightweight front carrier frame in July.

2004 Main frame hinge changed from forging to casting for auto-brazing, producing a longer wheelbase.

2005 Mark 4 introduced. C-type remains, but L and T types replaced by M, S and P variants, according to handlebar style. Many detail changes, including reach-adjustable brakes, a single-speed hub, a return to Sturmey-Archer hubs o n 3-speed models, new saddle, Pentaclip saddle clamp, XL lightweight titanium variants, new battery lights, SON dynohub option and smaller S-bag (obligatory on bikes with flat handlebars) .

Brompton adopts the World Championship series of public-entry Brompton races, held around the world.

Mark 4 Brompton

2007 New seat clamp quick-release, and optional rear frame clip.

2008 Will Butler-Adams becomes Managing Director. In May, the Brompton tyres are reconfigured with softer rubber on the shoulders, giving improved grip, but slightly inferior rolling resistance. Double-butted lightweight spokes introduced on the 1- and 2-speed rear wheel. New softer foamed polyurethane suspension block introduced.

The global credit crunch sees an ensuing period of significant folding bike price rises for Brompton and its competitors.

£1 million invested in the Brentford factory to increase efficiency and productivity.

2009 In January the **BWR 3-speed wide ratio hub** replaces the SRAM 3-speed on all 6-speed models. An optional hard suspension block is introduced, and all paint finishes are changed from gloss to satin. In May, Brompton introduced a new 'handgrip' saddle, non-folding right-hand pedal whose appearance matches the folding left-hand pedal, and a lightweight front wheel on selected models, featuring cartridge bearings and double-butted spokes.

In October Andrew Ritchie wins the Prince Philip Designer's Prize 'for outstanding achievement in design'.

2010 For the new model year, the bag range is completely revised, the old Cloth Pannier and Touring Pannier lightly restyled with in a smoother shape, zipped lap-top pocket, bright yellow interior and curved zip-top rear pockets, as the 'C-Bag' and 'T-Bag' respectively. Two new bags were the 'A-Bag' with leather attache case, and the 'O-Bag' - a custom-made Ortlieb pannier. Meanwhile, Brompton finally relented to pressure and added a hard case (the Brompton Pod) to the existing soft 'B-Bag' for protection in transit.

The long-established 'Yellow Flash' (non-Kevlar) tyre was withdrawn, as was the rather frail Schwalbe Stelvio, both these lightweight options being replaced by the Schwalbe Kojak. Rather surprisingly, the Schwalbe Marathon was also withdrawn, although still available from Schwalbe dealers.

From about this time, a little depression was formed in rear frames to increase tyre clearance, pre-empting a 2015 ISO ruling that tyre clearance must be at least 6mm. In October the titanium seat pillar fitted to XL models is discontinued and replaced with a nickel-plated aluminium pillar. The intention is to fit the pillar to all models later on.

2011 March sees the launching of the first Brompton Junction store in Kobe Japan. Many others follow. In May, Brompton releases a limited edition of **150 'Royal Wedding' bikes** for Korea, Japan, Singapore and Taiwan. The bikes sell out very quickly.

In June, the **alloy seat pillar is withdrawn** following flaking and surface pitting of the nickel plating. For the time being, all bikes are fitted with the standard steel seat pillar, with XL purchasers receiving a £35 rebate, but the alloy pillar is never sorted satisfactorily, and the steel pillar becomes a permanent fitting. In July, Brompton launches the **'Oratory' jacket**, the first in a proposed line of Brompton-branded cycle clothing. The company also launches the first public hire **Brompton Dock** at Guildford railway station. September sees the first new handlebar configuration for seven years, the **H type**. It caters for 'taller riders and for those wanting a markedly more upright riding position'. The height of the grips from the ground has been raised by 60mm compared to the classic M Type.

2012 In March, after two years of development, Brompton's neat frame-mounted Toolkit wins a Design & Innovation Award at the Taipei Cycle Show. Introduction is promised for early summer, then December, then April 2013. 2012 also sees a further **eight Brompton Dock openings**. In the summer of 2012, Brompton quietly withdraws the titanium folding pedal bolt from XL models, replacing it with an improved, but slightly heavier, steel bolt.

2013 Manufacture of titanium rear frames begins at joint venture **Brompton-Fletcher Ltd**. The long-established one-piece crank and chainring is replaced with separate cranks, allowing any 130mm chainring to be fitted. This meant a change to a different bottom bracket cartridge, JIS (Japanese Industrial Standards), from ISO (International Standards Organisation). The only serious difference is to the profile of the square-taper bottom bracket spindle. Although the taper angle is unchanged, mixing of components is not recommended.

More compact, but more powerful brake levers are introduced, and a double-walled wheel rim design, with angled spoke holes for rear wheels, increasing strength and reducing spoke stress. The rims also have a deeper well to make tyre fitment easier.

2015 In January Brompton launches a saddle height insert to make setting the right saddle height easy for riders.

Brompton announces it is working with Williams Advanced Engineering (part of Williams Formula One team) with the aim of developing an electric assist Brompton.

In May Brompton Dock rebranded as **Brompton Bike Hire**.

Entrepeneur Luke Johnson appointed a Brompton director in September.

2016 Brompton-Fletcher now producing 200 titanium rear frames a month.

Andrew Ritchie resigns as a director of Brompton in March.

New 84,000 square foot factory officially opened by the Duke of Edinburgh in November in **Greenford**. The company signs a 15-year lease on the building.

From November, the more powerful 2013 brake lever is incorporated into an integrated gear and brake lever cluster, subsequently fitted to all bikes, together with colour co-ordinated lock-on handlebar grips. The new design also brings about a slightly lower M and H-type handlebar profile and taller stem. Double-butted spokes are now only fitted on lightweight variants of 1- and 2-speed bikes.

2017 The long awaited **Brompton Electric** variant begins a very gradual 'soft' launch.

Brompton Electric

2018 Brompton drops the 'Green Flash' tyre, turning to Schwalbe to deliver a new 349mm version of the Marathon Racer as the standard tyre.

The official launch of the Brompton Electric takes place in June, some months after the first bikes are sold. Despite this caution, there are early failures, including noisy drive gears, overheating motors, and software speed-control issues. Reviews are generally kind, but the bike fails to match up to expectations due to the low-profile launch, high price (initially £2,595+) and these early technical issues. The bike cannot be fitted with existing bags and vice-versa, and upgrading an existing bike to Electric spec is not practical.

One useful feature of the software architecture is that upgrades can be introduced very rapidly and user- or dealer-downloaded onto existing bikes. There are at least three upgrades in the first year.

Concerned about the effects of Brexit, the UK's exit from the European Union, Brompton spends £50,000 renting a warehouse near Heathrow, to store £1 million worth of parts, enough to provide a four week buffer, should congestion at ports and customs delay parts. Brompton is heavily dependent on bicycle parts and accessories from Europe.

A more conventional introduction is the X-CHPT3, although this new model looks more like marketing hype than innovation. Specced in association with pro-cyclist David Millar, the bike is effectively a normal super-light model without mudguards, but including Fabric Slim grips, Fabric Scoop titanium-railed saddle, harder suspension, and tanwall Schwalbe Kojak tyres. Priced at £1,990, the bike is Brompton's most expensive variant.

2019 In February, the X-CHPT3 is officially launched with a new 349mm variant of the Schwalbe One tyre, which replaces the Kojak fitted to early examples. The tyre is sold as an exclusive fitment at first, but Brompton later relents to pressure and allows the tyre to be sold by third parties in the European Union.

Brompton Electric sales hit 2,500 after ten months, but it's barely more than 5% of total bikes sales. MD Will Butler-Adams still hopes that electric sales will ramp up to 6,000 in 2019/20 and eventually account for half of all the bikes sold.

In April, Brompton introduces the **B75**, basically a blue M3 fitted with an unusual list of parts, and without mudguards, folding pedal or carrier block for £745. Although marketed rather cheekily as a 'Limited Edition', cynics suggest the bike is a thinly-disguised marketing exercise to get rid of old heavy saddles, out-dated brakes and extended seat-posts. It does, however, provide a cheap lead-in to Brompton ownership.

In May, the unusual 'P'-type handlebars are withdrawn, after 14 years of modest sales. Brompton also announces that it will sell bikes through Halfords.

Meanwhile, Brompton remains bullish about the prospects for the Brompton Bike Hire scheme, putting a further £1 million into an expansion of the scheme, but the accounts tell a different story. After seven years, only 25 or so remain open, and some high-profile Docks in the Midlands and the North have clearly failed. Losses are revealed as £290,000 for 2018/19, up from £182,000 the previous year. Turnover continues to spiral downwards, from £640,000 in 2016/17, to £460,000 in 2017/18, and £304,000 in 18/19.

Some say the £1,525 Brompton Explore, announced in August, is yet another marketing exercise. The 'adventure bike' is aimed at those undertaking longer trips on unsurfaced roads, but it's basically a standard M6E in camouflage-style Forest Green, with matching luggage, tan grips and Brooks saddle. A 44-tooth chainring gives slightly reduced gearing, but tyres are conventional tanwall Schwalbe Marathon Racers.

2020 March accounts see record annual sales of 59,052, up by more than 10,000 on the previous year's results. Faced with the **coronavirus epidemic**, which hits London first and hardest, Brompton keeps production underway, thanks in part to the spares stockpiled to cover possible Brexit contingencies, although social distancing rules reduce productivity sharply. The closure of many retail outlets doesn't help, and in April, the company experiments with 'direct-to-home' deliveries. Things turn around quickly however, as 2020 becomes the start of the 'great bicycle boom', with bike shops deemed an 'essential service' and allowed to open and Brompton recruit an extra 150 staff throughout the year bringing its global total staff count to 600.

In June Brompton wins a Court of Justice of the EU case against Korean company Get2Get who produced a carbon fibre Brompton lookalike called the Chedech. Get2Get admitted it deliberately copied the Brompton fold because it was the most functional technical solution and claimed that they were within their rights to do so, as the original patent had expired. The court ruled that there was additional copyright in the area of design rights which Get2Get had infringed.

Brompton's new monthly subscription service launched in September

2021 March's financial results confirm both the **bike boom** and Brompton's ability to keep producing and selling bikes throughout it. March end accounts show an increase of 10,000 plus over 12 months, with sales at 69,696.

Supply chain difficulties dog the company throughout the year as it resorts to very expensive air freight to avoid production lines shutting down. Mid 2021 sees the start of a **global surge in inflation** with many economists linking it to the effects of the Covid epidemic which saw a huge injection of public money into people's pockets and massive supply chain disruptions engendering some goods shortages.

October sees a new naming system with **A Line and C line models** replacing the previous nomenclature. The **P line** follows in November with a redesigned titanium rear frame and new 4-speed derailleur.

A Brompton phone mount is released, compatible with A,C and P lines with a T line specific version following on later..

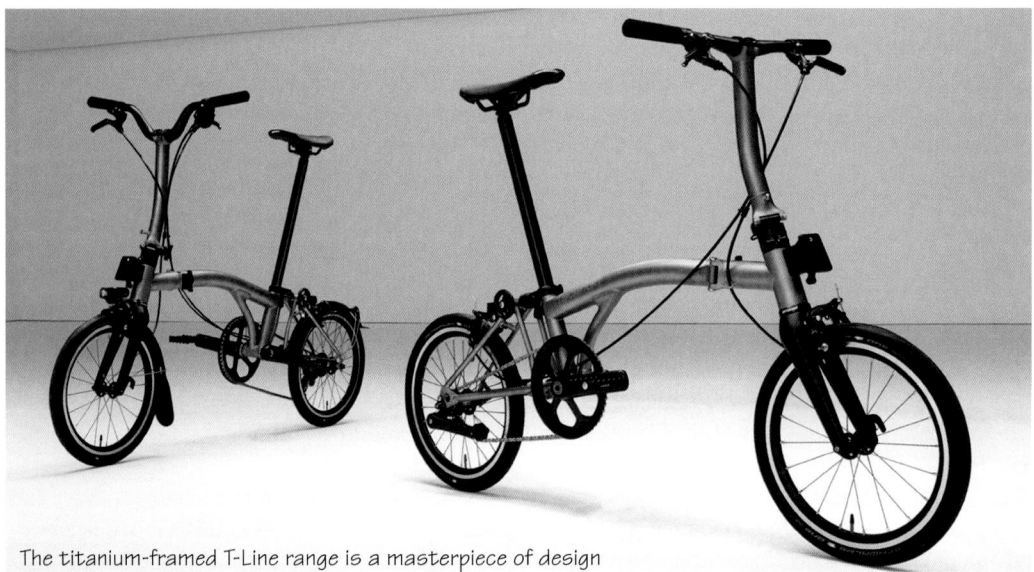

The titanium-framed T-Line range is a masterpiece of design

2022 Groundbreaking all titanium T-Line announced in January – a virtually new bike with a headline weight of 7.45kg for the single speed and 8kg for the four speed version

Russia invades Ukraine in February; both countries being sources of titanium for Brompton. More titanium is sourced from China and prices rise. Brompton announce plans to move to a new greenfield site in Ashford, Kent, citing space constraints and rental costs at their current location.

Late 2022 sees inflation peak at around 11% in the UK and it gradually starts to subside thereafter.

March end figures show a huge surge in sales to an all time high of 93,460 but costs have also surged to nearly £100 million and profits are down by almost a quarter to £7.3 million.

December sees the announcement of Brompton making its millionth bike ahead of its 2023 world publicity tour. The same month Brompton submit their **new factory plans to Ashford Borough Council.**

2023 Flexible mudguard set launched in February

Annual financial results to March 2023 show a decline in bike sales to 91,785, but an increase in both turnover - up 21% to £129.43 milllion - and pre-tax profit up some 46%% to £10.7 million. Great going when financial results across the bike industry generally showed falling profits - or even losses.

In May Brompton shareholders approve £19 million of investment from BGF, the high street bank-backed growth fund - an 8% stake based on a £180 million valuation.

June sees the introduction of the alloy-bodied Lezyne mini pump (with longer flexible hose). It comes as standard with the C Line Explore (6-speed) and C Line Electric model. The previous plastic-bodied Zefal pump was only previously supplied with the C line Explore (6-speed), the pre-May 2023 Brompton Electric and other pre-2022 bikes. For all the other models, the pumps are available as a bike accessory

A Brompton 12-speed model

2024 Launch of **12 speed versions of T Line, Electric P Line, P Line, and Electric C Line models**.

January also sees National Highways request a three month delay in making a decision on Brompton's Ashford factory application due to concerns over its impact on parking in the area. February sees funding from Innovate UK to optimise bicycle production through the development of robotic and automation solutions.

In June Brompton claims it has 'produced the world's first 100% recycled aluminium wheel-rim thanks to its strategic partnership with Hydro'. Hydro are based in Dormagen, Germany, where scrap sorting and final extrusion takes place with final assembly to happen at Brompton's Greenford factory. Although the rims are claimed to produce a weight saving, there is no detail by how much or when the first such rims will appear on Bromptons.

Appendix II - Gearing Options

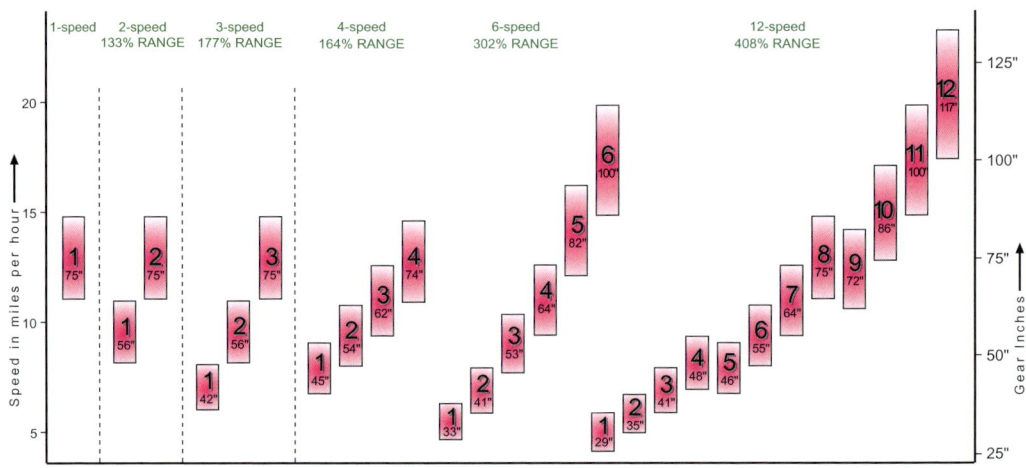

The chart shows optimal road speed for each gear with the six current Brompton variants (note that the Sturmey-Archer 3-speed gear option is now only available on the A-line and may not be continued). The 6- and 12-speed not only provide a much wider gear range than the 2- or 3-speed, but more overlap between the gears too, making changes smoother and progress more efficient. But don't write off the 1- and 2-speed bikes because a chart can never tell the whole story! In practice their lighter weight, improved efficiency and faster gear changes give excellent acceleration and hill-climbing. The gear ratios shown can be fine-tuned up (limited options on some variants) or down (all variants) to suit local riding conditions.

Note on Gear Inches: This British measurement (shown on the right hand side of the graph and elsewhere), dates back to mid-Victorian times, and indicates the diameter a 'Penny-Farthing' wheel would have to be to achieve the same gearing. An 85" gear, for example, would require a wheel 7' 1" (2 metres 16cm) in diameter. This comparison means little today, but the concept of gear-inches has remained popular in many countries as a guide to how 'easy' or 'difficult' it is to pedal in each gear. High gears are needed for speed and low gears for climbing hills and carrying loads. Gear-inches make a useful measurement because they can be applied to any bicycle, whatever the actual wheel size or gearing setup, allowing for easy comparison. But once again the size of the gear cannot tell the full story as it gives no indication of gear efficiency.

Special Brompton factory-fitted gearing options :
1-speed with 19% reduction = 61"
2-speed with 19% reduction = 46"-61"
3-speed with 14% increase = 42"-75"
6-speed with 8% increase = 36"-108"
12-speed with 8% increase = 31" - 126"

1-speed with 7% reduction = 69"
2-speed with 7% reduction = 52"-69"
3-speed with 23% increase = 52"- 92"
6-speed with 12% reduction = 29"-88"
12-speed with 12% reduction = 26" - 103"

(Mathematical note: The 19% reduction on 1- and 2-speed bikes is actually 18.52%. For simplicity it is described by Brompton as an 18% reduction, but marginally closer to 19% in reality.)

Gear 'range' is the difference between the lowest and highest gear, generally expressed as a percentage. On the graph below, Brompton's 'standard' gear ranges (shown in blue), are contrasted with non-standard options. For example, the 2-speed and 6-speed bikes have 12- and 16-tooth sprockets as standard. Replace the 16-tooth with a 19-tooth (the largest that can easily be squeezed on) and you get a 158% range on a 2-speed bike, and an impressive 388% range on the 6-speed. At the expense of some some rather odd gaps between gears, this conversion makes the bike suitable for loaded touring, even in very hilly areas.

However, some Brompton riders either want a wider range or don't feel comfortable with the twin-lever system. Alternative gear options fitted by such riders are shown here in pink, but all involve a loss of efficiency vis-a-vis the 6-speed bike, particularly in very high or low gears, and in most cases, extra weight. Also note if you fit a non-standard conversion yourself the manufacturer's warranty may be invalid, so the cost of professional fitting could well be worthwhile.

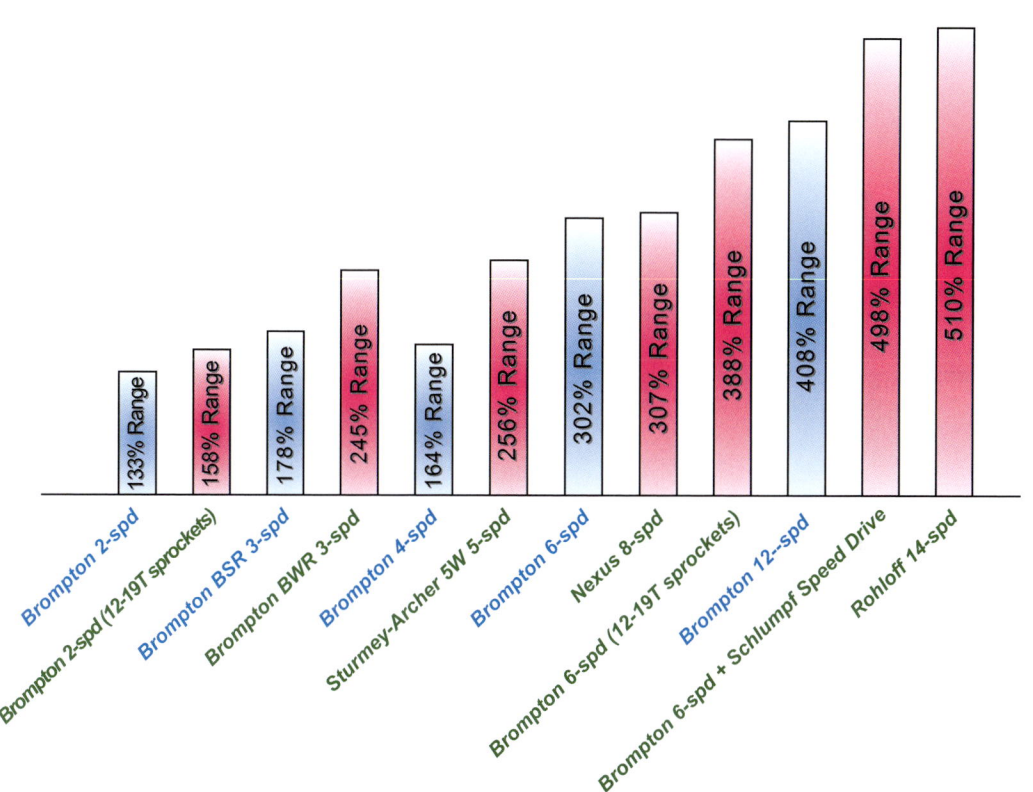

Appendix III - Brompton Naming System

Before the Mark 4 Brompton was introduced in 2005 Brompton used the relatively simple naming system of T,L or C followed by the number of gears. The letters indicated with rack, without rack and without rack or mudguards respectively. The graphic below is based around the system introduced in 2005 which accommodated the many new features of the Mark 4s.

Post-2005 the naming system became more complex to include the new titanium and extended lighting options, so bikes could now have up to six characters. The system was subsequently pared down so that by 2020, a three character description was standard, using only the first three characters of the system shown below.

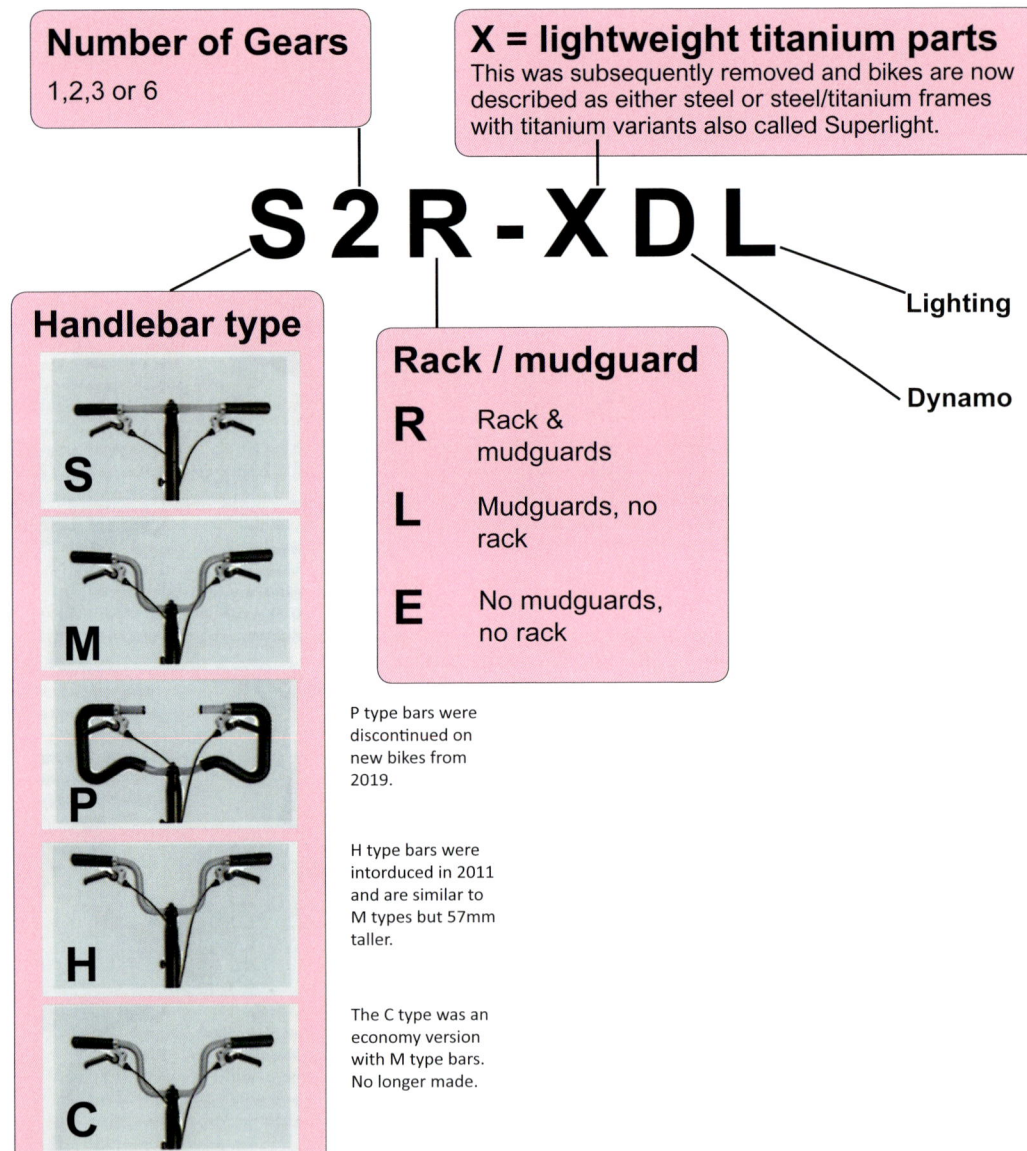

234

2021-2022 saw the rollout of new model lines based on the letters A, C, P and T - signifying basic, standard, light and superlight versions, with titanium making an appearance on the P and T lines. The previous letters that signified the presence of a rack or lighting are now in effect redundant; racks are a factory fitted option on the C and P lines (not avaialble on the A and T lines) whilst lights are purchased as a separate accessory.

Rather confusingly *Urban* and *Explore* were used to distinguish between models within the C and P line ranges; *Urban* models have two or four derailleur gears and *Explore* six or twelve gears thanks to the incorporation of the three speed wide-ratio hub gears.

	Weight	Frame / forks	Gearing	Rear rack / Mudguards	Other
A — The 'basic' model	11.5kg	Steel	3x Sturmey Archer hub gears	• No rack • No mudguards	• No front bag support or pump • Schwalbe Marathon Racer tyres • Platform, non-folding pedals • Plastic clamp handles
C — The 'standard' model	11.4kg - 12kg ⚡ 4 speed 14 - 17.4kg 12 speed 14.8 - 18.2kg (weights are without and with battery + charger)	Steel	2 & 6 speeds	• No rack on non-electric models • Mudguards as standard	• Schwalbe Marathon Racer tyres • Folding pedal • Electric option available - ⚡ hard-wired lights as standard with optional rack. 4 speed and 12 speed gearing only
P — The 'lightweight' model	10kg - 10.5kg ⚡ 4 speed 13.1-16.5kg 12 speed 13.4-16.8kg (weights are without and with battery + charger - racks add 341g)	Steel mainframe, titanium rear triangle and forks	4 & 12 speeds	• Mudguards as standard • Rack optional	• Continental Contact Urban tyres • Detachable pedal • No pump • Aero rims (not electric) • Electric option available - ⚡ hard-wired lights as standard with optional rack. 4 speed and 12 speed gearing only
T — The 'super-lightweight' model	7.5kg - 8.8kg	Titanium mainframe and rear triangle Carbon forks	1, 4 & 12 speeds	• Mudguards as standard • No rack	• Schwalbe One tyres • Detachable pedal • No pump • Aero rims

Appendix IV - Frame & Serial Numbers

The frame number can be found stamped on the main frame just above the rear frame pivot bearings. Rather confusingly, frames seem to have been stamped in batches of 500 within a set period, typically one or two months, but very often (especially in the early days) the batch would not be entirely used up before the next began, and in other months (particularly later) several batches might be running at once. In any event, the date might have been stamped some weeks or even months before the bike was actually shipped out of the factory, so the frame number can be no more than a guide to the date of sale. Appendix V should be used with other evidence, such as the Sturmey-Archer hub date, stamped on the steel shell, and chronology in Appendix 1.

From October 2001, bikes were also given a unique serial number as well as a frame number, but serial number stickers were not added to the bike immediately. The sticker can be found on the top back of the seat tube, or the bottom of the tube from 2013. The first four digits of this unique identifying number indicate the date of manufacture: the first pair the year, and the second pair the month. From late 2015, the sticker changed to a laser-etched plate.

Important Note: Frame numbers are only a rough guide to a bike's age. Neither Brompton, nor Excellent Books, nor the author is suggesting that a particular serial number guarantees a bike of a particular age.

Frame No.Range		Approx build date		Frame No.Range		Approx build date	
600	1103	Jan 88	Dec 88	36500	36999	Mar-97	Apr-97
1104	1674	Jan 89	Aug 89	37000	37499	Apr-97	Jun-97
1675	2234	Sept 89	Feb 90	37500	37999	Jun-97	Aug-97
2235	2760	Mar 90	June 90	38000	38499	Aug-97	Sep-97
2761	3290	July 90	Oct 90	38500	38999	May-97	Sep-97
3291	3814	Nov 90	Feb 91	39000	39499	Jun-97	Jul-97
3815	4837	March 91	Aug 91	39500	39999	Sep-97	Oct-97
4838	6086	Sept 91	April 92	140000	140499	Oct-97	Nov-97
6087	7249	May 92	Oct 92	140500	140999	Aug-97	Jan-98
7250	8316	Nov 92	Mar 93	141000	141499	Dec-97	Jan-98
8000	8499	May 93	Jul 93 *	141500	141999	Dec-97	Jan-98
8500	8999	Sep 93	Oct 93	142000	142499	Feb-98	
9000	9499	Aug-93	Nov-93	144000	144499	Jan-98	Feb-98
9500	9999	Oct-93	Jan-94	144500	144999	Feb-98	Jun-98
11000	11499	Jan-94	Mar-94	145000	145499	Mar-98	Jun-98
11500	11999	Mar-94	Apr-94	145500	145999	Mar-98	Aug-98
12000	12499	Apr-94	Jun-94	146000	146499	Apr-98	Aug-98
12500	12999	Jun-94	Jul-94	146500	146999	May-98	Oct-98
13000	13499	Jul-94	Aug-94	147000	147499	Aug-98	Nov-98
13500	13999	Aug-94	Sep-94	147500	147999	Sep-98	Dec-98
14000	14499	Sep-94	Oct-94	148000	148499	Oct-98	Jan-99
14500	14999	Nov-94	Dec-94	148500	148999	Oct-98	Mar-99
15000	15499	Nov-94	Feb-95	148000	148499	Oct-98	Jan-99
15500	15999	Feb-95	May-95	148500	148999	Oct-98	Mar-99
16000	16499	Mar-95	Jun-95	149000	149499	Jan-99	Apr-99
16500	16999	Jun-95	Sep-95	149500	149999	Feb-99	Apr-99
17000	17499	Jun-95	Sep-95	150000	150499	Mar-99	Jun-99
17500	17999	Jul-95	Sep-95	150500	150999	Nov-98	Jun-99
18000	18499	Aug-95	Sep-95	151000	151499	Oct-98	Jan-99
18500	18999	Sep-95	Oct-95	151500	151999	Nov-98	May-99
19000	19499	Oct-95	Jan-96	152000	152499	Feb-99	Jun-99
19500	19999	Nov-95	Dec-95	152500	152999	Jun-99	Sep-99
20000	20499	Jan-96	Mar-96	153000	153499	Jun-99	Sep-99
20500	20999	Feb-96	Jun-96	153500	153999	Jul-99	Sep-99
21000	21499	Mar-96	Jul-96	154000	154499	Aug-99	Oct-99
21500	21999	Mar-96	Jun-96	154500	154999	Aug-99	Nov-99
22000	22499	May-96	Jun-96	155000	155499	Sep-99	Dec-99
22500	22999	Jun-96	Aug-96	155500	155999	Oct-99	Dec-99
23000	23499	Aug-96	Sep-96	156000	156499	Oct-99	May-00
23500	23999	Aug-96	Oct-96	156500	156999	Nov-99	May-00
34000	34499	Sep-96	Nov-96	157000	157499	Dec-99	May-00
34500	34999	Oct-96	Dec-96	157500	157999	Dec-99	May-00
35000	35499	Nov-96	Jan-97	158000	158499	Apr-00	Jul-00
35500	35999	Dec-96	Jan-97	158500	158999	Apr-00	Jul-00
36000	36499	Feb-97	Mar-97	159000	159499	Apr-00	Aug-00

159500	159999	Apr-00	Aug-00		166500	166999	Feb-01	Apr-01
160000	160499	May-00	Sep-00		167000	167499	Mar-01	May-01
160500	160999	Jun-00	Sep-00		167500	167999	Apr-01	Jun-01
161000	161499	Jul-00	Sep-00		168000	168499	May-01	Jul-01
161500	161999	Jul-00	Sep-00		168500	168999	Jun-01	Aug-01
162000	162499	Aug-00	Oct-00		169000	169499	Jul-01	Aug-01
162500	162999	Aug-00	Nov-00		169500	169999	Aug-01	Sep-01
163000	163499	Sep-00	Oct-00		170000	170499	Aug-01	Sep-01
163500	163999	Oct-00	Dec-00		170500	170999	Aug-01	Sep-01
164000	164499	Nov-00	Dec-00		171000	171499	Sep-01	Nov-01
164500	164999	Nov-00	Jan-01					
165000	165499	Dec-00	Jan-01					
165500	165999	Dec-00	Feb-01					
166000	166499	Feb-01	Mar-01					

* **Note** There are discrepancies in the records regarding the precise manufacturing dates of these early frame numbers - certainly up until around July 1993.

Frame numbers aren't always easy to make out. This example, 162912, gives an approximate date for the bike's manufacture; between August and November 2000.

Appendix V - Profit & Sales Figures

Brompton's success has been helped by Andrew Ritchie's meticulous financial husbandry ("Call it meanness!", says Andrew). Growth has been remarkably steady, despite mixed trading conditions, and since the start-up years, achieved without borrowing. The company has been profitable since 1990, even during the Sturmey-Archer crisis of 2001-2002. A very notable achievement.

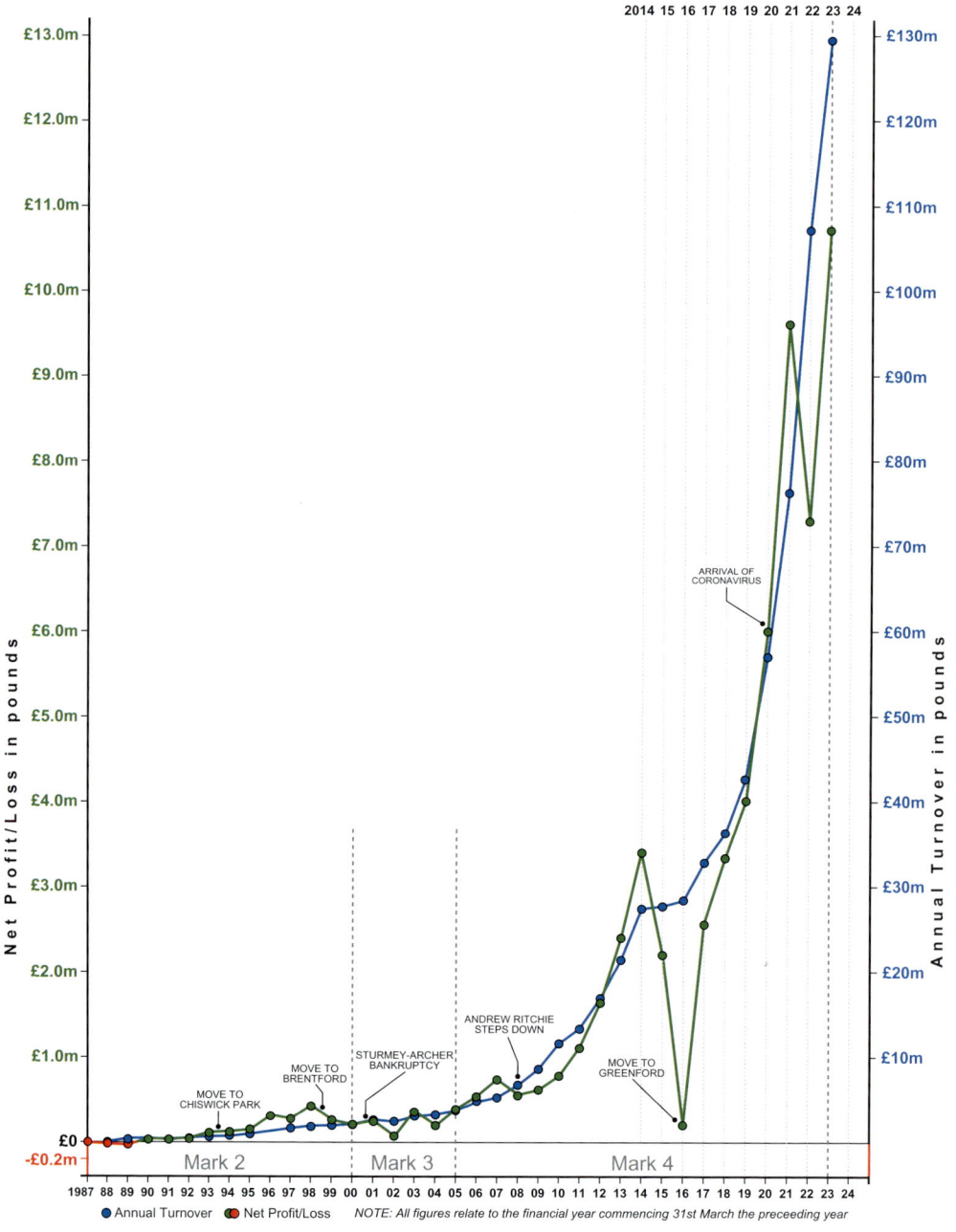

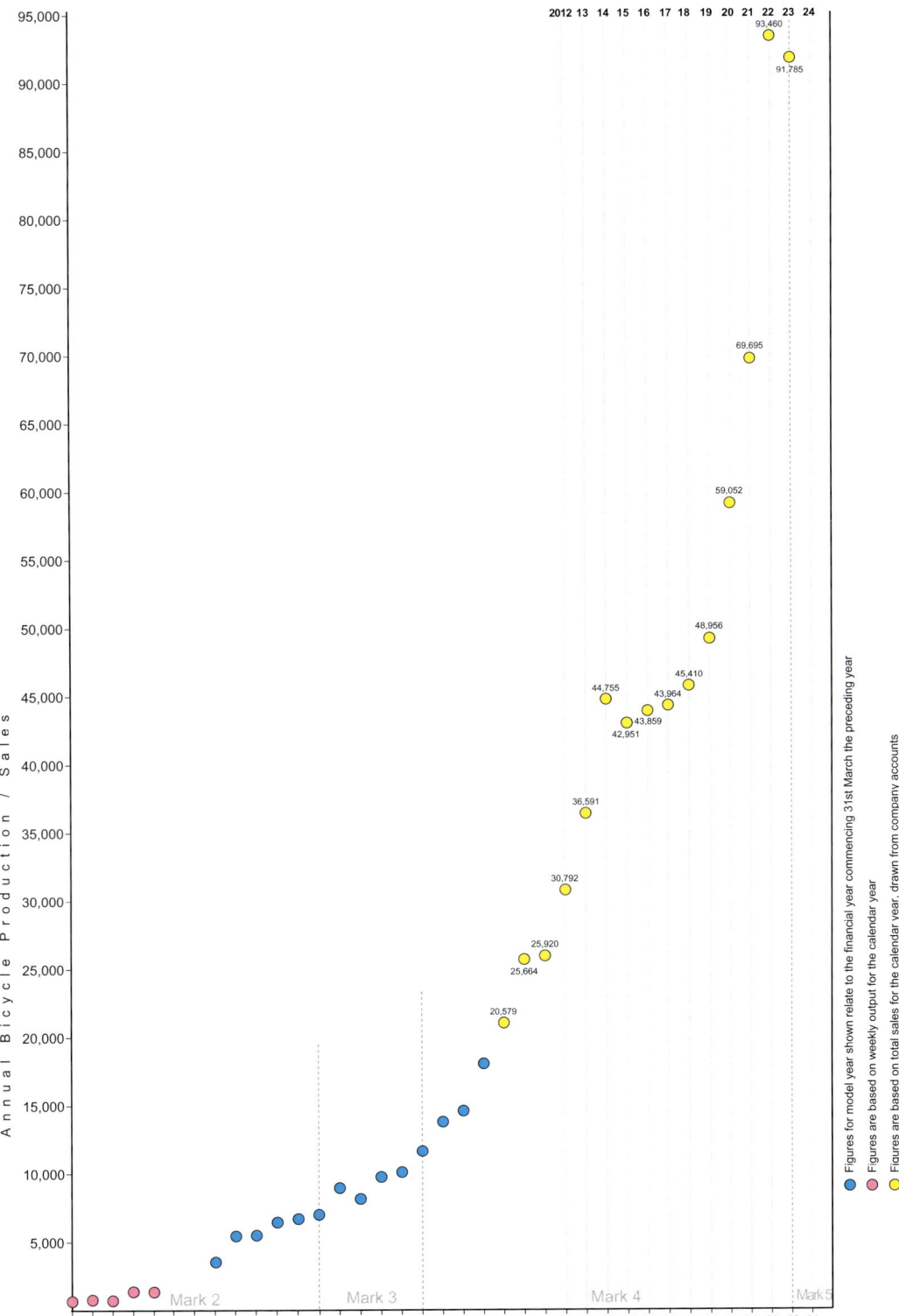

Appendix VI - Further Information

A to B
'Alternative' transport magazine run by Brompton Bicycle book author David Henshaw.
40 Manor Road
Dorchester DT1 2AX
01305 259998
www.atob.org.uk

The Hub of the Universe
The story of Sturmey Archer told in 368 beautifully printed and bound hard-back pages covering everything Sturmey-Archer ever made in considerable detail. Available from A to B (details above).
Also see www.sturmey-archerheritage.com

Diana Powell
Front cover from an illustration by Diana Powell. Various Brompton inspired prints available
dianampowell@gmail.com

Excellent Books
Brompton Bicycle book publishers and specialists in cycle publishing and journalism
07922 474233
richardpeacecycling.com

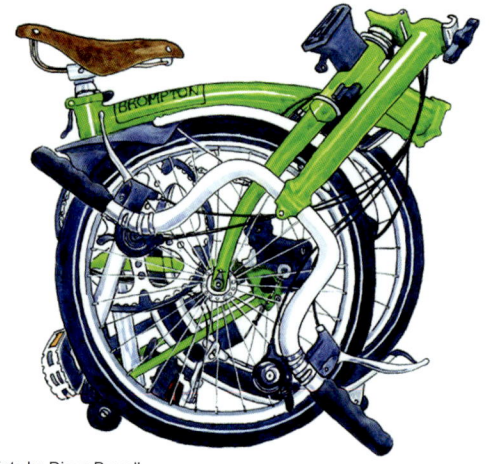

Prints by Diana Powell

Text Note: Victorian Prices Compared to Modern-Day Equivalent Prices

Throughout this story we have tried to show modern-day equivalent prices wherever possible. These take account of the increase (usually) in the Retail Price Index since the product or service was first advertised. However, they can seem unrealistically cheap today, because the RPI takes no account of the increase in Gross Domestic Product per capita in the intervening years. In other words, we're all much wealthier now, making discretionary purchases like bicycles less painful. This disparity is particularly striking with prices from the Victorian era, when the majority of working people would consider a bicycle a very major purchase.

Index

2-speed Brompton 84, 87, 90, 92, 184, 199
3-speed Brompton 37, 49, 50, 52, 53, 76, 77, 82, 83, 84, 87, 88, 90, 139
5-speed Brompton 49, 50, 52-53, 76, 83, 84, 87, 88, 153, 184, 186, 187, 198, 199, 200, 201, 205
6-speed Brompton 84, 87-88, 90, 92, 96, 138
12-speed Brompton 143, 144-145, 146, 149, 175, 176, 185, 195, 200, 210, 212, 214, 216, 231, 232-233, 235

A-bike, Sinclair 72, 73
A-Line 143, 145, 160, 185, 230, 232, 235
Accell 176
Aceoffix Flyer 186, 202
ADFC, Brompton Bike of the Year 74, 225
Agius, Marcus 20
Airframe 39, 62-63, 78, 98
Airnimal 78, 92
Airnimal Joey Move electric folder 164
AKM motor 172
alloy rims 197, 224, 225
Allso, Simon 83
Aluminium as frame material 12, 23, 69 140-141, 155
Aluminium supply 144
ARCC electric Brompton 166, 174
Arches factory, Brentford 48, 54, 57, 124, 137, 224
argon 109, 110
Ashford Factory project 151
assembly, of Brompton 46-48, 65-66, 74, 222-223
auto-brazing 223
automatic gearing 148
Avon Valley Cyclery, Bath 53
AW Sturmey-Archer hub 102, 143, 144, 146, 212

B75, Brompton model 131, 229
bags
  A-bag 227
  B-bag, padded bag 227
  C-bag 227
  O-bag 227
  T-bag 227

Barbour, Brompton (special edition) 203
Barts Charity 133
Bateman, Colin Sturmey-Archer MD 83, 84
belt drive 1, 148, 158, 176, 178
Bersaglieri, military use of folders by 2
Bickerton 12-15, 22, 39, 53, 57, 62, 63, 68, 185
Bickerton Californian 14
Bickerton Classic 13, 15
Bickerton Country 14, 15
Bickerton, Harry 12, 14, 22, 52, 62
Bickerton, Mark 14, 15, 72, 97, 100
Bicycle Doctor, Manchester 47
Bike Friday 25, 68, 78, 92, 153, 182, 208
Bike Friday All-Packa 179
Bike Friday Metro 69
Bike Friday Tikit 25, 99
BionX, electric assist system 164
Birdy (Riese & Muller) 60, 68-70, 78, 92, 100, 153, 182
Black & Decker Workmate 26-27
Boost electric kit 170, 171, 174
Bosch power tool batteries 166
Bottle dynamos 189, 195
Bowden cables 23, 25, 26, 99, 224
brake levers 118, 188, 197, 227, 228
brake maintenance 188-189, 196-197
brake weakness, Brompton 52, 57, 67, 76, 87, 155, 196-197
brazing 37, 46, 47, 48, 66, 81, 88, 89, 102, 107, 109, 124-127
Brecki, Brompton recumbent 152, 158-159
Brentford factory 74, 101, 108, 124
Brexit 129, 133, 134, 139, 146, 229, 230
briefcase holder for Brompton 51
British Cycling 133
British Standards 67, 81
Brompfication 107
Brompton company, established 26
Brompton Bike Hire Ltd 121, 122, 228, 229

Brompton Dock (B-Dock) 106, 120, 122-123, 227, 228
Brompton Electric 111-118, 150, 174, 228, 229
Brompton Electric, possible redesign 150
Brompton Fletcher Ltd 108-109, 111, 227, 228
Brompton, idea & prospectus 23
Brompton Junction stores 135, 182, 227
Brompton name, genesis 25-26
Brompton, original sketches 24
Brompton poster 119, 244
Brompton World Championships 118-120, 134, 156
Bromptonaut electric kit 172, 174
Brooks saddles 83, 88, 229
BSA 2-4
BSR Brompton Standard Ratio hub 90, 102, 143, 185, 233
Bubblegate design company 78
Busch & Muller lighting 116, 195
Butler-Adams, Will 81, 88, 101, 118, 120, 121, 133, 134, 136, 137, 151, 226, 229
BWR Brompton Wide Ratio gear hub 86, 102, 103, 143, 144, 145, 184, 186, 210, 212, 227, 232

C-Line 143, 145, 182, 183, 206, 230, 231
C-type Brompton 70, 76, 225-226, 234
cable problems & maintenance 89, 188-189, 196-197
Cannondale 135
Carbo folding e-bike 172
Carbon fibre 108, 140, 141, 147, 162, 172, 229, 230
Carradice bag for Brompton 51
cartridge bearings 67, 227
Castles, Tony electrical engineer 165, 166
Cateye battery lighting 195, 196
chain 29, 30, 87, 88, 183, 195, 198, 200, 206, 214, 215
chain tensioner 26, 47, 57, 87, 188-189, 215, 225
chain tensioner, maintenance 192-195
chainring 52, 88, 92, 183, 185, 195, 210, 212, 227, 229
Chambers Churchill handlebar manufacturers 67

241

Chedech carbon fibre copy 229
CHH CoNeX 121, 123
children, riding with 82, 197-199
child seat 153, 218-219
China 45, 47, 60, 90, 98, 108, 132, 134, 135-136, 139, 144, 230
Chiswick factory 62, 65, 74, 255
CHPT3, Brompton model 129-131, 134, 229
Chubb, Esther 48, 54
Clark C.H. Opposite 1, 5
CMM (Co-ordinate Measuring Machine) 223
Cobley, Dan 136
Colchester, Nico FT reviewer 37
Colchester Technical College 20
Compax Sports Traveler 6
Condor Cycles, London 47
Continental Urban tyre 148, 186, 202, 203, 214, 235
Cooper, Ben (Kinetics Brompton conversions) 178
Coronavirus (also Covid, pandemic) 118, 121, 122, 124, 132-134,136, 139, 140, 230 209
Cranage, Derek 136, 154-155
Cranium, Petre (Hummingbird) 173
Cresswell Fold-it 70-71
Cresswell Micro 70-71, 76
Cresswell, Richard 70-71
Crowdfunder 133
Crystalyte front hub motor 168, 174
Cyclecare Olympia, London 47
CycleDock 120
Cyclex trade show, 1987 47, 48, 50, 53, 62, 224
Cytronex electric system 111, 114, 116, 162, 170-171, 173, 174, 209

Dahon 14-15, 16-17, 50, 57, 63, 72, 74, 78, 89, 96, 97, 98, 100, 135, 136, 164, 176
Dahon Boardwalk 72
Dahon Boost 164
Dahon Cadenza 17
Dahon Ciao 17,
Dahon Curve 16
Dahon Formula S18 164
Dahon Helios SL 16
Dahon Ikon 164
Dahon IZIP E3 Compact 164
Dahon Jack 17
Dahon Roo EL electric assist 164
Dahon Tailwind 72
Dahon Unio E9 & E20 164
Dawes 9, 28, 39, 57, 65, 136
Dawes Kingpin 9, 38
Dawes Newpin 9
D-Day, folding bike use on 4

derailleur, Brompton 2-speed 84, 87, 90, 92, 102, 103, 144, 148, 184, 199, 214, 226, 228, 232-233
derailleur, Brompton 4-speed 142, 143, 144, 145, 200, 212
Derby Cycle Corporation 83-84, 88
Direct-to-Home service 133
disc brakes, fitted to Brompton 148-149, 155, 157
Donald, Edward 89, 96
Drakes bike shop, Cambridge 53
dual-pivot brakes 76, 196-197, 225
Duomatic, 2-speed automatic hub 148
Dunlop 7, 8
Dursley-Pedersen 2, 3
Dwyer Folding Bicycle Company 5
dynamo lighting on Bromptons 37, 49, 51, 67, 88, 92, 93, 155, 189, 195, 196, 212, 225, 226, 234,

E type Brompton 90
Ealing Cycles, London 47
Eazy Wheels 91, 178, 208
Ebike Solutions 172
Eerder Metaal 176-177
Electric Transport Shop, Cambridge 111, 166
Electric Wheel Company 166
Elliott Automation 20
Engineering Solutions 20
ETRTO 8
Eurotai, builders under licence 57-58
Explore six-speed, Mark 5 variants 143, 145, 231, 235
Explore special edition, Brompton model 132, 229

Faun 1
financial performance summary 238-239
Financial Times, article 37, 38
fi'zi:k saddle 90, 91
Fletcher (C W, Ltd) 108-109, 111, 227, 228
FLIT electric folder 173
folding basket 51
folding pedal 38, 58, 77, 90, 108, 131, 143, 180, 182, 184, 185, 186, 189, 204-205, 227, 229, 235
Folding Society 214, 220-221
Forks 67, 90, 93, 108, 141, 147, 154, 166, 176, 177, 184, 197, 235
Form consultancy 121
frame bush 88, 141, 186, 191, 205
frame failures 39, 82, 183, 206

frame hinge Brompton 18, 23, 25, 29, 34, 47, 89, 226
frame hinge forgings shortage, Mark 1 Bromptons 38-39, 45, 224
frame numbers see 'serial numbers'
Franklin family 104
Freedom E-bike, Israel 111
front mudguard stay hook 205
Fulham Cycles, London 37

GB Cycles, handlebar manufacturers 67, 81, 204, 224
Gates belt drive 176
gearing 1, 52, 72, 76, 198-201
gearing future designs 149
gearing options 210-211
gear shifters / triggers 52, 67, 77, 87,118, 199-200
Get2Get court case 229
Gibbs, Caroline 41, 44
Goldhawk Road 137
Goode, Richard 23, 26, 29, 90
Goodwin Hartshorn 108
Goodwood racing circuit 118
Green Flash tyre 202, 228
Greenford Factory 124-128, 134, 151, 223, 228
  paintshop 127
Greenspeed 131
  Scorcher tyre 131, 203
GRIN Technologies 168, 172, 174
Grosvenor, Frances 30, 31, 41, 44,
Grosvenor, Steve 33, 35, 37, 44,
Grosvenor-Reeve 33, 34, 35, 36, 45,
Grout Portable 1 (and opposite 1), 16
Grout, William 1
Guinness, Tim 19, 21, 22, 23, 75, 78, 88, 96, 101, 103, 225
gyroscopic action, of small wheels 181, 209

H-type bars 204, 227, 228, 233
H&H titanium seat pillar 107
Haden Brothers, Brompton suppliers 46
Hadland, Tony cycle historian 104
handlebars, adjustment & maintenance 204
handlebar brace (crossbar) 82, 204, 225
handlebar catch 88, 141, 169, 188, 205, 215, 226
handlebar failures 68, 81, 82, 204, 206

handlebar stem hinge Brompton 30, 88, 181, 191
Hart-Davis, Adam 82
headset & bearings 29, 34, 57, 180, 189, 225
Heathrow, warehouse stockpile 129, 133, 229
Hesson, Mike Brompton wheel builder 84
Hickman, Ron Workmate inventor 26
high bicycles 1
Highpath wide range sprockets 92
hinges, maintenance 191-192
Holloways Studios 151
Hon, David 16-17, 30, 57, 63, 72, 100
Hon, Joshua 100
hub gear, maintenance and repair 188, 189, 198-201
hub gear upgrades 186
Hughes Aircraft Corporation 16
Hummingbird 108
Hummingbird Electric 172-173
Humpert handlebars 81, 204, 225

ICFC venture capitalists 29, 30, 34
indicator chain, hub gears 189, 198, 215-215
Ingram, Bill 22
Interbike show, Las Vegas 89
IS disc brake mounts 178
IT Chair child seat 155, 218
IZIP E3 Compact 164

Japanese Kaizen 128
Japanese market 16, 57, 60, 89, 96, 98, 135, 227
jig 33, 109, 110, 222, 223
Johnson, Boris 105, 120
Johnson, Luke 136-137, 228
Junik-HPV 158, 168
Junior Brompton 42, 217

KEYIN hub 225
Khan, Sadiq 120
Kinetic Energy Recovery 111
Kinetics, Glasgow 148, 155, 178, 197
Klein mountain bikes 15
Korn, Simon Netherlands distribution 54

L-shaped M style handlebars 204
Lawrence-Tune engineers 33, 34, 35
Lenark 83, 84

lighting, Brompton 37, 49, 51, 54, 77, 92, 93, 94, 113, 116, 145, 174-175 189, 195-196, 209, 212, 225, 226, 234, 235
London Bridge station 27
London Evening Standard 37, 38
London House Plants 21, 22, 23, 46
Love London Go Dutch 120
L type Brompton 49, 51, 76, 77, 88, 90, 234
lubrication diagram 189
luggage & touring 7, 8, 37, 40, 208-209, 211-215
Lynch motor 35, 37

M-type bars 91, 132, 210, 227, 234
Mark 1 Brompton 27, 31, 32, 39, 40, 41, 45, 50, 182, 187, 196, 198, 224
Mark 2 Brompton 27, 42, 47-53, 160, 183, 184, 186, 187, 192, 197, 224
Mark 3 Brompton 64, 76-79, 81, 186, 187, 225
Mark 4 Brompton 80, 89-95, 96, 98, 184, 196, 197, 226, 234
Mark 5 Brompton 185
Marylebone station 55, 187
Matthews, Gary Derby Cycles chief executive 88
McGregor, Nicola 65, 74, 224
 early life & career 54
 role at Brompton 55
Mezzo 96-97
MicroBike 72
military use of folding bikes opposite 1, 2-6
Millar, David 129, 130, 229
Mitsubishi 60, 89, 96
Mizutani, Japanese bike producer & distributor 60, 89, 96
Mobiky Genius 72
Moulton 7-11, 12, 23, 27, 28, 43, 47, 51, 53, 76, 153, 166
Moulton, Dr. Alex 7, 8, 11, 12, 28, 69
Mountain Drive gearing, Schlumpf 92, 190
MTBrompton, off-road conversion kits 178
mudguard stays 92, 212
Muller, Heiko engineer 69

Naim Audio 43, 74
Nakane, Mac Mitsubishi 60, 96
Nano-Brompton electric assist kit 105, 111-112, 165-167, 175
NASA 16
Nascimento, Rafa 144

Neobike 58-61,67, 74, 81, 89, 204, 225
Neuß, Juliane, Brompton conversions 102, 152, 158-159, 168
New York 5, 58
Newland, David engineer 11, 12
NHS staff 133, 134
the North, Brompton coverage in 52
Nottingham City Council, role in Sturmey affair 84
NYCeWheels 107, 111, 166

Office of Fair Trading, Brompton's referral to 53
Old Oak Common HS2 124
OPEC oil embargo 1973-4 33
Oratory jacket 227
Ouroussoff, Nick engineer 33-35
Oxsilan 127

P-Line 143, 145, 160, 164, 185, 206, 230, 231, 235
P-type bars 91, 226, 234
Pacific Cycles (Birdy licencees) 60, 179
Panasonic Traincle 16
Panasonic Will electric assist folder 164
parachutists, folding bike use by 4
Parry, Steve engineer 153-157, 212
Pashley 65, 70, 136
patents 1, 5, 6, 9, 11, 16, 26, 30, 41, 45, 71, 83, 111, 164, 174, 229
Patrick, Brompton brazer 37-39, 53, 65
pedal maintenance 188, 189, 204-205
Peddlers bike shop, Worcester 53
Pedersen 2-3
Pendix electric-assist 168, 169, 175
penny-farthings 1, 232
Pentaclip saddle adjuster 90, 91, 226
Phillips, Richard 111
Pod case, for air travel 208-209
Pope Manufacturing Company 5
powder-coating process 65, 127, 222
power assistance 28, 164-175, 209
Powerhouse factory 35-37, 46, 48
pre-production bikes 34-35
Primo tyres 70, 76, 131, 148, 186, 202, 203

Prince Philip, Duke of Edinburgh 124, 228
  Designer's Prize 104, 227
production line manufacture 107, 124-128, 223
prototypes:
  P1 24-25, 224
  P2 25-26, 27, 224
  P3 18, 26, 27, 224
  P4 18, 26, 224
Puch Pic-Nic 12
puncture proof tyres 148-149
Putin, Vladimir 140, 143

Queen's Award for Export Achievement 67, 225

R type Brompton (with rack) 90, 94, 206, 211-212
Radical Designs Cyclone Chubby trailer 212-213
Radnall, Peter 70
Rae, Ed US agent 222
Raleigh 10, 11, 12, 28, 35, 37, 38, 39, 47, 50, 57, 65, 83, 85, 88, 100, 136
Raleigh Record tyre 70, 76, 203
Raleigh RSW / Compact variant 10, 11
raw laquer finish 89
rear hinge Brompton 29, 155, 188, 189, 192-193
rear rollers 40, 67, 178, 189, 192, 206, 209
rear sprocket 30, 52, 87, 92, 103, 183, 194, 195, 198, 201, 210
Recalls 41, 144
Reekie, Caroline 39, 41
Reeve, Tim engineer 33, 35, 37
Removable pedal 142, 235
Rickels, Steve designer 84, 90, 98, 103
riding characteristics, Brompton 30, 39, 167, 181, 209
Riese & Muller, bike manufacturers 60, 69
Riese, Marcus engineer 69
Ritchie, Andrew 11, 43, 44, 46, 47, 52,53, 54, 55, 58, 60, 62, 65, 66, 74, 75, 78, 81, 84, 87 , 101, 103, 111, 134, 143, 148, 153, 164, 184, 206, 227
  achievements 104,
  Brompton, idea for & early development of 22-31
  early life & career 19-22
  Mark 1 bikes 32-39, 41, 45
  Mark 2 bikes 48, 50, 57
  Mark 3 bikes 76-78
  Mark 4 bikes 90
  resignation 136-137, 228
  Sturmey-Archer affair 84

Taiwanese Brompton 57,58, 60, 61
Roberts, Emerson marketing manager 101
Rohloff hubs 153, 155, 157, 160, 178, 179, 233,
rolling resistance, tyres 7, 11, 17, 70, 148, 176, 210, 213, 226
routine checks diagram 188
Rowlinson, Steve 14
Rubin, Len lightweight conversions 160-162
rumbling machine 128, 136
Russia 90, 108, 111, 134, 139, 140, 144, 230
Ryan, Michael B. 5

S-bag 94, 211, 226
S-shaped M style handlebars 204
S-Sun lighting 196
S-type bars 91, 92, 211, 217, 226, 234
Saccon brakes 67, 204, 225
Sachs 67, 82, 225
Saddle Height Insert 210, 228
safety bicycle 1, 7
Sanders, Mark Strida designer 62, 72, 99
Sanders, Nick of Sturmey-Archer 84
Santander bike hire 122
Schlumpf bottom bracket gearing 233
Schwalbe tyres 129, 130, 131, 132, 179, 184, 186, 215, 235
  Almotion 203
  Kojak 148, 202, 203, 214, 227, 229
  Marathon Plus 148, 202, 203
  Marathon Racer 132, 202, 228, 229, 235
  One 130, 203, 229, 235
  Stelvio 202, 203, 227
  Winter 203
Scientific American magazine 5
Scotland, limited Brompton coverage in 53
seat clamp 39, 188, 189, 226
seat pillar 12, 23, 25, 26, 34, 88, 90-91, 107, 108, 141, 147, 155, 188, 189, 190, 205, 206, 227
seat pillar binding 191
seat pillar slippage 191
seat, using the Brompton as 206-207, 208
secondhand prices 182-185
Selle Royal saddles 88
serial numbers (frame numbers) 236-237
Sheffield factory 108, 141, 143, 151
Shepherd, Charles 'Chuck' Brompton sales rep 48, 50, 53

Sherwen, Ellie 116
Shimano Nexus hub 82-83, 96, 102, 153, 158, 233
shopper bike 11, 12
Silkmead engineering 98
Simpsons bike shop, London 47
Sims, Ian 130-131
Sinclair, Sir Clive 72-73
single-speed Brompton 67, 70, 90, 143, 153, 160, 162, 185, 230,
Skoot 79
SON hub dynamo 92, 93, 195, 226
Sonny, Brompton brazer 48
South Pole, Brompton use at 82, 181, inside rear cover
South West Trains 120
SP Brompton conversions 153-157
SP (Shutter Precision) dynamos 195
Spa cycles, Harrogate 53
Spaninga rear lighting 195-196
Sparta 176
Sparticle e-conversion 158, 165
Speed Drive gearing, Schlumpf 92, 233
spokes 7, 76, 77, 83, 160, 188, 214, 215, 226, 227, 228
SRAM 70, 77, 82, 84, 87, 90, 103, 144, 155, 184, 186, 198, 199, 225, 227
SRAM Sparc electric assist hub 164
SRAM Torpedo gear shifter 77, 199
Stevens, Colin, military vehicle expert 4
Stewart-Smith, Christopher 75
stop disc, lower 205
Street Associates 123
Strida folding bike 62, 72, 78, 98-99
Sturmey, Henry 1
Sturmey-Archer 12, 50, 52, 66, 76, 77, 82, 83, 84, 86, 87, 88, 89, 90, 98, 102, 103, 124,143, 144, 148, 149, 153, 184, 185, 186, 199, 200, 201, 204, 225, 226, 232, 233, 235, 236, 238, 240
Sunrace gear manufacturers 88, 103
Sunstar motor assist 164
Superlight bikes 107, 108, 162, 143, 234
suspension 7, 8, 9, 11, 23, 25, 26, 30, 43, 69, 176, 179, 192, 229
suspension block 189, 190, 226, 227
Swytch 169, 170, 175

T type Brompton 49, 51, 57, 65, 76, 88, 90, 94, 224, 234
T-Line (all titanium) 140-143, 146, 147, 150, 160, 162, 170, 173, 174, 175, 176, 181, 182, 185, 200, 205, 230, 231,
Taiwan 14, 16, 63, 67, 69, 85, 88, 98, 100, 108, 144, 184, 227
Taiwanese Brompton see 'Eurotai' and 'Neobike'
tandem, SP conversion 155, 156
TCK 14
Tannus tyres 149
telescopic seatpost, Brompton 23, 176, 210,
Tern 100,
  Vektron 172
titanium parts 90, 91, 92, 93, 100, 107, 108, 109, 110, 118, 160-162, 227
  Sheffield manufacture 107-111
titanium, supply of 90, 107, 108, 140, 143-144, 147, 151, 230
titanium welding 109-110
Tongxin, electric hub motor 111, 165-166
toolkit, Brompton branded 108, 227
touring emergency kit 214-215
trailer bike, SP conversion 155
trailers 190, 192, 193, 196
Transit Travel bag 209
TranzX front hub motor 164
tricycle, SP conversion 155-156
tyre size 7-9, 11, 12, 14, 17, 26, 30, 70, 72, 76
  larger sizes 176-179
tyres 6, 70, 76, 77, 96, 149, 197, 202-203, 210, 214-215, 226, 227

Ukraine 140, 143, 230 160, 174, 235
Ultimate Folding Bike & UFB Adventurer lightweight Bromptons 160-162
United States 5-6, 16, 41, 60, 68, 83, 88, 89, 99,120, 129, 131, 134, 139, 151, 160, 174, 220, 222
universal rear frame 186, 199, 201
Urban, Brompton range 143, 145,
Utility range 145

V-brakes, fitted to Brompton 155, 160
van Eerd, Vincent 176-177
Velospeeder (Velogical) friction drive 116, 168-169, 175
Vereker, Julian 48, 50, 53, 54, 55, 65, 67, 101, 224, 225
  early life & career 43
  becomes involved with Brompton 41,
  43-45
  Mark 2 bikes 48, 50, 53, 55
  illness & departure from Brompton 74-76
Voss, Hans German distributor 54

Walton, Clive 83
Warlands bike shop, Oxford 53
Wasson, Channell, US distributor 88, 220
Waterloo Station 120
weight & Bromptons 39, 51, 76, 87, 90, 92, 93, 102, 122, 147, 160-163
Westfield-Columbia 6
wheel hub bearings 189, 201
wheelbase, Brompton 23, 26, 30, 89, 197, 204, 226
Wheels for Heroes 133, 134
WhizzWheelz 131
Williams Advanced Engineering 111, 114, 228
Williams, Paul, Brompton Specialist Products Design Manager 108, 111
wire basket for Brompton 51

X-bike, Sinclair 72-73
X-CHPT3, Brompton model 129-131, 134 229
Xplorer, off-road Brompton conversion 176, 177

yachting, role as Brompton market 43, 44, 90
Yellow Flash tyre 77, 202, 203, 227
York Cycleworks 47, 48

Zyro, Dahon distributors 100

These original posters were produced by Philippa Steward in the late 1980s when Brompton was still struggling to find its niche, and amounted to pretty much the sole thrust of the company's marketing at the time. But the 'Go Anywhere... Take Anywhere' slogan was spot on, summing up the adaptability that would later become the cornerstone of the company's phenomenal success. Like the bike, the posters have become a design classic.